PUBLIC FINANCE AND ECONOMIC DEVELOPMENT IN GUATEMALA

PUBLIC FINANCE AND ECONOMIC
DEVELOPMENT IN GUATEMALA

By John H. Adler, Eugene R. Schlesinger
and Ernest C. Olson

In collaboration with the Research Department
of the Banco de Guatemala

GREENWOOD PRESS, PUBLISHERS
WESTPORT, CONNECTICUT

INTRODUCTION

THE PURPOSE of this study is, as the title indicates, twofold: it attempts to analyze the fiscal operations of the Guatemalan government in the course of the last decade in order to determine their impact on the Guatemalan economy. In addition, it tries to evaluate these operations with a view toward determining to what extent they have affected the rate of economic development and to what extent the fiscal system can contribute, in its present form or with suitable modifications, to the success of the government's policy of encouraging and actively supporting those improvements in the country's material and social welfare which are generally summed up under the term *fomento*.

The interaction between fiscal operations and economic development has always been recognized as an important subject of discussion and inquiry. But the expansion of government activities in recent years has resulted in renewed emphasis on the role of fiscal operations with regard to a country's economic progress and well-being. The new techniques of aggregative analysis which have been developed in the last two decades are designed primarily, though by no means exclusively, to throw significant light on the interaction of fiscal operations and the rhythm of economic life of the community.

The present study of the fiscal structure of Guatemala and its impact on the country's economic development is, in a limited sense, an application of the techniques 'of analysis and experience in research and presentation which one of the authors and Henry C. Wallich gained in the preparation of a report on the fiscal system of El Salvador.[1] The publication of that report led

[1] H. C. Wallich and J. H. Adler (with the collaboration of E. R. Schlesinger, P. W. Glaessner and F. Nixon), *Public Finance in a Developing Country—El Salvador, a Case Study* (Cambridge, Mass.: Harvard University Press, 1951). A Spanish translation of the study was published by the Fondo de Cultura Económica, in Mexico City, 1949.

to an invitation by the Banco de Guatemala to undertake a similar study of the fiscal structure of Guatemala. From the outset it was clear, however, that what the authors were requested to do was more than a mere repeat performance. Although the economies of Guatemala and El Salvador have many similarities, the differences in institutions, policies, and—as we soon found out—problems were marked. The pattern of the El Salvador study, therefore, had to be substantially modified to take account particularly of one aspect of the Guatemalan economy which, at the time of the preparation of the El Salvador study, was absent in that country. In the last five years, the Guatemalan government has devoted close attention, and a constantly growing proportion of its financial resources, to the country's long-run economic and social development. It has established a new central bank, a development institute, and a social security system; it has passed laws to promote private investment in new lines of production; and there are many other indications that the promotion of economic development and the government's participation in it have become the main issues of economic policy for the present and undoubtedly for many years to come. Although Guatemala's *fomento* experience is limited, and many development activities did not commence until 1949 (which year is only partly covered in this study), numerous fiscal problems peculiar to the process of fostered development have already arisen and many more are bound to arise. Therefore, the impact of the fiscal structure upon the long-run growth of the economy has been made the focal point of our inquiry.

Since the concept of *fomento* policy itself is relatively new, a study of fiscal problems of *fomento* must of necessity venture into unfamiliar and unconventional grounds. In spite of the forward-looking subject matter and the inducement to engage in broad speculations and generalizations which it holds, we have attempted to base our conclusions and observations on statistical data and other factual information pertaining to the experience of recent years. Moreover, we have come to the conclusion that the ultimate purposes of this study are best served if we refrain from presenting our conclusions in the form of cut-and-dried recommendations. The dangers inherent in the presentation of a set of firm recommendations in a period in which many of the structural and institutional factors on which our analysis is based may rapidly change, seem to outweigh the formal advantages of positive results. A number of recommendations are, however, implicit in the analysis of the fiscal system and it is our hope that those of our findings which continue to be pertinent will be taken into consideration in the shaping of fiscal policies in future years.

The study is based on such statistical data and other factual information as were available in the summer of 1950. In some instances it has been possible to take account of later developments; but no systematic attempt has been made to bring the manuscript up to date to the time of publication. The study was submitted to the Banco de Guatemala at the end of 1950. In the meantime, significant changes in the revenue structure have been made, several of them in line with suggestions advanced in this study. The large increase in the price of coffee and the rise in earnings of coffee producers have enabled the government to raise the coffee export tax first to 6, and later to 8 quetzales per quintal. The income tax proposal, which is discussed in detail in the text, has been modified and improved in many respects; the discriminatory treatment of corporate earnings, which was criticized in the study, has been virtually eliminated, and capital gains have become taxable under the new proposal. The increased tax receipts, resulting in part from a further growth in national income and in part from the increases in the coffee export tax and upward adjustment of some import duties, have been offset, however, by a rise in administrative expenditures. Perhaps the most significant development in the field of public finance was the establishment, in the fall of 1951, of a Tax Commission, composed of representatives of all sectors of the economy and charged with the responsibility of investigating the entire tax structure. The formulation of economic development policies of the government has made considerable progress through several policy statements by the government elected in 1951. It benefited also from a report of a survey mission sponsored by the International Bank for Reconstruction and Development, which submitted in July 1951 a study on the Economic Development of Guatemala (Washington: International Bank for Reconstruction and Development, 1951). A Citizens' Committee, which was appointed by the President to study the report, endorsed most of the recommendations which, among other things, call for several major revisions of the fiscal system; these recommendations are largely based on the findings of our study.

In one—and, we believe, not unimportant—respect, the present study lays claim to be a novel experiment in inter-American intellectual co-operation. In order to expedite the preparation of this study and to obtain the full benefit of the factual knowledge of local experts, it was agreed from the outset that the Research Department of the Banco de Guatemala would bear the burden of a major portion of the statistical and factual research which has gone into the preparation of this book. The authors must leave to the judgment of the reader the decision as to how far this form of co-operation has been successful.

From the point of view of the authors themselves, who as guests of the Banco de Guatemala had the opportunity to work for long periods in intimate intellectual association with the management and research staff of the bank, it was a unique and most gratifying experience. For this we wish to express our thanks to Dr. Manuel Noriega Morales, then president of the Banco de Guatemala and now Minister of Economy and Labor, Dr. Alberto Velazquez, vice-president, and Dr. Max Jimenez Pinto, general manager. In the Research Department, we enjoyed the efficient and tireless co-operation of Julio Gonzales del Solar, director, and of Dr. Theodore A. Sumberg, his successor. Antonio Cerezo R., Ing. Mario Dalponte, and Edgar Picciotto of the research staff of the Banco de Guatemala and Miss Hilda Gadea and Francesco Fernandez of the Production Development Institute devoted many weeks of arduous work to the collection and preparation of statistical data without which the study would not have materialized. The sections on the public debt and on money creation are based on memoranda prepared by Michael Zuntz of the Credit, Securities, and Exchange Department of the bank, who was greatly aided in his undertaking by the advice and the experience of Manuel Benfeldt J., the department's director.

The successful completion of the study would have been impossible without the energetic and untiring co-operation of Ing. Jorge Ahumada, adviser of the Production Development Institute, who for many months carried the main burden of time- and effort-consuming research which forms the basis of this study; the development of the national income series in particular was the result of his efforts. The authors have greatly benefited from his knowledge of the Guatemalan economy and his counsel on many problems of analysis. His departure to join the staff of the Economic Commission for Latin America deprived us of our most important collaborator and the study of a fourth author.

Numerous officials of various departments of the Guatemalan government provided us with information and advice. The late Dr. Antonio Goubaud Carrera, director of the Indian Institute and subsequently Ambassador to the United States, and Ing. Jorge Arias of the General Statistical Office were particularly helpful.

Henry C. Wallich, formerly chief of the Foreign Research Division of the Federal Reserve Bank of New York and now Professor of Economics of Yale University, Theodore A. Sumberg, Michael Zuntz, Dr. Manual Chavarria, adviser of the Production Development Institute, and Arthur I. Bloomfield, senior economist of the Federal Reserve Bank of New York, gave us the benefit of their comments on the preliminary draft of the study. We are indebted to all of them for pointing out to us factual errors and analytic weaknesses; they are not to be held responsible, however, for whatever faults remain in the manuscript.

Winthrop W. Case of the Federal Reserve Bank of New York and Mrs. Maria Wilhelm of the International Bank for Reconstruction and Development were kind enough to help us in the preparation of the English text. The difficult task of translating the study into Spanish was undertaken, with technical competence and helpful understanding, by Dr. Carlos A. D'Ascoli, technical adviser of the Production Development Institute. To them and to our secretaries and those of the Banco de Guatemala, who spent many hours on the preparation of the manuscript, likewise go our thanks.

J. H. A.

E. R. S.

E. C. O.

December 1951

TABLE OF CONTENTS

LIST OF TABLES

xvii

PUBLIC FINANCE AND ECONOMIC DEVELOPMENT IN GUATEMALA

I

SUMMARY AND EVALUATION

INTRODUCTION

In the course of the last two decades, economists have been increasingly concerned with fiscal policies and fiscal operations. This development was largely the result of the expansion of government activities into fields which one or two generations ago were considered outside the proper scope of government responsibilities. In consequence, government now absorbs, and produces, a much larger share of the gross national product of virtually every country than it did a few decades ago.

The growth of government is partly the cause and partly the result of a reappraisal of the role of fiscal operations in the economic life of a country. In addition to its traditional function of providing administrative, protective, and certain types of communal services, government has assumed an increased share of responsibility for the social and cultural development of the country. It has been charged with the task of enhancing the growth of the country's economy and the economic well-being of the population through governmental initiative and the encouragement of private efforts. Moreover, the financial operations of the government have been recognized as a powerful tool for offsetting or, at least, mitigating periodic variations in the level of economic activity.

For these reasons an analysis of fiscal operations can no longer concern itself exclusively with the level and the composition of public receipts and expenditures. It must deal with the impact of these operations on the level of production, consumption, savings, investment, the volume of foreign trade, international movements of capital, the supply of money, and the behavior of prices. In the case of a country whose natural and

3

human resources are not yet utilized to the full extent which modern technology permits, particular attention must be devoted to the impact of the fiscal system on the rate of economic development.

The present study describes and analyzes the fiscal system of Guatemala in the broad setting of the Guatemalan economy, in order to determine how well it serves the government in the discharge of its manifold responsibilities and thereby the economy as a whole. Since one of the primary objectives of government policy is the acceleration of economic development, the fiscal system and the government's fiscal policies are appraised particularly from the point of view of their suitability and efficiency in this respect. Throughout the study, an attempt has been made to present the factual material and the conclusions derived from its analysis in quantitative terms. This was relatively easy in the case of fiscal data proper, although the accounts of the government did not always lend themselves readily to the rearrangements necessary to arrive at analytically meaningful concepts. In other instances, this was more difficult, since it was necessary to collect basic data of uncertain accuracy or to rely on incomplete samples or crude estimates. In consequence, some parts of the study rest on quantitatively uncertain grounds. Nonetheless, the statistical material at our disposal proved sufficient, in volume and in reliability, to determine with reasonable accuracy the most significant quantitative relationships.

The disadvantage of limited quantitative information is partly offset by the relative simplicity of the structure of the Guatemalan economy. Its well-defined export sector, its primitive techniques of agricultural production, and its heavy dependence on foreign sources for manufactured articles are typical of many countries in Latin America and other parts of the world. The rather sharp and economically and socially significant distinction between the native-Indian and urban-*ladino* sectors somewhat complicates the analysis; but because of similar social and economic cleavages in many other countries, the analysis of the interplay of fiscal policies and economic development in such a setting is the more significant for the reader who is not primarily concerned with Guatemala.

The study is divided into three parts. The present chapter summarizes the major findings. The next three chapters present a description of the Guatemalan economy, the system of government revenues, and the pattern of government expenditures and the public debt. The remaining seven chapters form the analytical sections of the study. Beginning with an appraisal of the incidence of taxation, the study proceeds to a discussion of the problem of fiscal administration and an analysis of variations in the level of government receipts and expenditures. The final chapters deal with the impact of the fiscal system on the national income and its distribution, on the money supply, on the balance of payments, and on the long-run economic development of the country. Several of the chapters are followed by Statistical Notes which provide detailed information on sources of statistical data and methods of computation.

SUMMARY OF FINDINGS

In the fiscal year 1947/48, the last year for which complete data are available, the gross national product of Guatemala amounted to 335 million quetzales.[1] Almost 60 percent of this amount represented income of the agricultural sector of the economy; coffee and bananas, the most important export crops of the country, accounted for 13 percent of the national product (chapter ii). Public receipts of 45.6 million quetzales absorbed 14 percent of the gross national product, while public expenditures, amounting to 51.1 million quetzales, accounted for 15 percent of gross income. By far the most important fiscal authority of the country has been the national government, which in recent years received approximately 90 percent of all public revenues. The national government's share in public expenditures has been somewhat smaller since it transferred a certain

[1] One quetzal (Q) equals one United States dollar.

proportion of its receipts to municipalities and autonomous entities.

In 1944/45 the Guatemalan government repaid almost all of its foreign debt, so that only an insignificant amount of Q670,000 was outstanding at the end of the fiscal year 1948/49. But the internal debt, which had been completely paid off before the war, expanded rapidly in the course of the last three years, reaching almost 14 million quetzales at the end of the fiscal year 1948/49 (chapters iii and iv).

The Impact of the Fiscal System on Business (chapter v)

During the fiscal year 1947/48, Guatemalan industrial, commercial, and agricultural enterprises paid approximately 97 percent of all taxes collected by the government. It is estimated that about 80 percent of this total was shifted to the consumer in the form of higher prices, and the remainder was borne by the business firms themselves. Although all types of taxes affect personal incomes, consumer purchases, and therefore the receipts of the business community, business, on the whole, is undoubtedly better off under the present system with its high proportion of shifted taxes than it would be under one which would permit less extensive shifting. Because of the great shiftability of taxes levied upon business firms, attempts by the government to increase the tax burden of business relative to that of the consumer are not likely to be completely successful. As a consequence of the shifting process, a certain proportion of the additional revenue would undoubtedly come out of the pockets of consumers. There is, however, one important practical reason for continuing the prevailing practice of *collecting* the bulk of tax receipts from business: the task of revenue administration is thereby greatly simplified.

Although the Guatemalan tax system has a relatively small direct incidence on business, it affects the operations of business firms in several significant respects. Taxes which lower consumption (because they are borne by those income groups which in the aggregate spend their entire income for consumption purposes) result in a substitution of government goods and services for the production of private goods and services; this decline in the demand for private production affects the business community as a whole adversely. The prevailing system also influences the composition of private production: agricultural producers, building contractors, textile and clothing manufacturers, and food processors in particular are benefited, while importers, liquor manufacturers, and producers of such nonessentials as are consumed by low-income groups get a smaller share of total consumers' expenditures than they would get if taxes were lower.

In view of the government's policy of fostering economic growth, the effects of the tax system on business investment are of particular interest. As a result of the relatively low direct incidence of taxes on domestic business enterprises, taxes do not appreciably reduce the volume of business profits which are available for reinvestment. The influence of the tax system on the desire to invest is likewise believed to be quite insignificant since taxes borne by business are low and there are no taxes on personal income which could not be shifted. Through the industrial development law, moreover, the government has attempted to encourage business investment by a policy of granting tax exemptions of limited duration to certain classes of industries. Fifty-nine enterprises have availed themselves of this privilege during the first two and one-half years of the law's operation. This indicates that the policy of fiscal encouragement appears to have been moderately successful, although it is difficult to determine how many of the new firms would have been founded if tax exemptions had not been granted.

The most serious weakness of the tax system with respect to investment is that it favors speculative rather than productive ventures; the absence of a tax on capital gains offers incentives to engage in real estate, land, or inventory speculation, rather than in the production of goods and services. The business profits tax also may impede capital investment in certain instances. The provision exempting firms with a capital of less than Q2,500 may deter small firms from increasing their invested capital.

The effects of the tax system on foreign capital are more complex than those on domestically owned businesses, for they are influenced by the economic conditions and tax policies of other countries as well as those of Guatemala. A prospective foreign investor is less concerned with the absolute level of Guatemalan taxes than with the net addition that these taxes make to his total international tax liability. In the past, the government has attempted to encourage foreign investment by granting companies contractual safeguards which explicitly stipulated all taxes for which they would be liable. Although this tax-exemption policy proved to be quite successful, it appears questionable whether it is suitable under present conditions, except in so far as foreign capital participates in the benefits of the industrial development law. Guatemalan tax legislation does not, for the most part, take advantage of those provisions in the revenue codes of other nations which tend to stimulate the export of capital.

The influence of the fiscal system on the business community has extended beyond the effects of the government's power to tax, for the government itself is a large business unit which engages in buying and selling activities. The government supplies services to business enterprises and is an important customer of several industries; importers and the producers of foodstuffs, textiles, feedstuffs, cattle, and construction materials particularly benefit from its purchases. On the other hand, the operating costs of some private industries have risen as a result of government competition for construction materials and the services of day laborers.

The Tax System and Private Income (chapter vi)

Since it seems reasonably clear that business firms bear only a small portion of the total tax burden, an analysis of the impact of the Guatemalan tax system on individuals and individual households in their dual capacity as income recipients and consumers is very revealing. A broad correlation appears to exist between the source and size of the incomes of Guatemalan families; therefore the over-all incidence of the Guatemalan tax system can be determined with some accuracy by comparing estimates of the tax burdens of typical households in various income groups.

Total taxes borne vary greatly, ranging from 5 percent of household income in the case of a small indigenous farmer to 28 percent for the family of a coffee grower with an income of Q20,000. The system is progressive up to the upper-middle-income brackets irrespective of the source of income; the progression continues in the case of those households which earn industrial and commercial incomes subject to the business profits tax, but the tax system becomes decidedly regressive for families who earn agricultural, professional, and salary incomes. The proposed general income tax law which has been before the Guatemalan Congress for some time would eliminate this tax discrimination between sources of income and would increase the progressiveness of the system as a whole.

Differences in tax burdens also exist between families with similar incomes but with different income-disposal patterns. Differential tax burdens are revealed, for example, by a comparison of taxes borne by large consumers of taxed commodities with those borne by smaller consumers of such articles; this is indicative of one of the weaknesses of a tax system which relies primarily on consumption taxes. Of much more basic significance are the differences in the tax burden of indigenous and *ladino* families. As would be expected, an indigenous household bears less taxes than an urban family with the same income, although this discrimination narrows somewhat in the higher-income brackets. The greater rate of progression among indigenous households is explained by the fact that with an increase in family income, the ratio of home-produced to total income declines and the participation of the family in the tax-burdened market economy increases.

The Government and the Budget (chapter vii)

An appraisal of the methods and costs of collecting the various groups of taxes shows that much can be done to better the efficiency of tax administration in Guatemala. Among the most important of the improvements that appear to be indicated are: (*a*) the completion of the real estate reassessment begun in 1945; (*b*) the curtailment of the illegal production of alcoholic beverages through a strengthening of the special police force in charge of enforcing the prohibition against uncontrolled production; (*c*) the simplification of the complicated customs-duty schedules by reducing the excessive number of individually listed items and consolidating all taxes on imports into one schedule; (*d*) better training of the personnel who administer the business profits tax; and (*e*) a review of the profitability of the large number of minor taxes for the purpose of determining whether they should be continued or abolished, or whether their administration could be made less expensive.

The government's ability to maintain or expand its functions depends in part on movements of the prices, wages, and salaries which it has to pay. Of the total increase of 360 percent in government expenditures which occurred between 1937/38 and 1947/48, approximately three-fifths may be attributed to an expansion of government activities; the remainder was due to a rise in the unit cost of government which amounted to 86 percent in the period under review. This relatively small increase in unit costs was largely the result of the slow rise of government salaries and wages, which have on the average absorbed two-thirds of government expenditures. Government salaries and wages rose respectively by 63 percent and 53 percent during the period, as contrasted with a 97 percent increase in the cost of living in Guatemala City. Although economy in the setting of salary and wage scales has enabled the government to expand its activities without raising substantial additional tax revenues or incurring heavy deficits, it is bound to result in a gradual deterioration of the average efficiency of the government's labor force, particularly since the salaries paid to competent white-collar workers by the business community are generally higher than those paid by the government. An attempt has apparently been made by the government to compensate for the unavailability of experienced personnel by the employment of a large number of unskilled or partly trained employees; the decline in over-all efficiency which was probably caused by this policy may disappear in due course if the turnover of personnel is kept low.

Variations in Government Receipts and Expenditures (chapter viii)

Seasonal fluctuations of the Guatemalan government's receipts and expenditures normally produce two seasonal peaks in the Treasury's cash balances and deposits. One results from the seasonally low rate of disbursements at the beginning of the fiscal year in July and August. It indicates that with the current level of Treasury balances there is no need for seasonal borrowing by the government. The other is caused by the concentration of coffee export tax receipts in the first three months of the calendar year; its seasonal nature should be taken into consideration in the preparation of the annual budget which is normally undertaken during this period.

The problem of the behavior of receipts and expenditures under the impact of cyclical changes in income and price is more significant than the question of seasonal variations. Although the built-in flexibility of the revenue system has been increased as a result of the modifications of the tax structure since 1937/38, it is still only moderate; if the 1947/48 tax rates had been in effect throughout the period, the fluctuation of tax receipts would have been slightly smaller than that of national income. In the case of expenditures, the expansion of government activities in recent years has resulted in a growing inflexibility in the downward direction, at least in the short run. A curtailment of investment activities would, of course, be possible if revenues fell, but it would obviously be undesirable to curtail government investment simply because ordinary administrative expenditures proved to be inflexible. It seems of paramount importance, therefore, to oppose a further growth of administrative expenditures, since there is danger that such an expansion may ultimately be at the expense of investment expenditures.

The long-run or growth flexibility of the tax system also merits attention. Since the most important groups of Guatemalan taxes (i.e., consumption and import taxes) are levied upon a specific basis, the level of the government's fiscal revenues depends primarily upon the volume of production and consumption in *real* terms; and since there are reasons to believe that real imports and real consumption (of taxed commodities) increase more than proportionately with an increase in national income, the present revenue system is sufficiently flexible for a process of gradual expansion of general economic activity *without* inflationary price increases. If, on the other hand, an increase in money income over and above that in real income takes place, the present fiscal structure would prove to be unsuited to stem an inflationary tide.

The growth flexibility of the present tax system notwithstanding, it may be necessary to supplement it with new sources of revenue, particularly in view of the government's policy of financing development projects that require expenditures over and above the "normal" yield of the prevailing tax structure. Opportunities for higher tax revenues appear to lie in an improvement of the administration of existing taxes, the imposition of higher rates on such existing taxes as the property tax and coffee export tax, and the imposition of a personal income tax.

The Fiscal System and the National Income (chapter ix)

The fiscal system affects the national income in three distinct ways, through (a) the level of government receipts and expenditures, (b) the difference between government expenditures and receipts which may cause an expansion or contraction of national income, and (c) the composition of receipts and expenditures, which causes a redistribution of national income among the various income groups.

During the last decade, government receipts and expenditures have not risen significantly in relation to national income, particularly if allowance is made for the inclusion since 1945/46 of receipts from, and expenditures of, the nationalized plantations. Since tax receipts amounted to 11 percent of the gross product of the private sector of the economy in 1947/48, as against 10.9 percent in 1937/38, it is clear that the relative cost of government, in so far as it is represented by taxation, has not risen appreciably in recent years; this bears out the previous observation that an increase in the over-all level of taxation will be necessary if the government intends to continue its policy of fostering economic development through public investment expenditures.

Government deficits and surpluses appear to have acted as an accentuating and mitigating force rather than a primary causal factor in Guatemalan income and price movements. Although the cash surpluses of the war years were unable to stem the inflationary expansion caused by export surpluses, they unquestionably held down the upward pressure to some extent. Similarly, the government deficits of 1947/48 and 1948/49 do not appear to have been the primary cause of the inflationary updrift that took place in the postwar period; this is borne out indirectly by the experience of 1946/47 when prices rose by 18 percent in spite of a large accumulation of Treasury balances. It is clear that in a country such a Guatemala neither a business recession originating from abroad nor an export boom caused by an increase in the foreign demand for Guatemala's exports can be cured solely by fiscal policies. But such expansions and contractions can be alleviated to some extent by proper fiscal policies, particularly if they are supplemented by appropriate monetary policies. Given a stable level of expenditures and an adequate equilibrium level of receipts, the built-in flexibility of the revenue system should produce relatively minor Treasury surpluses in a period of moderate expansion, and some deficits in a contraction. If necessary, this built-in rhythm of fiscal operations can be accentuated, of course, by net borrowings from the banking system in periods of contraction and net debt retirements in a period of expansion. But it must be kept in mind that the government's freedom of action is limited—at least in a period of declining business activity—by movements of the country's foreign exchange reserves. The economy can afford an accentuation of the loss of foreign exchange through the incurrence of a Treasury deficit only to the extent to which the central bank is able to build up exchange reserves in an upswing while the government accumulates Treasury balances.

The current tax structure, together with the present pattern of government expenditures, produces a moderate redistribution of the national income in favor of indigenous and urban families with annual incomes of less than Q1,200. Indigenous households participate in the benefits of expenditures to a smaller extent than their urban counterparts, but this disadvantage is offset by the fact that they have a commensurately smaller tax burden. The redistribution of income in Guatemala is largely the result of the high proportion of the benefits of social and cultural expenditures that accrues to the lower-income groups, and thus tends to stimulate a gradual increase in the productivity of a large part of the population; better schools, more hospitals, and similar social improvements are bound to enhance the productivity of the economy in the final result. The withdrawal of income from the upper-income groups may, on the other hand, adversely affect the formation of private capital, but in view of the moderate extent of the income redistribution under the present fiscal system, this factor does not appear significant.

Fiscal Operations and the Monetary System (chapter x)

Fiscal operations have had important effects on Guatemala's monetary system and balance of payments in recent years. In Guatemala, as anywhere else, government financing, along with the balance-of-payments and business financing, is one of the principal factors determining the aggregate means of payment of the economy. In the period under consideration, significant changes occurred in government borrowing and repayment of loans to the banking system. After a decline of 3.4 million quetzales between June 30, 1937, and June 30, 1946, the government's fiscal and nonfiscal liabilities to the banks increased by 7.4 million quetzales in the following three years; they amounted to 8.5 million on June 30, 1949. Despite these relatively wide movements, however, fiscal operations appear to have been a secondary rather than a primary causal factor in the variations in the money supply which have occurred since 1937. When movements in Treasury cash balances and official deposits are taken into account, it appears that changes in the balance-of-payments and business borrowing from the banks have had greater significance than fiscal operations for fluctuations in the net means of payment in the hands of the public.

Although the absence of a fully developed government-securities market did not materially affect the stability of the currency during the period under review, there is no guaranty that continuous borrowing from the banking system may not do so in the future; an examination of those forces which have tended either to retard or further the development of a government bond market in Guatemala is thus of prime importance. As of the end of 1949, nonbank investors held none of the direct fiscal debt of the national government, but owned some 1.3 million quetzales of securities guaranteed by the government. In the past, this limited acceptance of government securities by Guatemalan savers has been explained to a large extent by three factors: (1) a deep-rooted fear of the devalorizing effects of inflation on fixed denomination savings in liquid form; (2) the higher yields which may be obtained from others forms of domestic investment, particularly during periods of rising prices; and (3) the relative illiquidity of government securities which results from the state of the government bond market. The government has taken steps to counteract the latter two of these factors; it has attempted to increase the liquidity of its securities by authorizing the Banco de Guatemala to conduct price-supporting operations in the open market and has acted to raise the effective rate of return on its direct and contingent obligations by exempting their ownership, transfer, and yields from all present and future taxes. As the deficits of recent years indicate, however, the authorities have not as yet attacked the psychological root of the trouble, namely, the fear of inflation.

Fiscal operations, of course, also have an important influence on the "money of external origin." If extraordinary payments for the retirement of the external debt in 1944/45 are disregarded, it appears that government expenditures abroad absorbed approximately the same share (about 12 percent) of total government expenditures in 1948/49 as in 1937/38; the substantial reduction in foreign debt service was counteracted by increased purchases of imported merchandise associated with the government's expanded investment program. "Real" government imports averaged about 3.5 percent of total "real" government expenditures in the prewar and early war years, declined to an average of 2 percent in the late war and early postwar years, and then rose to a new level of about 9.5 percent in 1947/48 and 1948/49.

The net effect which the expanded government-investment program has had on the propensity of Guatemala to import also depends on the ratio of "real" private imports to the "real" gross product of the private sector of the economy. In 1947/48, private imports—which had absorbed a smaller percentage of private income in the war and early postwar years than in the prewar years—accounted for about the same share (20 percent) as in the prewar years. If account is taken of (a) the abnormally large imports which were associated with the commencement of large-scale operations at the United Fruit Company's Pacific Coast installations during 1937/38 and 1938/39, and (b) that part of the increase in "real" private income which is explained by the growth of the indigenous labor force, the private sector's marginal propensity to import appears to be slightly larger than its average propensity. It seems evident, however, that the marginal propensity of the government to import is at present significantly higher than that of the private sector. Although the statistical evidence is not absolutely conclusive, it suggests that as taxation curtails the consumption of imported goods, additional government purchases abroad will exceed the curtailment of private imports by a considerable margin, and thus result in a higher total volume of imports.

The Fiscal System and Economic Development (chapter xi)

Total capital formation in Guatemala in 1947/48 is estimated to have amounted to 34.3 million quetzales, or 10 percent of the gross national product. The government provided 48 percent of this total, while the private sector appears to have accounted for the remainder. If allowance is made for unproductive and indirectly productive investment and attention is focused on directly productive investment only, the rate of investment in 1947/48 becomes significantly smaller; productive investment amounted to only 6 percent of the gross national product.

A reasonably stable and high rate of capital formation is not only a sign of the economic vitality of any country, but in the case of Guatemala, like that of other less developed countries, is also one of the basic prerequisites for a rise in the standard of living and economic well-being. Another equally important condition is a rise in the productivity of human effort through improvements in the methods of production, achieved through better training, better supervision, and improved diet without the application of additional capital in the usual sense of the term.

The limited scope of private initiative outside the customary investment channels was one of the main reasons for the establishment of the Production Development Institute (INFOP). Although this autonomous agency has been functioning only since the beginning of 1949, it is noteworthy that it has been accepted by the business and financial community as a valuable and useful addition to the institutional framework of economic development. This favorable reception must be ascribed in part to the absence of direct government intervention in the operations of the Institute, which apparently has managed to translate into reality the legal concept of administrative autonomy. The concentration of INFOP's credit and development activities in the field of agricultural production has also contributed to its acceptance by the business community; observers believe that the Institute was right in its decision to refrain from major manufacturing ventures of the spectacular and politically appealing variety and to avoid capital investment that would strain its limited resources.

The administrative autonomy of the Production Development Institute, which essentially has worked to good advantage, has, however, certain shortcomings. Although close and effective cooperation exists between INFOP and the monetary authorities, the experience of the first year of operation seems to indicate that the fiscal policy of the government, particularly with respect to the timing and financing of public works, has not been co-ordinated with the credit and investment activities of INFOP. It also appears of paramount importance that the government should systematically maintain and replenish the resources of INFOP by carrying out its commitment to allocate a certain proportion of the annual receipts of the Treasury to the Institute. This does not mean that the rate of disbursements for loans and direct purchases by INFOP should be maintained at a constant level. Quite to the contrary, changes in the rate of disbursements by INFOP should be made an important tool of monetary and general economic policy which can exercise a valuable stabilizing influence upon the level of production and real income and assure an adequate rate of economic growth.

Private capital expenditures and government expenditures for economic development also affect the balance of payments. The initial outlays for capital investment purposes usually include a high proportion of foreign expenditures, since machinery and certain classes of construction materials have to be imported; besides, the disbursements for domestic capital formation in the form of wages, salaries, and purchases of domestically produced materials may cause an expansion of income that results in an increased demand for imported consumers' goods. The experience of recent years suggests that more than seventy centavos of each quetzal of investment expenditures eventually find their way abroad, while only eighteen or twenty centavos of each quetzal of consumption expenditures are spent for imports. Even if a rise in investment may involve a commensurate decrease in consumption expenditures, it causes balance-of-payments pressures.

From the standpoint of the long-run growth and balance of the Guatemalan economy, the development and expansion of export industries is the most desirable method of relieving these pressures. Partial reliance upon foreign capital, either through loans or in the form of direct investments, is also likely to be of major practical significance in the years immediately ahead. Fiscal and monetary policies are only two of the factors which determine the attractiveness of Guatemala as an area for foreign investment since political conditions and official labor policies are obviously of equal, or greater, importance in this respect. Three fiscal and monetary factors are likely, however, to influence the attitudes of foreign investors favorably: (1) the maintenance of a free and stable foreign exchange market, (2) the co-ordination of Guatemalan tax policies with the tax laws of other countries, particularly those of the United States, and (3) the avoidance of double taxation of corporate dividends at progressive rates, as stipulated in the proposed income tax law.

Certain forms of social overhead capital (e.g., road construction, technical training facilities, irrigation projects, etc.) are not readily susceptible to private commercial exploitation. Therefore the task of providing such forms of capital falls upon the government or INFOP. It is from the standpoint of the foreign currency cost of such projects that official foreign borrowing is important. As of the end of 1948/49, the external debt amounted to only $670,000, and the service charges were of negligible size. Guatemala could quite easily absorb the foreign-exchange cost of servicing new foreign loans of moderate amounts, provided that a sufficiently large proportion of total investment led to an eventual expansion of exports or replacement of imports. Besides, an increase in social capital would tend to attract additional private funds from abroad, and to encourage domestic private investment.

OVER-ALL EVALUATION

In the course of the last five years, the Guatemalan government has laid the institutional groundwork for its announced policy of supporting the development of new industries, fostering improvements in methods of agricultural production, and providing the country with sufficient social capital to stimulate and assure its continued economic growth. It has reorganized the country's monetary system through the establishment of a new central bank; it has established the Production Development Institute as an autonomous agency of the government to plan and manage a more economic utilization of the country's resources; it has set up the framework of a broad social security system to provide protection against the hazards of disease, accidents, old age, and industrial unemployment.

These new activities put a heavy strain on the fiscal system. The strain has been mitigated in recent years through the availability of Treasury balances accumulated in the course of the war years and by exceedingly favorable conditions in the country's export trade. It is only too obvious, however, that the fiscal system, on the receipts side as well as on the expenditures side, is not yet adapted to cope with the additional tasks which the government is committed to undertake. The government has been reluctant to increase the over-all level of taxes because it did not wish to curtail the level of consumption of the low- and middle-income groups which bear the largest share of the tax burden. It has failed, on the other hand, to gain access to the savings of the relatively small group of the well-to-do.

The fiscal experience of the last few years has shown that the level of tax receipts may be too low if the government intends to carry out its *fomento* objectives. Additional sources of revenue may have to be tapped. In considering new taxes, as well as other changes in the tax structure, two fundamental issues must be faced and resolved. One is the problem of determining to what extent the growth in the level of consumption of the population as a whole can be, and should be, retarded in order to devote a larger proportion of the gross national product to the formation of capital. The other issue pertains to the use to which the resources available for investment can, and should, be put. The latter is probably the key issue of Guatemala's development policy. Its solution involves, on the one hand, a reconsideration of expenditure policies of the government and an improvement of its administrative practices, particularly in the case of the enterprises administered by the Department of National Farms. On the other hand, it suggests the formulation of tax policies which would discourage the investment of private savings in speculative and traditional lines, such as urban real estate and landed property, and encourage the expansion of industrial activities. It must be realized, however, that even the most efficient fiscal practices cannot assure the success of the government's development policies, unless they are accompanied by, and coordinated with, proper monetary policies.

II

THE STRUCTURE OF THE GUATEMALAN ECONOMY

GENERAL DESCRIPTION

GUATEMALA is the most populous, and in territorial extent the third largest, of the Central American republics. Its territory of 42,052 square miles (108,889 square kilometers) extends between the Atlantic and Pacific oceans; it has common borders with Mexico, British Honduras (Belize), Honduras, and El Salvador.

In 1950 Guatemala had a population of 2,786,369.[1] The average density of population is therefore sixty-six persons per square mile (twenty-six per square kilometer). Some areas of the country, however, have a much lower density; the Atlantic coastal region and the partly unexplored northernmost department of El Peten in particular are very sparsely populated. The population is concentrated in the highlands—the heartland of the country. This concentration, together with a net rate of increase of almost 3 percent per year, causes a certain amount of concern regarding the possibility of overpopulation in the more temperate areas in the not too distant future.

The population consists of two socially and culturally distinct groups; by far the larger is the indigenous population of Indian origin, which comprises about two-thirds of the total. The remainder, known as *ladinos*, is of partly European extraction. The Indian population forms the bulk of the rural population in the highlands. The nonindigenous population resides partly in urban centers, partly in rural areas. The largest concentration of urban population (283,100) is found in the capital of the country, Guatemala City, which is also the center of business activity.

[1] Preliminary results of the official population census conducted in April 1950 by the Bureau of the Census (Oficina.Permanente del Censo).

22

THE NATIONAL INCOME OF GUATEMALA[2]

In spite of the growing significance of manufacturing activity and the rather important share of the gross national product originating in services, agricultural production continues to be the principal source of income in the Guatemalan economy. An estimate of the composition of the gross national product in 1947/48, presented in Table 1, shows that agriculture (including cattle raising, fishing, and forestry production) accounts for almost 60 percent of the gross national product. Agriculture is also important as the structural basis for food-processing industries, which account for one-third of the industrial sector of the economy. As a consequence of the predominance of agricultural production, the economy is heavily dependent upon imports as a source of manufactured consumers' and producers' goods. The importance of foreign trade is in turn reflected in the relatively large shares of commercial and transportation services in the gross national product.

From a structural point of view, three major sectors of the economy can be distinguished:

1. Food and crude-material production for domestic consumption. This sector includes the production of such staple crops as corn, beans, rice, vegetables, sugar, meat, and dairy products. It forms the principal form of livelihood for the bulk of the indigenous population.

2. The export crops, i.e., coffee, bananas, and chicle. These commodities account for about one-fourth of total agricultural production and for more than 90 percent of the country's exports.

3. The industrial sector, which is devoted mainly to food processing. In recent years there has been an expansion in the direction of nonfood consumers' goods, such as textiles, leather goods, etc.

These main sectors are supplemented by construction activi-

---

[2] It should be noted that data on the country's national income are not available. The term "national income" is used in this study as synonymous with "gross national product," although it is, of course, realized that the two concepts differ.

ties and by the production of services such as transportation, trade, banking, and an expanding tourist industry.

THE INDIGENOUS SECTOR

More important than the preceding classification of the sectors of the economy is the distinction between the economic ac-

TABLE 1

ESTIMATE OF GROSS NATIONAL PRODUCT, 1947/48[a]

Source		Millions of Quetzales[b]	Percent of Total
Agriculture (including fishing and forestry production)		*189.8*	*56.7*
Corn	45.0		13.5
Coffee	26.1		7.8
Bananas	18.2		5.4
Beans	12.4		3.7
Cattle raising	35.1		10.5
Fishing	0.8		0.2
Other agriculture	52.2		15.6
Manufacturing and mining		*46.3*	*13.8*
Food and beverages	16.0		4.8
Textiles	8.7		2.6
Lumber	4.2		1.2
Other manufacturing, mining, and handicraft	17.4		5.2
Private construction		*4.2*	*1.3*
Private services		*61.1*	*18.2*
Wholesale and retail trade	23.5		7.0
Transportation	11.0		3.3
Housing	17.5		5.2
Other, including professional and domestic services	9.1		2.7
Government		*33.6*	*10.0*
National	30.4		9.1
Municipal and autonomous entities	3.2		0.9
Total gross national product		*335.0[c]*	*100.0*

[a] For a brief description of the sources and methods of computation of the estimates, see the Statistical Note to chapter ii.

[b] One quetzal (of 100 centavos) equals one United States dollar.

[c] This estimate of gross national product represents the total output of goods and services produced in Guatemala. Since it was derived from production rather than expenditure data and since for purposes of fiscal analysis a measure of total output rather than total expenditure is desired, no adjustment has been made to allow for the balance of the transactions of the Guatemalan economy with the rest of the world. The figure thus represents the national product produced and not the product available.

tivities of the indigenous and the nonindigenous or *ladino* population. The basic difference between these two social classes and racial groups lies in the fact that the indigenous population participates only partly, or seasonally, in the market economy. Although living conditions and social habits vary somewhat from region to region, the typical Indian family derives its livelihood in considerable part from a household economy which consists of the production of staple crops and of textiles for the family's own use. The household-economy aspect of the indigenous way of life is somewhat modified by the exchange of foods that takes place in the local produce markets where surplus stocks of food and other products are sold and deficiencies made up by purchases from other families. The income from the household production is usually supplemented by the seasonal employment of one or more members of the family in the "commercial" sector of the economy, primarily in coffee plantations. Money wages (of an average of thirty-five centavos per day) are supplemented by payments in kind, consisting primarily of corn, beans, and rice. A certain proportion of the Indian population resides permanently on plantations where the Indians are allowed to cultivate small areas for a part of their food requirements; but this does not basically change the dual character of the indigenous mode of living as partly agricultural worker and partly small-scale agricultural producer.

As a result of the limited interaction of the indigenous population with the commercial sector of the economy, together with the prevalence of very primitive methods of production, there is a substantial difference between the per capita income and standard of living of the indigenous and the nonindigenous populations. On the basis of the gross national product estimates presented above, it appears that the aggregate share of the indigenous population in the gross national product amounted in 1947/48 to 121 million quetzales, or slightly less than Q70 per capita. This contrasts sharply with an average per capita income of Q246 for the nonindigenous population.

The differences which distinguish the indigenous from the nonindigenous sector of the Guatemalan economy are obviously of great importance for the purpose of this study. As will be shown in detail later, the limited participation of the indigenous population in the market economy results in a substantially smaller incidence of taxation upon them; conversely, it seems reasonably clear that the indigenous population benefits to a smaller extent from the services that the government provides than does the nonindigenous population.

THE GROWTH OF THE ECONOMY

On the basis of incomplete information regarding prices and the volume of production in various sectors of the economy, a series of estimates of the value of the gross national product was prepared covering the period from 1936/37 to 1947/48.[3] This series has been supplemented by an index of the value of production of the economically more advanced "commercial sector" of the economy. This index, which is based on industrial production and international trade data, undertakes to show the changes in the gross product of the private sector of the economy, which is engaged in the production of goods and services for the national and international markets. The index, it should be stressed, is not an index of the gross product of the nonindigenous sector of the economy, since the indigenous population takes part in the production of some of the more important segments of this "commercial sector," i.e., in the production of coffee and chicle.

Table 2 conveys the impression that the gross national product remained fairly stable during the first half of the period under consideration but in subsequent years increased rapidly. This acceleration, however, is largely accounted for by price increases in the postwar years. It may be noted in passing that the composition of the gross national product has not undergone any major significant changes. The ˉare of agricultural production

---

[3] With the exception of three years for which agricultural production data proved to be too unreliable to form the basis for such estimates.

has increased somewhat in the last year, but this increase was primarily due to the larger price increases that occurred in the agricultural sector; conversely, the rise is accounted for by the depressed level of agricultural prices that prevailed in the prewar years.

TABLE 2

ESTIMATES OF THE GROSS NATIONAL PRODUCT, BY MAJOR SECTORS
1936/37 TO 1947/48

(*In millions of quetzales*)

Fiscal Year	Gross National Product	Agri-culture	Meat and Dairy Products	Manu-facturing and Mining	Govern-ment	All Others
1936/37	120.3	51.7	13.8	20.4	8.8	25.5
1937/38	113.6	38.0	13.0	19.6	9.4	34.2
1938/39	98.8	41.2	12.3	13.9	8.7	22.8
1939/40	113.6	53.9	11.9	14.0	8.4	24.7
1940/41	114.9	52.5	11.8	15.4	8.9	26.1
1941/42	132.7	63.7	14.6	19.4	8.8	25.7
1942/43	178.2	92.3	18.1	22.3	9.5	34.4
1943/44 ....*	.....	18.0	21.4	11.1	....	
1944/45	.....	24.4	25.5	11.9	....	
1945/46	239.9	108.2	26.9	32.3	21.9	50.3
1946/47	.....	30.9	35.7	26.0	....	
1947/48	335.0	153.9	35.1	46.3	33.6	66.1

* Not available.

A comparison of changes in the gross national product with those of the commercial sector (see Table 3) discloses that the movements of the gross national product were somewhat more erratic than changes in the product of the commercial sector, although, of course, there was a considerable degree of correlation. The gross national product went through a depression of substantial proportions between 1936/37 and 1941/42; the movements of the commercial sector lagged one year behind this cycle, presumably because they were strongly influenced by the prewar expansion and subsequent contraction of international trade as a result of the war. The impact of the war is also reflected in the divergence of the figures in 1942/43 and 1945/46. Difficulties originating from abroad beset and retarded the expansion of the commercial sector, while the noncommercial sector apparently benefited money-income-wise from the war-caused scarcities.

In order to present a measure of the real social and economic progress of the Guatemalan economy in the course of the last

TABLE 3

INDEXES OF GROSS NATIONAL PRODUCT AND PRODUCT OF COMMERCIAL
SECTOR AT CURRENT PRICES, 1936/37 TO 1947/48

(1936/37 = 100)

Fiscal Year	Gross National Product	Product of Commercial Sector
1936/37	100.0	100.0
1937/38	94.6	105.5
1938/39	82.3	94.0
1939/40	94.4	84.2
1940/41	95.7	82.1
1941/42	110.4	93.1
1942/43	148.3	105.3
1943/44	*	112.9
1944/45	.....	134.3
1945/46	199.6	154.3
1946/47	.....	213.3
1947/48	278.8	287.6

* Not available.

decade, changes in the price level have been eliminated in the figures shown in Table 4. The resulting series of estimates of the "real" gross national product shows that between 1936/37 and 1947/48 the sum total of goods and services produced by the Guatemalan economy rose 47 percent, or at an average annual rate of approximately 4 percent. The largest growth occurred in the government sector, which more than doubled in "real" terms.[4] The next largest "real" expansion was recorded in "All Others," reflecting a rapid growth of most service industries, such as transportation (particularly air transportation), hotels, etc.

Table 5 concludes the quantitative description of the domestic

[4] Government data shown in this chapter pertain to income payments (wages, salaries, pensions) only. They do not give a direct indication of the "size" of government.

aspects of the Guatemalan economy. It shows estimates of the average per capita income of the total population in money as well as in "real" terms. In evaluating these figures, it must be kept in

TABLE 4

ESTIMATES OF THE "REAL" GROSS NATIONAL PRODUCT, BY MAJOR SECTORS
1936/37 TO 1947/48

(In millions of quetzales at 1947/48 prices)

Fiscal Year	Gross National Product	Agri- culture	Meat and Dairy Products	Manufac- turing and Mining	Govern- ment	All Others
1936/37	227.8	105.1	24.4	39.4	14.3	44.4
1937/38	208.0	94.0	27.9	36.1	14.4	35.4
1938/39	224.5	111.1	25.0	28.0	14.2	44.6
1939/40	240.9	124.4	26.1	28.6	14.5	45.3
1940/41	259.0	135.1	25.8	30.9	16.2	48.9
1941/42	266.3	148.8	28.4	32.6	14.5	39.4
1942/43	289.1	151.6	30.5	34.7	16.7	48.9
1943/44 ....*	.....	28.6	32.6	18.2	....
1944/45	.....	28.5	33.5	16.2	....
1945/46	278.4	135.6	29.7	39.9	22.0	50.3
1946/47	.....	32.2	40.2	26.0	....
1947/48	335.0	153.9	35.1	46.3	33.6	66.1

* Not available.

TABLE 5

PER CAPITA INCOME, IN MONEY AND "REAL" TERMS, 1936/37 TO 1947/48

Fiscal Year	In Million Quetzales			In Quetzales	
	In Money Terms	In "Real" Terms[a]	Population[b] *(In thousands)*	In money Terms	In "Real" Terms[a]
1936/37	120.3	227.8	2,184.6	61.4	104.3
1937/38	113.6	208.0	2,221.1	51.1	93.6
1938/39	98.8	224.5	2,255.0	43.8	99.6
1939/40	113.6	240.9	2,283.8	49.7	105.5
1940/41	114.9	259.0	2,325.5	49.4	111.4
1941/42	132.7	266.3	2,364.7	56.1	112.6
1942/43	178.2	289.1	2,390.8	74.5	120.9
1943/44 ....*	.....	2,422.1	....	.....
1944/45	.....	2,461.2	....	.....
1945/46	239.9	278.4	2,508.2	95.6	111.0
1946/47	.....	2,555.2	....	.....
1947/48	335.0	335.0	2,610.0	128.4	128.4

[a] At 1947/48 prices.
[b] Annual projection based on 1947/48 estimate and on data of annual birth and death rates.
* Not available.

mind that their intrinsic meaning is limited since aside from the wide range of the income distribution which prevails in every country of the world, the Guatemalan average actually lumps together the mean income of two distinct social and economic classes. This fact, together with the technical and conceptual difficulties involved in international income comparisons in general, narrowly circumscribes the validity of the comparison of the Guatemalan figure with the statistics of other countries. Nevertheless, the average per capita income figures for a group of other countries presented in Table 6 are believed to give a rough indication of the relative state of the economic development of Guatemala.

According to the table, the Guatemalan per capita income

TABLE 6

PER CAPITA INCOME IN SELECTED COUNTRIES, 1947/48[a]

(*In United States dollars*)

Country	Per Capita Income
Ecuador (1948/49)	$ 64
Dominican Republic (1946)	86
El Salvador[b] (1946)	87
Peru	105
Brazil[c] (1948)	125
Guatemala[b]	128
Colombia	169
Mexico	190
Spain (1946/47)	314
Uruguay	316
Cuba	325
Netherlands	460
United Kingdom	755
Switzerland	870
Canada	916
Sweden	998
United States	1,472

[a] Except as otherwise indicated.
[b] Per capita gross national product.
[c] Original data converted at average between free and official rates of exchange.
General Note: Original data converted at official rate of exchange.
Sources: For national income data: International Monetary Fund, *Financial Statistics* (monthly), and unpublished official and private estimates. For population data: United Nations, *Monthly Bulletin of Statistics*.

ranks approximately at the median level of the Latin-American republics for which data are shown. But since it is probable that data are lacking for more countries with a lower-income level than for countries with higher incomes, Guatemala's income may actually be somewhat higher in relative terms than its position in the table indicates. Moreover, because of unrealistic exchange rates, the estimates for some countries seem to be somewhat too high.

The Guatemalan "real" per capita income has risen during the period under consideration by 23 percent. The average annual rate of increase thus was slightly more than 2 percent. This rate of increase compares rather favorably with that prevailing in economically more mature countries and, in all probability, also with that of most underdeveloped countries. It remains to be seen, however, to what extent the rise in "real" per capita income in recent years represents a lasting gain, and to what extent it has been due to temporarily favorable circumstances, such as the high prices that Guatemala's chief export, coffee, brings in foreign markets. In order to pursue this question further and to appraise the significance of foreign trade to the Guatemalan economy in general, we now turn to a brief description of Guatemala's international transactions.

THE INTERNATIONAL ACCOUNTS OF THE GUATEMALAN ECONOMY

Data on merchandise trade are shown in Table 7. A comparison of these figures with the national income estimates reveals the importance of foreign trade to the Guatemalan economy, a situation which is the result of a large part of the gross national product originating in agricultural production both for export and for domestic food requirements. From an examination of Table 8, which summarizes the commodity pattern of Guatemalan trade, it is clear that the country is heavily dependent upon foreign sources for finished manufactures. Such goods accounted for nearly three-fourths of the value of all imports in 1948 and an even larger part of the total during the preceding decade. The economy is largely self-sufficient in foodstuffs, however; food imports, consisting mostly of nonessential foodstuffs of a luxury and semiluxury variety, account for only a minor part of total imports.

TABLE 7

BALANCE OF TRADE OF GUATEMALA, 1936 TO 1949

(In thousands of quetzales)

Year	Value of Exports[a] (f.o.b.)	Value of Imports (c.i.f.)	Trade balance
1936	16,926.7	14,389.9	+ 2,536.8
1937	17,905.0	20,928.6	− 3,023.6
1938	18,232.5	20,951.7	− 2,719.2
1939	18,781.8	19,119.7	− 337.9
1940	12,039.5	15,833.7	− 3,794.2
1941	14,502.8	16,098.9	− 1,596.1
1942	20,437.6	13,671.6	+ 6,766.0
1943	20,154.2	17,849.5	+ 2,304.7
1944	23,856.7	20,702.6	+ 3,154.1
1945	30,435.8	23,348.8	+ 7,087.0
1946	36,679.1	36,203.6	+ 475.5
1947	52,032.9	57,319.3	− 5,286.4
1948	50,165.5	68,349.9	−18,184.4
1949	51,932.6	67,983.8	−16,051.2

[a] Trade return data; unadjusted for undervaluation of banana exports.

Source: General Statistical Office (Dirección General de Estadística).

Exports are dominated by three commodities: coffee, bananas, and chicle, which together form approximately 85 percent of the total value of exports. Coffee is by far the most important export commodity, accounting for considerably more than half of total export receipts. While such a degree of dependence upon a single crop has often exposed a country to considerable risks, Guatemalan coffee exports are less susceptible to misfortune in the market than would appear to be the case merely from a consideration of the relative importance of coffee exports. There are two principal reasons for this: first, the United States market, which in recent years has absorbed nearly all of the coffee exported by Guatemala, has greatly expanded over the last decade because of a growing per capita consumption of coffee which apparently repre-

TABLE 8

COMMODITY PATTERN OF GUATEMALAN TRADE, 1936 TO 1948

(As percent of total value of exports[a] and imports)

	1936	1937	1938	1939	1940	1941	1942	1943	1944	1945	1946	1947	1948
Percentage composition of exports by commodity:													
Bananas	25.0	26.7	29.1	32.3	48.2	33.0	17.3	8.5	13.3	19.4	23.7	22.4	20.6
Chicle	0.9	1.9	3.1	4.6	5.1	7.9	6.3	5.8	5.8	8.4	8.0	7.6	4.9
Coffee	69.5	65.2	61.3	56.1	39.0	51.3	64.8	66.8	63.6	58.2	55.6	61.2	61.2
Essential oils	0.3	0.4	0.3	0.4	0.9	1.2	1.8	1.7	1.7	2.0	2.7	1.0	1.7
Other	4.3	5.8	6.2	6.6	6.8	6.6	9.8	17.2	15.6	12.0	10.0	7.8	11.6
Total	100.0	100.0	100.0	100.0	100.0	100.0	100.0	100.0	100.0	100.0	100.0	100.0	100.0
Percentage composition of imports by economic classes:													
Crude foodstuffs	0.4	0.4	0.6	0.3	0.4	1.3	0.4	1.9	1.2	1.0	1.2	0.9	0.7
Manufactured foodstuffs	8.6	8.8	7.8	7.6	8.1	7.7	8.0	9.9	9.3	12.5	9.4	10.3	10.2
Crude materials and semimanufactures	10.9	9.0	9.8	11.1	15.8	15.9	15.4	14.8	12.8	11.9	12.2	12.0	14.5
Finished manufactures	79.9	81.5	81.1	80.8	75.7	75.0	75.7	71.5	74.7	74.5	77.0	76.8	74.6
Other[b]	0.2	0.3	0.7	0.2		0.1	0.5	1.9	2.0	0.1	0.2		
Total	100.0	100.0	100.0	100.0	100.0	100.0	100.0	100.0	100.0	100.0	100.0	100.0	100.0

[a] Export values unadjusted for undervaluation of bananas; the percentage figures therefore understate the importance of banana exports and overstate that of other commodities.
[b] Primarily art objects.

sents a permanent change of consumption habits; and second, Guatemala, like El Salvador and Colombia, produces a mild "blue" coffee which, because of its outstanding quality and its use for blending with hard Brazilian coffee, has a much more elastic demand than hard varieties. As a consequence, Guatemala has rarely experienced difficulty in disposing of its entire exportable production of coffee at comparatively satisfactory prices.

Banana exports are also a significant source of foreign exchange. Although accounting for a somewhat smaller share of export receipts in recent years than before the war, they amounted to some 20 percent of the total in 1948. It should be noted, however, that as a result of an undervaluation of banana exports, this percentage, shown in Table 8, understates the true importance of banana exports (and, by the same token, overstates the value of other exports). The undervaluation occurs in the banana exports of the United Fruit Company, which ships the bananas to its own sales organizations in the United States and in Europe. United Fruit reports a fictitious export price which is substantially below the market price at which independent exporters report their sales.

Chicle ranks third in value among Guatemalan exports but is of much less importance than coffee and bananas. In the period under consideration, chicle exports achieved their greatest relative importance in 1945 when they accounted for somewhat more than 8 percent of the total. By 1948 this proportion had declined to less than 5 percent.

Estimates of the Guatemalan balances of payments for the years 1947 through 1949, prepared by the Research Department of the Banco de Guatemala, are presented in Table 9. They present a more accurate statement of the value of exports and also provide information on interest and dividend payments, service transactions, and capital movements. The most important foreign-owned enterprises whose investment is estimated at $140 million are those of the United Fruit Company, the Electric Company, and the International Railways of Central America. In 1947, substantial interest and dividend payments were made on these invest-

TABLE 9

BALANCE OF PAYMENTS OF GUATEMALA, 1947 TO 1949

(*In thousands of quetzales*)

	1947		1948		1949	
	Debit	Credit	Debit	Credit	Debit	Credit
Current Transactions:						
Merchandise f.o.b. (adjusted)	50,880.5	76,653.4	61,509.5	71,823.9	60,909.0	62,315.1
Services:						
Freight	5,597.0	.....	6,941.4	.....	7,715.9	.....
Tourist	559.8	1,866.1	502.2	2,511.0	383.2	1,196.0
Films	260.8	.....	315.3	.....	408.7	.....
Insurance	1,823.1	710.4	2,209.0	937.7	2,505.4	1,098.5
Banking commissions	7.5	1.4	9.7	1.0	3.2	0.3
Diplomatic and consular services	688.2	1,087.3	793.6	1,232.9	830.9	1,864.4
Government services (including international contributions)	161.4	2,278.1	125.1	2,145.5	532.0	1,788.8
Other services	225.0	27.5	251.4	.....	405.1	.....
Remittances:						
Family	80.3	.....	79.7	102.4	89.5	128.8
Student	36.4	.....	14.2	.....	38.3	.....
Interest and dividends:						
Public debt	28.1	.....	21.1	.....	17.7	.....
Private companies	14,060.9	36.7	8,700.2	30.5	2,005.8	23.9
Total current transactions	74,409.0	82,660.9	81,472.4	78,784.9	75,844.7	68,415.8
Capital Transactions:						
Capital movements	4,797.2	1,082.9	1,173.7	1,302.9	920.8	5,993.1
Monetary gold movements	1.6	.....	1.0	.....	.....	.....
Foreign exchange movements	4,151.1	.....	.....	5,878.7	.....	9,021.7
Total capital transactions	8,949.9	1,082.9	1,174.7	7,181.6	920.8	15,014.8
Errors and omissions	384.9	.....	3,319.4	.....	6,665.1	.....
Total international transactions	83,743.8	83,743.8	85,966.5	85,966.5	83,430.6	83,430.6

Source: Bank of Guatemala.

ments, exceeding receipts under the same heading by more than 14 million quetzales. They declined sharply, however, in 1948 and 1949 to 8.7 and 2 million quetzales, respectively. The movements were not large enough, however, to offset the postwar rise in imports, which continued through 1948, and the fall in export proceeds in 1949. The changes in the merchandise and service accounts together resulted in a shift from a substantial current account surplus in 1947 to a deficit in 1948 which increased further in 1949.

The figures shown under the heading of capital transactions reveal that in 1947 a net outflow of capital of 3.7 million quetzales took place; in 1948 an insignificant inflow of capital occurred; in 1949, however, a substantial net inflow of long-term private investment, which in most instances took the form of imports of capital equipment, was recorded. These transactions were accompanied by an increase in Guatemala's foreign-exchange holdings in 1947 and considerable losses in 1948 and 1949. The large amounts recorded as "errors and omissions" seem to indicate that at least a part of the decline in foreign-exchange holdings was due to transfers of private Guatemalan funds to foreign countries, particularly to the United States.

A measure of the "real" returns to Guatemala from its international trade is provided by the index of the terms of trade presented in Table 10. The war years were characterized by a considerable deterioration of the terms of trade owing to the imposition of price controls in the United States. Because coffee prices rose less rapidly than the prices of Guatemalan imports from the United States in the period before controls were imposed, the initial differential was perpetuated in the years immediately following. Since the end of the war, however, Guatemala's exports have appreciated substantially in terms of their purchasing power over imports—by two-thirds over the entire period and by more than half since the end of the war. In view of the pronounced rise in the price of coffee which occurred during the last year (1949/50) and the comparatively stable prices of Guatemala's imports in the same period, it appears certain that a further improvement in the terms of trade has taken place.

TABLE 10

INDEX OF TERMS OF TRADE OF GUATEMALA, 1936 TO 1949

(1936 = 100)

Year	Index of Import Prices[a]	Index of Export Prices[b]	Index of Terms of Trade[c]
1936	100.0	100.0	100.0
1937	105.6	107.0	101.3
1938	100.8	100.8	100.0
1939	98.8	118.9	120.3
1940	106.7	77.2	73.4
1941	112.4	104.1	92.6
1942	139.3	140.1	100.5
1943	153.1	145.2	94.8
1944	176.7	154.6	87.5
1945	175.3	184.9	105.5
1946	160.5	232.3	144.7
1947	192.5	268.5	139.5
1948	201.4	283.9	141.0
1949	187.6	312.7	166.6

[a] Based on the price indexes of United States exports by economic classes, compiled by the United States Department of Commerce. The component indexes were weighted by the value of the corresponding classes of Guatemalan imports in 1949. The original United States crude-material and semimanufacture indexes were combined in order to conform to the Guatemalan classification.

[b] Index of unit values of five leading Guatemalan export commodities (coffee, bananas, chicle, essential oils, and lumber), weighted by value of exports in 1949.

[c] Index of export prices divided by index of import prices. A rise in the index means an improvement in the terms of trade for Guatemala.

Another significant aspect of Guatemala's international position is the regional distribution of its trade, shown for the years 1936 through 1948 in Table 11. During the entire period the United States has been both the principal source of imports and the chief purchaser of Guatemalan exports. Before the war, various European countries, especially Germany, also accounted for a considerable part of Guatemala's exports and imports; but with European sources and markets isolated by the war, the United States became an even more important trading partner, a position it has retained, more or less, in the postwar period. For the period as a whole, the United States share of imports increased

TABLE 11

GEOGRAPHICAL PATTERN OF GUATEMALAN TRADE, 1936 TO 1948

(*As percent of value of total exports and imports*)

	1936	1937	1938	1939	1940	1941	1942	1943	1944	1945	1946	1947	1948
Percentage composition of exports by destination:													
Canada	0.4	1.4	0.5	0.8	1.3	4.0	0.7	0.5	5.4	2.7	4.8	5.7	3.9
France	1.5	1.3	0.6	0.4	...	...	...	...	...	...	...	...	...
Germany	18.5	17.4	14.1	11.5	...	...	...	...	...	...	...	...	...
Netherlands	6.7	4.5	5.2	5.2	...	...	...	...	...	...	0.2	0.7	0.5
Sweden	4.6	4.1	4.3	5.6	3.0	1.0	...	...	...	...	4.0	2.1	0.6
United Kingdom	2.3	0.6	0.3	0.4	2.0	0.1	0.1	0.1	0.5	0.5	...	0.4	1.4
United States	59.3	64.1	69.4	70.7	91.0	92.3	92.1	89.3	87.0	90.7	86.5	86.5	88.9
All other countries	6.7	6.6	5.6	5.4	2.7	2.6	7.1	10.1	7.1	6.1	4.5	4.6	4.7
Total	100.0	100.0	100.0	100.0	100.0	100.0	100.0	100.0	100.0	100.0	100.0	100.0	100.0
Percentage composition of imports by origin:													
Canada	0.5	0.3	0.9	0.7	1.3	1.5	1.4	1.5	1.8	1.5	2.8	2.1	2.1
El Salvador	0.8	0.3	0.4	0.3	0.8	2.0	4.5	5.0	2.2	1.6	2.8	1.6	2.3
Germany	31.0	32.4	35.0	27.0	2.8	0.3	...	...	...	...	...	...	...
Mexico	3.2	1.6	0.9	1.1	2.0	2.4	7.3	16.6	18.0	14.6	10.8	5.3	2.7
Netherlands West Indies	...	...	0.5	1.2	4.0	2.9	1.3	1.7	1.5	1.0	2.4	2.2	2.4
Peru	1.3	1.5	1.4	1.7	2.2	3.2	4.0	3.7	3.0	2.9	3.1	2.3	0.8
United Kingdom	8.6	8.0	6.0	3.7	1.6	2.3	2.5	2.6	1.6	1.0	0.3	1.7	2.2
United States	42.4	45.3	44.7	54.5	73.9	78.5	70.5	60.6	61.6	67.4	67.7	74.7	76.2
All other countries	12.2	10.6	10.2	9.8	11.4	6.9	8.5	8.3	10.3	10.0	10.1	10.1	11.3
Total	100.0	100.0	100.0	100.0	100.0	100.0	100.0	100.0	100.0	100.0	100.0	100.0	100.0

Source: Ministry of Finance; General Statistical Office.

from 42 percent in 1936 to 76 percent in 1948, while the proportion of exports taken by the United States rose from 59 percent to 89 percent.

STATISTICAL NOTE

Agriculture.—The estimates of agricultural output were largely based on production figures published by the General Statistical Office. Some of the commodity statistics were derived from consumption data contained in a sample survey of 222 indigenous families, made by the Indigenous Institute (Instituto Indigenista) under the direction of Antonio Goubaud Carrera (hereafter referred to as the Goubaud Carrera study). Another source was a cost-of-living study prepared by Jorge Arias B. for the General Statistical Office (*Estudio sobre las condiciones de la vida de 179 familias en la ciudad de Guatemala*) and published in June 1948 (Arias study).

Manufacturing and Mining.—These estimates, based on the industrial census of 1946, were adjusted for certain omissions and changes that occurred between 1946 and the fiscal year 1947/48. The data were supplemented by estimates of the handicraft production of textiles, footwear, tools, and household goods of the indigenous population. The figures shown are estimates for value added, i.e., the value of raw materials and fuel of domestic agricultural or foreign origin are not included.

Private Construction.—These figures are based on data published by the General Statistical Office on construction activities in Guatemala City, supplemented by estimates of the value of rural construction. The latter estimates were provided by the Production Development Institute (Instituto de Fomento de la Producción). As in the case of manufacturing and mining, the cost of construction materials has been excluded.

Private Services.—"Value added" of wholesale and retail trade was based on payroll data of commercial enterprises supplied by the Guatemalan Social Security Institute (Instituto Guatemalteco de Seguridad Social). These data were supplemented by additional estimates in order to account for enterprises not yet covered by the social security scheme, and for business profits. Transportation services were estimated in part on the basis of payroll data published by the International Railways of Central America (IRCA), partly on the registration and gasoline consumption of trucks and partly on data of gross receipts of autobus transportation enterprises supplied by the General Statistical Office. The estimate of housing includes imputed rents, as well as rentals actually paid; it was partly derived from the Goubaud Carrera and Arias studies.

Government.—These estimates pertain only to salary and wage payments by the national government, municipalities, and autonomous entities, since government expenditures for material purchases are already included in the agricultural and industrial production estimates. It should be noted that the data shown in the estimate cover only one part of the government's share in the gross national product.

III

GOVERNMENT RECEIPTS

INTRODUCTION

HAVING presented in the preceding chapter a brief description of the salient features of the Guatemalan economy, we now proceed to the subject matter proper of this study—the receipts and expenditures of the Guatemalan public authorities. In this and the following chapter, the volume and composition of public revenues and expenditures in the last twelve years are analyzed and their administration described.

Total expenditures and receipts of the national government, the municipalities, and the autonomous entities established by the national government are shown in Table 12. The very large increase in the fiscal operations of the public authorities, which the figures reflect, must not be taken as an indication of a major ex-

TABLE 12

PUBLIC RECEIPTS AND EXPENDITURES IN GUATEMALA, 1937/38 TO 1948/49ᵃ

(In thousands of quetzales)

Fiscal Year	Receipts	Expenditures
1937/38	14,066.5	12,718.5
1938/39	15,120.1	15,289.0
1939/40	14,030.2	13,014.9
1940/41	13,610.4	12,580.8
1941/42	14,049.6	12,936.9
1942/43	16,334.9	15,279.5
1943/44	19,983.9	16,874.9
1944/45	19,937.8	25,838.7
1945/46	33,619.9	32,430.5
1946/47	44,328.6	40,016.0
1947/48	45,554.7	51,113.3
1948/49	52,480.2	53,797.5

ᵃ Figures include receipts and expenditures of the national government, municipalities, San Carlos University, Social Security Institute, National Olympic Committee, and Production Development Institute. Revenues and expenditures of the national government are shown on a cash basis; they include loan receipts and debt payments.

41

pansion of the role of government in the Guatemalan economy. A large proportion of the rise, particularly in the last five years, is accounted for by increases in the price level as well as by the expansion of government activities through the acquisition by expropriation of a large number of plantations and other enterprises; the assumption of additional functions in the field of social security and economic development by the government was responsible for only a relatively small share of the increase.

TOTAL RECEIPTS

Table 13 shows a breakdown of total public revenues by the various fiscal authorities for the period 1937/38 through 1948/49. The most striking change reflected in the table was the establishment of autonomous entities. Two of the latter, the Social Security Institute (Instituto Guatemalteco de Seguridad Social) and the Production Development Institute (Instituto de Fomento de la Producción) are new institutions; until 1946, San Carlos University was under the administrative jurisdiction of the Ministry of Public Education, and all its receipts (and expenditures) were included in the fiscal accounts of the government.[1] In spite of the growth of these autonomous entities, whose fiscal significance is likely to increase in the future, the receipts of the national government have remained of paramount importance; with the exception of the war years, they accounted for approximately 90 percent of all public revenues. The relative importance of municipal revenues, on the other hand, has declined. Until 1945/46 their receipts ranged between 11 and 16 percent of total public revenues; in the last three years, however, their relative share has declined to around 7 percent.

[1] The Banco de Guatemala and the National Mortgage Credit Institute (Credito Hipotecario Nacional) are also autonomous entities, but since their receipts and expenditures are primarily of a nonfiscal nature, they are not included in this or subsequent tables. The corresponding table on expenditures includes another autonomous entity, the National Olympic Committee; but since the committee did not obtain any receipts aside from the transfer of funds from the national government, it does not appear in Table 13. In 1949, the Department of National Farms (Departamento de Fincas Rusticas Nacionales e Intervenidas), whose receipts and expenditures were in part heretofore included in the accounts of the national government, was reorganized as an autonomous agency.

TABLE 13

Receipts of National Government, Municipalities, and Autonomous Entities, 1937/38 to 1948/49

Fiscal Year	Total		National Government		Municipalities		San Carlos University		Social Security Institute		Production Development Institute	
	Q1,000	Percent of Total	Q1,000	Percent of Total	Q1,000	Percent of Total	Q1,000	Percent of Total	Q1,000	Percent of Total	Q1,000	Percent of Total
1937/38	14,066.5	100.0	12,452.2	88.5	1,614.3	11.5	....	...	....	...	...	...
1938/39	15,120.1	100.0	13,456.3	89.0	1,663.8	11.0	....	...	....	...	...	...
1939/40	14,030.2	100.0	12,144.0	86.6	1,886.2	13.4	....	...	....	...	...	...
1940/41	13,610.4	100.0	11,612.0	85.3	1,998.4	14.7	....	...	....	...	...	...
1941/42	14,049.6	100.0	12,065.4	85.9	1,984.2	14.1	....	...	....	...	...	...
1942/43	16,334.9	100.0	12,855.1	84.8	2,479.8	15.2	....	...	....	...	...	...
1943/44	19,983.9	100.0	16,824.2	84.2	3,159.7	15.8	....	...	....	...	...	...
1944/45	19,937.8	100.0	17,000.1	85.3	2,937.7	14.7	....	...	....	...	...	...
1945/46	33,619.9	100.0	30,136.3	89.6	3,413.6	10.2	70.0	0.2	....	...	...	...
1946/47	44,328.6	100.0	40,823.1	92.1	3,365.5	7.6	140.0	0.3	....	...	...	...
1947/48	45,554.7	100.0	41,918.7	92.0	3,166.0	6.9	220.0	0.5	250.0	0.5	...	...
1948/49	52,480.2	100.0	47,041.2[a]	89.6	3,842.8	7.3	190.3	0.4	1,401.6	2.7	4.3	0.0[b]

[a] Excluding proceeds of sale of United States government bond of $1 million.
[b] Less than 0.05 percent.

RECEIPTS OF THE NATIONAL GOVERNMENT

The data on the receipts of the Guatemalan government that are published in the annual reports (*Memoria*) of the Court and Control Office of Accounts (Tribunal y Contraloría de Cuentas) pertain to revenues provided for in the annual budget. They do not include nonbudgetary receipts such as the proceeds of loans, or the annual contributions of the United States government to the construction of the Roosevelt (Pan American) Highway, or certain amounts of tax revenues that are assigned to autonomous entities, or for the accumulation of sinking funds; moreover, they do not make allowance for the fact that certain receipts, primarily from import duties, are not immediately received when they are recorded. The differences between these budget liquidation figures and cash receipts are relatively insignificant in earlier years; but, as a comparison of the figures shown in Table 14 indicates, they assume major proportions in the last three years.

The cash receipts data include the following amounts of loan proceeds:[2]

Year	Thousand Quetzales
1938/39	1,000.0
1946/47	121.7
1947/48	1,178.7
1948/49	1,736.8

The "loan" obtained in 1938/39 was actually an advance payment of taxes by the United Fruit Company; it was used to repay an earlier loan obtained from the Bank of London and South America and was offset by the tax and other liabilities incurred by the United Fruit Company in the same and in the following year. The data shown for the last three years represent proceeds of loans obtained from the Banco de Guatemala and the National Mortgage Credit Institute.[3]

[2] The sources of the data on cash receipts, and cash expenditures are shown in the Statistical Note at the end of this chapter, which also contains references to the sources of other data shown here.

[3] For a more detailed discussion of the government's credit operations, see chapter iv.

Receipts from all other sources are further analyzed in Table 15. Taxes are of course the principal source of national government receipts, accounting for more than three-fourths of the total in 1948/49. But the inclusion of gross receipts of the nationalized farms since 1945/46 has greatly enhanced the significance of receipts from government enterprises. Noncommercial revenues are also derived from public services, consisting chiefly of the postal and communications system.

TABLE 14

RECEIPTS OF THE NATIONAL GOVERNMENT, 1937/38 TO 1948/49

(In thousands of quetzales)

Fiscal Year	Budget Liqui-dation Receipts	Cash Receipts[a]
1937/38	12,497.5	12,452.2
1938/39	13,410.7	13,456.3
1939/40	12,150.2	12,144.0
1940/41	11,589.8	11,612.0
1941/42	11,956.0	12,065.4
1942/43	13,711.8	13,855.1
1943/44	16,818.0	16,824.2
1944/45	16,876.6	17,000.1
1945/46	29,393.4	30,136.3
1946/47	40,536.1	40,823.1
1947/48	39,631.0	41,918.7
1948/49	44,452.5	47,041.2[b]

[a] Including nonbudgetary receipts from loans.
[b] Excluding proceeds of sale of United States government bond of $1 million.

Historical Survey

As Table 15 indicates, government receipts have grown steadily except during the depression years 1930–33 when declining incomes and prices were reflected in substantially lower tax yields. Somewhat similar movements in the revenues derived from public services and business enterprises of the national government also occurred during the same interval. In general, the relative importance of the various sources of revenues throughout the period showed little change, with the exception of receipts from government enterprises. Another exception to the generally

TABLE 15
NATIONAL GOVERNMENT RECEIPTS, EXCLUDING LOANS, BY SOURCES, 1927/28 TO 1948/49
(In thousands of quetzales)

Fiscal Year	Total Q1,000	Total Percent of Total	Taxes Q1,000	Taxes Percent of Total	Public Services Q1,000	Public Services Percent of Total	Government Enterprises Q1,000	Government Enterprises Percent of Total	Other Receipts Q1,000	Other Receipts Percent of Total
1927/28	13,849.8	100.0	12,412.3	89.6	745.0	5.4	99.3	0.7	593.2	4.3
1928/29	15,397.7	100.0	13,024.5	84.6	1,072.1	7.0	283.9	1.5	1,062.2	6.9
1929/30	13,426.3	100.0	11,759.1	87.6	1,109.3	8.3	257.1	1.9	300.8	2.2
1930/31	10,653.0	100.0	9,354.0	87.8	852.2	8.0	173.6	1.6	273.2	2.6
1931/32	9,219.4	100.0	8,164.2	88.6	647.8	7.0	140.5	1.5	266.9	2.9
1932/33	8,266.0	100.0	7,185.6	86.9	685.9	8.3	194.0	2.4	200.5	2.4
1933/34	8,623.4	100.0	7,645.9	88.7	690.8	6.8	215.8	2.5	170.9	2.0
1934/35	9,643.6	100.0	8,423.0	87.3	665.2	6.9	203.0	2.1	352.4	3.7
1935/36	10,488.5	100.0	9,336.6	89.0	655.6	6.3	233.8	2.2	262.5	2.5
1936/37	11,605.4	100.0	10,272.8	88.5	739.6	6.4	274.3	2.4	318.7	2.7
1937/38	12,497.5	100.0	11,141.9	89.2	670.6	5.4	417.3	3.3	267.7	2.1
1938/39	12,410.7	100.0	10,928.4	88.0	670.3	5.4	579.6	4.7	232.4	1.9
1939/40	12,150.2	100.0	10,862.0	89.4	674.2	5.5	420.0	3.5	194.0	1.6
1940/41	11,589.8	100.0	10,089.2	87.1	667.5	5.8	501.2	4.3	331.9	2.8
1941/42	11,956.0	100.0	10,572.8	88.4	706.5	5.9	461.9	3.9	214.8	1.8
1942/43	13,711.6	100.0	11,975.4	87.3	789.9	5.8	620.9	4.5	325.4	2.4
1943/44	16,818.0	100.0	14,511.0	86.3	882.8	5.2	826.5	4.9	597.7	3.6
1944/45	16,880.0	100.0	14,625.7	86.6	959.9	5.7	791.0	4.7	503.4	3.0
1945/46	29,393.4	100.0	20,853.7	70.9	1,069.6	3.6	6,573.7	22.4	896.4	3.1
1946/47	40,536.1	100.0	28,271.7	69.7	1,288.4	3.2	9,611.1	23.7	1,364.9	3.4
1947/48	39,631.0	100.0	31,234.5	78.8	1,384.2	3.5	6,393.4	16.1	618.9	1.6
1948/49	43,452.5	100.0	33,853.1	77.9	1,383.1	3.2	7,713.6	17.7	502.7	1.2

Note.—The figures appearing in this and the next table are based on liquidation data; therefore assigned revenues and certain other receipts are not included, because it proved impossible to incorporate the adjustments made in Table 12 in the breakdown shown here.

stable proportions of the various revenue sources was the public service revenues, the relative importance of which declined slowly but quite steadily after 1933.

An examination of the movements of various tax receipts, as shown in Table 16, reveals that since 1927/28 direct taxes, though still of decidedly minor significance, have steadily increased in importance as sources of revenue in both relative and absolute terms. Whereas in that year such taxes provided only 0.2 million quetzales, or 1.6 percent of national tax revenues, a little more than two decades later they yielded 3.2 million quetzales or more than 10 percent of the total, and 16 times their revenue yield in the earlier year.

Domestic consumption taxes also increased notably, particularly after the beginning of the war. The influence of the depression is evident in the declining yields of these taxes during 1930/31 through 1933/34. Their movements during this period followed the cyclical pattern of other taxes. While consumption taxes experienced a fourfold increase since 1927/28, their share of total tax revenues rose at a much slower rate.[4]

Although receipts from import duties have tended in general to increase since 1927/28, they have been subject to rather wide fluctuations. Two movements are discernible: a steady and severe decline between 1927/28 and 1932/33 reflecting the world-wide economic dislocations of that period, which was followed by a virtually uninterrupted rise until the outbreak of the war; and a subsequent decline during the war when many imports were unobtainable or available only on a very limited scale, followed in the postwar period by a sharp increase to levels greatly in excess of those for any other years during the period under consideration. Import taxes, however, have shown a clear tendency to decrease in relative importance, although with some fluctuation from year to year.

Export taxes have fluctuated considerably, and although their

---

[4] The data on consumption taxes somewhat understate their yield in recent years since the bulk of assigned revenues consists of additional taxes on alcoholic beverages and cigarettes.

TABLE 16

Composition of National Government Tax Receipts, 1927/28 to 1948/49

Fiscal Year	Total Taxes Q1,000	Per cent of Total	Direct Taxes Q1,000	Per cent of Total	Property Taxes Q1,000	Per cent of Total	Consumption Taxes Q1,000	Per cent of Total	Import Taxes Q1,000	Per cent of Total	Export Taxes Q1,000	Per cent of Total	License and Other Business Taxes Q1,000	Per cent of Total	Fines and Fees Q1,000	Per cent of Total	Other Tax Receipts Q1,000	Per cent of Total
1927/28	12,412.3	100.0	200.2	1.6	271.5	2.2	2,248.7	18.1	6,781.8	54.7	2,249.0	18.1	511.0	4.1	64.2	0.5	85.9	0.7
1928/29	13,024.5	100.0	212.6	1.6	290.2	2.2	2,240.3	17.2	7,516.2	57.7	2,126.2	16.4	551.0	4.2	68.2	0.5	19.8	0.2
1929/30	11,759.1	100.0	244.4	2.1	290.8	2.5	2,125.7	18.1	5,997.8	51.0	2,289.0	19.4	681.1	5.8	104.4	0.9	25.9	0.2
1930/31	9,354.0	100.0	192.5	2.0	284.2	3.0	1,729.1	18.5	4,358.5	46.6	2,065.5	22.1	570.5	6.1	127.9	1.4	25.8	0.3
1931/32	8,164.2	100.0	224.4	2.8	311.4	3.8	1,666.2	20.4	3,813.8	46.7	1,463.2	17.9	556.1	6.8	122.9	1.5	6.2	0.1
1932/33	7,185.6	100.0	174.7	2.4	362.2	5.0	1,357.8	18.9	3,254.2	45.3	1,402.5	19.5	514.5	7.2	92.7	1.3	27.0	0.4
1933/34	7,645.9	100.0	178.1	2.3	407.6	5.3	1,282.3	16.8	3,316.8	43.4	1,636.1	21.4	614.1	8.0	154.7	2.0	56.2	0.8
1934/35	8,423.0	100.0	335.3	4.0	433.5	5.1	1,514.7	18.0	4,083.9	48.5	1,254.9	14.9	623.7	7.4	120.5	1.4	56.5	0.7
1935/36	9,336.6	100.0	294.3	3.2	445.3	4.8	1,730.0	18.4	4,104.2	44.0	1,940.3	20.7	630.3	6.8	139.2	1.5	53.0	0.6
1936/37	10,272.8	100.0	486.5	4.7	469.6	4.6	1,928.4	18.8	4,759.9	46.4	1,739.4	16.9	646.0	6.3	147.0	1.4	96.0	0.9
1937/38	11,141.9	100.0	705.5	6.3	460.5	4.1	2,032.3	18.2	5,144.6	46.2	1,735.9	15.6	830.6	7.5	187.2	1.7	45.3	0.4
1938/39	10,928.4	100.0	639.5	5.9	418.4	3.8	2,005.4	18.4	4,836.9	44.4	1,888.3	17.3	852.9	7.8	233.0	2.1	37.0	0.3
1939/40	10,862.0	100.0	835.9	7.7	434.7	4.0	2,076.4	19.1	4,739.6	43.6	1,694.6	15.6	842.6	7.8	205.7	1.9	32.5	0.3
1940/41	10,089.2	100.0	821.6	8.1	437.9	4.3	1,916.1	19.0	4,108.7	40.8	1,759.1	17.4	834.5	8.3	178.5	1.8	32.8	0.3
1941/42	10,572.8	100.0	904.1	8.6	467.3	4.4	2,085.5	19.7	4,222.8	40.0	1,745.7	16.5	959.1	9.1	152.8	1.4	35.5	0.3
1942/43	11,975.4	100.0	1,137.8	9.5	504.3	4.2	2,568.2	21.4	3,835.6	32.1	2,719.7	22.7	969.5	8.1	200.0	1.7	40.3	0.3
1943/44	14,511.0	100.0	1,750.8	12.1	555.6	3.8	3,442.9	23.7	4,286.2	29.6	3,097.5	21.3	1,087.3	7.5	227.7	1.6	63.0	0.4
1944/45	14,625.7	100.0	1,519.4	10.4	488.6	3.3	4,304.7	29.5	4,802.2	32.8	2,166.2	14.8	1,166.8	8.0	99.1	0.7	78.7	0.5
1945/46	20,854.7	100.0	1,999.8	9.6	532.5	2.6	6,206.0	29.8	7,030.3	33.6	2,951.1	14.2	1,883.1	9.0	170.5	0.8	80.4	0.4
1946/47	28,271.7	100.0	3,110.6	11.0	578.4	2.0	7,951.3	28.2	10,414.4	36.8	2,999.6	10.6	2,861.4	10.1	250.4	0.9	105.6	0.4
1947/48	31,234.5	100.0	3,215.5	10.3	597.1	1.9	8,286.2	26.5	13,072.5	41.9	2,664.0	8.5	2,957.7	9.5	293.1	0.9	148.4	0.5
1948/49	33,853.1	100.0	3,637.1	10.7	668.6	2.0	8,879.6	26.2	14,359.4	42.4	2,618.0	7.7	3,234.0	9.6	292.4	0.9	164.0	0.5

annual yield since the end of the war has been larger than in nearly every other year during the last two decades, increases in receipts from this source have not approached the increases in direct taxes, import duties, and consumption taxes. Relative to total tax collections, moreover, export taxes in recent years have shown a marked decline in importance. The slow growth of export tax receipts appears to be explained by the fact that the basic coffee export tax, which is the most important revenue source in the group, has not undergone a major change in rate for many years and is levied on a specific basis, as is the tax on banana exports. Fluctuations in tax receipts are therefore due to variations in quantities of these products exported.

Property taxes have somewhat more than doubled since 1927/28 and business taxes and business and vehicle licenses have increased nearly sixfold. Both groups have shown steady growth, with very little fluctuation from year to year.

As a general observation, it may be noted that the Guatemalan tax system since 1927/28 has undergone certain structural changes which are rather clearly reflected in the record of tax revenues. The government is somewhat less dependent upon indirect taxes for revenue than it was twenty-odd years ago, direct taxes having increased in importance at a rapid rate, particularly in recent years, but even now providing for no more than one-tenth of the total receipts. Import taxes have shown a tendency to decline in importance, while consumption taxes have until recently been producing an increasing share of government revenues. The significance of these trends for the Guatemalan economy will be discussed in later chapters.

The Present Tax Structure

The present Guatemalan tax structure appears to conform closely to the tax structures of other Latin-American republics: import taxes and consumption levies yield by far the largest share of total tax receipts. In 1948/49 over 40 percent originated in import duties and related fees, and more than 25 percent in consumption taxes. In sharp contrast to these percentages, only 10 percent of total tax receipts were derived from direct taxes. Export duties and business license taxes contributed smaller amounts, while property taxes and other levies yielded only insignificant returns.

Import taxes.—Import duties, both specific and ad valorem, are applied to a wide range of merchandise. Gasoline imports, which have both essential and nonessential aspects, are subject to a very high special duty (*vialidad*), which more than doubles the price of gasoline to the consumer. In 1947/48 this tax provided over 13 percent of the revenues arising from imports. Besides gasoline, the most heavily taxed imports are alcoholic beverages, clothing, certain textiles, and machinery.

Import taxes consist of: the customs duty, which is a specific duty in nearly all cases; consular fees, which constitute a 4 percent ad valorem tax assessed on the f.o.b. value of merchandise; and the assigned taxes (*rentas consignadas*), which are a 6 percent ad valorem, f.o.b. tax applied to those imports on which the specific duty amounts to less than 6 percent ad valorem. There have been a number of changes in duties since the law regulating such taxes was passed in December 1935, but there have been about as many downward as upward revisions. In 1948/49 import taxes yielded over 14 million quetzales.

Consumption taxes.—The two most important consumption taxes are those assessed on alcoholic beverages and tobacco. The tax on liquors is 90 centavos per liter, that on beer 14 centavos per liter; in addition, a tax on industrial alcohol is levied at Q1.28 per liter. The most important tobacco taxes are production taxes on cigarettes, which are assessed at Q2.25 per thousand cigarettes selling for one-half centavo each or more, Q1.00 per thousand cigarettes selling for less than one-half centavo each, and a tax of one centavo per package selling for 15 centavos or more, in addition to the tax of Q2.25. A tax of 50 centavos per thousand is assessed on handmade cigarettes. In 1947/48 taxes on alcoholic beverages amounted to about 6.2 million quetzales, or nearly 75 percent of all consumption taxes. Tobacco taxes yielded a little less than 22 percent of the total, while other consumption taxes furnished less than 4 percent. The total yield of consumption taxes was about 8.3 million quetzales.

Direct taxes.—By far the most important tax in the relatively unimportant category of direct taxes is that on business profits (*impuesto sobre utilidades de empresas lucrativas*). In 1947/48 this tax provided nearly 95 percent of all direct tax revenues, which amounted to 3.2 million quetzales. This tax is a progressive tax levied on the incomes of business enterprises with a capital exceeding Q2,500. The first Q500 of net annual income is exempt, but amounts in excess of this exemption are taxed at rates ranging from 5 percent for the lowest bracket to 43 percent for the highest bracket of Q300,000 and above. Noncorporate farming enterprises are exempt from the law, as are all mining and insurance companies, but the latter are subject to a special tax assessed in lieu of the business profits tax. Capital gains are not subject to the tax. Under contracts entered into by the government in connection with the original granting of operating concessions, the three largest foreign companies doing business in Guatemala —the United Fruit Company (including its subsidiary, the Compañía Agrícola), the Electric Company (Empresas Eléctricas), and the International Railways of Central America (IRCA)—are also exempt from this tax.[5]

The business profits tax was established in 1938. In 1943 and 1944 the rates provided in the original law were changed, and again in 1946 when the present more steeply progressive rate structure was established.

In the last three years, efforts have been made to enact a general income tax which would subject income from sources other than business enterprises to approximately the same rates

[5] See chapter v.

of taxation as those that were imposed by the present business profits tax.

Direct taxes next in importance to the business profits tax, but yielding only a fraction as much revenue, are the gift and inheritance taxes. The inheritance tax is regulated at present by a decree issued in 1947, which established a series of progressive rates varying not only in accordance with the amount involved but also with the degree of relationship between the parties. Rates range from one percent for smaller amounts bequeathed to close relatives, to 25 percent for amounts greater than Q500,000 bequeathed to beneficiaries not related by blood or marriage. Exemptions vary from Q500 to Q1,000 according to the degree of relationship between the heir and the deceased.

Export taxes.—Export taxes are derived from three principal sources: the export of coffee, bananas, and chicle. The coffee tax, which has not been changed in many years, is Q1.50 per quintal.[6] The banana tax is one centavo per bunch for bananas grown on the Atlantic Coast and two centavos per bunch for those grown on the Pacific. In the past, taxes on chicle ranked ahead of the tax on bananas as a source of revenue, but with the development of synthetic chicle there is some uncertainty as to the amount of future revenue from this source.

Property taxes.—The property tax, established in 1921, applies to persons whose rural and urban land and real estate holdings are valued at Q100 or more. Property is taxed at the rate of Q3 per Q1,000 valuation. In 1945 an office was established to reassess property values, but during the interval since its establishment it has reassessed only 25,000 urban holdings, rural holdings still remaining to be reassessed. In addition to the tax on property holdings, there is a tax on the turnover of real estate. The former, however, is the more important, yielding more than 80 percent of property tax revenues in 1947/48.

[6] Exporters also pay a five-centavo tax which accrues to the Central Coffee Office; in addition, a surcharge of ten centavos per quintal for the construction of the national stadium has been levied since 1947.

BUDGET AND ADMINISTRATION OF GOVERNMENT RECEIPTS

The Receipts Budget

The annual budget, which is prepared by the Budget Department (Departamento de Presupuesto) of the Ministry of Finance and Public Credit, contains, in addition to expenditure authorizations, detailed estimates of all receipts of the government. The estimate of government receipts is prepared by the Court and Control office of Accounts (Tribunal y Contraloría de Cuentas). The budget and the annual budget liquidation in which collections are compared with the original estimates, distinguish seven or eight sources of receipts:

1. Income from property
2. Public services
3. Sales of monopoly articles and commercial products of the government
4. Taxes and contributions, group A
5. Taxes and contributions, group B
6. Taxes and contributions, group C
7. Various receipts
8. Extraordinary receipts

The first seven comprise "ordinary" receipts; they appear every year. "Extraordinary" receipts are those from loans, surpluses from previous years, and in 1948/49 the proceeds of the sale of a United States government bond of $1 million.[7]

The budget estimates of receipts are to be based primarily upon the collections of the last five years for which data are available, but the budget law (Ley Organica del Presupuesto)[8] also provides that "the various factors that influence the economy of the country" should be taken into consideration in the preparation of the estimates. As Table 17 shows, the annual estimates have

---

[7] Although the budget law stipulates that proceeds of credit operations are to be included in the budget (or at least in the liquidation data) the practice of recent years has been to show loan proceeds only in Treasury accounts.

[8] Government Decree 1920 of February 12, 1937.

TABLE 17

COMPARISON OF BUDGETED AND ACTUAL GOVERNMENT RECEIPTS, 1937/38 TO 1948/49

(In thousands of quetzales)

Fiscal Year	Total Receipts			Collections as Percent of		Tax Receipts[a]			Collections as Percent of	
	Original Budget Estimates	Revised Budget Estimates	Actual Collections[b]	Original Estimates	Revised Estimates	Original Budget Estimates	Revised Budget Estimates	Actual Collections[b]	Original Estimates	Revised Estimates
1937/38	9,788.5	9,964.5	12,497.5	127.8	125.4	8,607.8	8,684.4	10,957.5	127.2	126.2
1938/39	10,332.6	10,512.1	12,423.6	120.3	118.2	8,983.0	9,058.7	10,720.6	119.3	118.0
1939/40	10,555.2	10,555.2	12,203.8	115.6	115.6	9,277.9	9,277.9	10,696.5	115.0	115.0
1940/41	10,258.5	10,414.2	11,596.1	113.0	111.3	9,012.2	9,012.2	9,915.1	110.0	110.0
1941/42	10,223.1	10,233.1	11,943.1	116.1	116.7	8,946.4	8,946.4	10,367.2	115.9	115.9
1942/43	10,033.2	10,033.2	13,711.8	136.7	136.7	8,788.9	8,788.9	11,788.7	134.1	134.1
1943/44	10,575.0	10,665.0	16,732.0	158.2	156.9	9,300.8	9,383.8	14,190.5	152.5	151.2
1944/45	13,824.0	15,257.5	16,879.6	122.1	110.6	11,960.2	13,061.2	16,879.6	141.1	129.4
1945/46	22,049.4	26,058.4	29,393.4	133.3	112.8	14,545.4	17,054.4	20,699.6	142.3	121.4
1946/47	26,500.0	28,978.3	39,765.1	150.0	137.2	18,729.6	19,160.4	27,471.4	146.6	143.4
1947/48	33,556.0	34,587.7	39,631.0	118.1	114.6	22,258.0	23,289.6	30,640.0	137.6	131.6
1948/49	44,646.0	46,140.8	44,452.5	99.5	96.3	30,920.3	31,569.0	33,282.0	107.6	105.4

[a] Receipts reported as taxes and contributions (*impuestos y contribuciones*) in the original classification of receipts.
[b] Recorded collections (*rentas recaudadas*), excluding assigned revenues (which also do not appear in the budget figures).

always been very conservative, in most years even below the five-year average.

In the course of the fiscal year, usually in connection with additional expenditure appropriations, the estimates are revised, either to take account of more recent collection experience or to include new sources of revenue. Nevertheless, in all except the last year, total receipts as well as tax receipts exceeded both the original and the revised estimates by substantial margins.

The deficiency that occurred in 1948/49 was due to an over-estimation of income from government property, particularly of the proceeds of the operations of the national farms, which fell 3.6 million quetzales short of the estimate. The annual report of the Court and Control Office of Accounts states that the over-estimate occurred because the budget figure failed to take account of the average of the receipts from this source in preceding years.

Administration of Receipts

Receipts of the national government are administered by the National Treasury (Tesorería Nacional) and four revenue offices—the General Customs Office (Dirección General de Aduanas), the General Revenues Office (Dirección General de Rentas), the Control Office of the Profits Tax (Contraloría del Impuesto sobre Utilidades), and the Tobacco Excise Administration (Administración de la Renta de Tabaco). All of these offices are agencies of the Ministry of Finance and Public Credit. The General Customs Office maintains customs offices in Guatemala City and at the borders; it assesses and collects all export and import taxes and operates customs warehouses. The General Revenue Office is subdivided into eight sections and administers all internal revenues except the business profits tax and the various tobacco taxes. Local tax offices (Administración de Rentas) are maintained in all political subdivisions of the country.[9]

[9] A more detailed account of the administration of the most important groups of taxes will be found in chapter vii.

MUNICIPAL REVENUES

In view of the limited importance of municipal finances, only a few observations on them will be presented. Receipts of municipalities are derived primarily from charges for public services, such as street illumination, water supply, sanitation, and cemetery services. They also include collections from license fees, fines, certain consumption and export taxes, and a per capita improvement tax (*contribución de ornato*) designated for the maintenance and improvement of public parks and buildings. The most important consumption taxes are those imposed on alcoholic beverages.

Local taxes, generally referred to as *arbitrios municipales*, are determined by the municipal authorities but must be approved by the Ministry of the Interior (Ministerio de Gobernación). The tax structure and the tax rates vary from municipality to municipality. Some typical municipal export taxes (the purpose of which is the protection of the locality against the diversion elsewhere of essential foodstuffs and raw materials) are shown in the following table:

Corn	2 centavos per quintal
Beans	3 centavos per quintal
Bananas	2 centavos per stem
Hides	20 centavos per piece
Cattle	15 centavos per head
Lumber	2 quetzales per 1,000 cubic feet
Firewood	5 centavos per wagonload

A government decree (*acuerdo*) of October 1948 sought to abolish the municipal taxation on cattle and basic foodstuffs. According to the decree, municipal taxes on these articles must be explicitly approved by the Ministry of Economy; they are to be imposed only in the case of acute local shortages and for periods not to exceed three months. According to information provided by the Ministry of Economy, however, the decree has not yet become fully effective.

INTERNATIONAL COMPARISON

The preceding sections of this chapter have been concerned with a description of the various sources of government receipts in Guatemala and with their relative importance in the Guatemalan revenue structure. The purpose of this section is to compare the Guatemalan revenue system with that of other countries. The introduction of such an international dimension provides a further basis for appraising the composition of government revenues by bringing out the differences and similarities in the various revenue systems. It should be noted, however, that intercountry comparisons are only rough measures of the relationships they portray. Economic differences as well as differences in other national characteristics limit to broad generalities the conclusions which may be drawn from such comparisons.

Because receipts other than taxes, fees, and fines are primarily the result of institutional peculiarities of each individual country, the comparison is confined to tax revenues and receipts from fees and fines. In so far as possible, the data have been compiled on a uniform basis; in addition to the receipts of Guatemala, those of the governments of Chile, El Salvador, Haiti, Mexico, Peru, Venezuela, the United Kingdom, the United States, Denmark, and New Zealand are shown. The Latin-American countries were included because their economic, political, and social institutions are in many respects similar to those of Guatemala. The United States and the United Kingdom were selected to represent fully industrialized economies, while Denmark and New Zealand were included as examples of non-Latin-American nations comparable to Guatemala in respect to size and the importance of agriculture in their economies.

Receipts from taxes, fees, and fines are shown in eight distinct classes. Total and per capita receipts are given in absolute terms, but in order to facilitate intercountry comparisons their composition is presented as a percentage of the total. The relation between receipts of taxes to income is also shown. In the grouping of individual taxes into the various classes, more or less arbitrary decisions had to be made in certain instances; therefore, some of the computations are subject to considerable margins of error.

Revenues from Taxes, Fees, and Fines

From an examination of Table 18, it will be seen that direct taxes formed 10.3 percent of total Guatemalan tax receipts in 1947/48. Among the other countries shown, only in El Salvador were direct taxes a smaller proportion of the total, while in the United States, the United Kingdom, and New Zealand they ranged from 45 to 56 percent. Among the Latin-American countries, Chile and Peru, with ratios of approximately 33 percent, showed the greatest dependence upon direct taxes. The explanation for the relative unimportance of direct taxes in Guatemala is discussed in subsequent chapters, but it may be noted in passing that one of the contributing factors, which also serves to explain the experience of El Salvador, is the large proportion of non-monetary income in the gross national product. In both countries the prevalence of small-scale agricultural units producing largely for their own consumption requirements, and the large number of small business units in general, have discouraged the adoption of adequate income-accounting procedures and have undoubtedly retarded the development of a more comprehensive system of direct taxes which would provide a larger share of total revenues. The growth of direct taxation in other Latin-American countries (e.g., Chile, Mexico, Peru, and Venezuela) in recent years indicates, however, that the structural and institutional factors retarding the expansion of direct taxation can be overcome.

Property and property transfer taxes contributed only a minor share of tax receipts in most of the countries under consideration. Guatemalan revenues from this source are comparable with those of the other Latin-American countries, although Chile, Mexico, and Peru derived larger shares of their total tax receipts from this source. The low percentages recorded for the United States and the United Kingdom are explained by the fact that in those countries property taxes are levied and collected primarily by

TABLE 18

COMPOSITION OF TAX RECEIPTS[a] OF SELECTED COUNTRIES

(Fiscal year ended with month indicated)

	Total Taxes, Fees, and Fines (Millions of national currency)	Percentage Composition of Total Receipts from Taxes, Fees, and Fines							
		Direct Taxes	Property and Property Transfer Taxes	Export Taxes	Transactions and Business License Taxes	Import Taxes	Consumption Taxes	Other Taxes	Fees and Fines
Guatemala (June 1948)	31.3 quetzales	10.3	1.9	8.5	9.5	41.9	26.5	0.5	0.9
Chile (December 1946)	4,730.6 pesos	33.6	9.7	4.3	8.1	30.1	11.2	0.8	2.2
El Salvador (December 1947)	50.4 colones	7.5	2.0	14.3	4.3	48.7	21.2	1.2	0.9
Haiti (September 1948)	75.3 gourdes	12.6	1.7	19.6	1.1	57.6	3.3	0.1	3.8
Mexico (December 1946)	1,580.6 pesos	23.7	10.8	15.7	1.2	15.1	26.8	3.7	3.0
Peru (December 1946)	451.7 soles	33.0	6.2	38.3	…	14.4	5.6	1.3	1.2
Venezuela (June 1946)	384.2 bolivares	25.7	…	…	5.5	42.1	25.5	…	1.2
United Kingdom (March 1947)	3,020.2 pounds	45.7	1.3	…	13.4	20.6	19.0	…	…
United States (June 1948)									
Federal only	42,375.8 dollars	51.7	0.2	…	24.0	1.0	17.3	5.7	0.1
Federal and state	50,167.8 dollars	45.0	0.7	…	21.4	0.8	22.6	7.4	2.1
Denmark (March 1947)	1,896.4 kroner	39.5	2.4	…	…	7.4	47.8	2.4[b]	0.5
New Zealand (March 1947)	113.0 NZ pounds	56.5	9.2	…	…	13.9	20.2	0.2	…

[a] Including fees and fines. The data for most of the countries shown were derived from Henry C. Wallich and John H. Adler, *Public Finance in a Developing Country: El Salvador—A Case Study* (Cambridge, Mass.: Harvard Univ. Press, 1951). The data for Guatemala, El Salvador, Haiti, and the United States, however, were compiled expressly for this study. The data shown refer in each case to receipts of the national government; state as well as federal government receipts have been included for the United States.

[b] Including fees.

municipal and county governments, and therefore do not appear in the table.

As in most Latin-American countries, import and export taxes contribute a major part of total tax revenues in Guatemala. In 1947/48 these taxes together furnished more than one-half of the Guatemalan government's total tax revenues. A much larger share of total receipts was derived from such taxes in Haiti and El Salvador, where their yields were 77 and 63 percent, respectively. In Chile, on the other hand, where direct taxes contribute a larger part of total tax revenues than in most other Latin-American countries and where import and export tax revenues are supplemented by exchange profits, taxes on foreign trade yielded 34 percent of total tax revenues. In the non-Latin-American countries included in the table there are no export taxes, and taxes on imports are relatively unimportant, with the exception of the United Kingdom, where they have served to restrict the consumption of imported goods. In the case of Venezuela, royalties on petroleum exports took the place of export taxes. As noted above, export taxes in Chile were supplemented by revenues derived from discriminatory exchange rates for certain exports.

Consumption taxes account for fairly substantial shares of total tax receipts in most of the countries compared. Among the Latin-American countries, those most dependent upon such revenues were Guatemala, El Salvador, Mexico, and Venezuela with percentages ranging from 21 percent in the case of El Salvador, to nearly 27 percent for Guatemala and Mexico. The share of total revenues provided by consumption taxes in Chile was only 11 percent, whereas in Haiti such taxes were comparatively insignificant, accounting for only a little more than 3 percent of the total. Consumption taxes in the United States, the United Kingdom, and New Zealand were of comparable significance in relation to total tax receipts, but in Denmark such revenues formed nearly half of the total. In most countries, taxes on the production and sale of nonessential goods, such as tobacco and alcoholic beverages, were important sources of consumption tax revenues. The more comprehensive general sales or excise taxes, which are major components of consumption revenues in the United Kingdom, New Zealand, Denmark, and the United States, were not used in any of the Latin-American countries shown, with the exception of Mexico. It may be observed in passing that, from the point of view of the consumer, taxes classified in the above comparison as consumption taxes understate the actual extent of taxes on consumption, since most import duties and many business taxes to a large extent are shifted to the consumer. This aspect of the Guatemalan taxation of consumption will be presented in detail in chapter vi.

The remainder of government revenues presented in Table 18 consist of receipts from transaction and business license taxes, fines, and fees. In Guatemala and Chile, revenues from these sources amounted to about 11 percent of the total, whereas in most other Latin-American countries shown the relative importance of such revenues was only half as great.

Per Capita Income and Tax Burden

Table 19 presents an international comparison of per capita taxes and the ratio of taxes to income. The dollar equivalent of tax collections in all probability does not accurately depict the actual tax burden of individuals in each country because the prevailing exchange rates do not adequately reflect the relative purchasing power of the various currencies. For purposes of general comparison, however, they will serve to approximate the magnitudes of individual tax liabilities in the countries shown.

The per capita tax burden in Guatemala appears to have been less than half as great as that in Chile and Venezuela but of about the same order of magnitude as that of Mexico and Peru, as shown in Table 19. In relation, however, to tax burdens in the United States, the United Kingdom, New Zealand, and to a lesser extent Denmark, even the comparatively large burdens in Chile and Venezuela appear small. In the former countries, per capita taxes were five to ten time as large as in Chile and Venezuela. But this comparison is not very revealing.

TABLE 19

PER CAPITA INCOME AND TAXES[a] OF SELECTED COUNTRIES[b]

(Fiscal year ended with month indicated)

	Per Capita Income (U.S. dollars)[c]	Per Capita Taxes (U.S. dollars)[c]	Taxes as Percent of Income
Guatemala (June 1948)	128	12.0	9.3
Chile (December 1946)	247	28.1	11.4
El Salvador (December 1946)	87	7.4	8.4
Haiti (September 1946)	...[d]	2.8	....
Mexico (December 1946)	117	14.3	12.2
Peru (December 1946)	84	10.0	10.9
Venezuela (June 1946)	306	27.3	8.9
United Kingdom (March 1947)	662	246.8	37.3
United States (June 1948)			
Federal only	1,472	291.0	19.8
Federal and state	1,472	345.0	23.4
Denmark (March 1947)	676	96.4	14.3
New Zealand (March 1947)	688	205.8	29.9

[a] Also includes fees and fines.

[b] With the exception of Guatemala and the United States, the data for which were compiled expressly for this study, the estimates presented in this table were derived from Henry C. Wallich and John H. Adler, *op. cit.* The data are for national governments only. State as well as federal data, however, have been included for the United States for purposes of comparison.

[c] Values in national currencies were converted into dollars at par values announced by the International Monetary Fund.

[d] Not available.

A more meaningful relationship for the appraisal of comparative tax burdens is a comparison of the ratios of taxes to income. In all of the Latin-American countries shown, for which income data were available, the relationship between taxes and income exhibited only a very narrow spread, ranging from 8.4 percent in El Salvador to 12.2 percent in Mexico. In contrast to the experience of these Latin-American countries, the four countries outside Latin America were subject to levies which taxed away a considerably larger part of incomes. This larger tax burden in relative terms confirms the fact that only with a high level of per capita income can an economy devote a large proportion of its total resources to the production of government services; that is to say, the ability to pay taxes rises more than proportionately with an increase in income. Conversely, the share of government in total income is necessarily more limited in countries with a small per capita income.

STATISTICAL NOTE

Receipts of the national government.—Data shown in Tables 12 and 13 represent cash receipts of the national government. They were computed from annual data on Treasury movements (*cuenta general de la caja*) in such a way as to reflect, as accurately as possible, only actual receipts; debits not resulting in cash receipts, transitory receipts, and receipts on custody accounts (the movements of which affect Treasury balances, but not the amount of annual regular revenues) are excluded.

Table 20 shows an abstract of the original accounts. Budgetary receipts shown in the table are identical with revenues collected (*rentas recaudadas*) of the national government. Assigned revenues are tax and nontax receipts that are transferred by the government to certain autonomous entities and other institutions. They appear as assigned revenues (*rentas consignadas*) and additional taxes (*impuestos adicionales*) in the Treasury accounts. "Net change in tax and other receivables" corresponds to the entry "debtors" in the original debit and credit accounts. An excess of debits of "debtors" over the corresponding credits reflects a net addition to cash receipts; in years in which credits exceeded debits, the difference was subtracted from receipts.

"Nonbudgetary loan receipts" are the amounts shown as debits of loans. It should be noted that the figures shown here differ somewhat from the loan receipts shown in the next chapter. The contributions of the United States government, shown as debits under the entry, "Approvals or reimbursements" (*legalizar o reintegrar*), are included under cash receipts.

"Net receipts on custody accounts" are the difference between the debit and credit entries of deposits (*depósitos*), excluding assigned revenues (*impuestos adicionales*) which are shown separately. Similarly, "Other nonbudgetary receipts (net)" represent the excess of debits over credits of the following accounts: bank bills (*valores circulantes*), bond premiums; donations; various creditors (*acreedores varios*); approvals or reimbursements, excluding receipts for the Roosevelt Highway and

TABLE 20

ANNUAL TREASURY MOVEMENTS, 1937/38 TO 1948/49

(In thousands of quetzales; by fiscal years)

	1937/38	1938/39	1939/40	1940/41	1941/42	1942/43
Receipts:						
Budgetary receipts	12,497.5	12,410.7	12,150.2	11,589.8	11,956.0	13,711.8
Receipts of assigned revenue	81.3	80.2	75.1	72.1	109.5	125.4
Net change in tax and other receivables^a	−126.6	−34.6	−81.3	−49.9	−0.1	−268.7
Nonbudgetary loan receipts	....	1,000.0	....	....	....	....
United States contribution to Roosevelt Highway^b	....	....	....	....	....	....
Net receipts on custody accounts	....	29.4	30.5	....	....	....
Other nonbudgetary receipts (net)	....	55.6	62.7	96.6	131.7	....
Decrease in Treasury balances	....	145.1	....	....	....	....
Total	12,452.2	13,686.4	12,237.2	11,708.6	12,197.1	13,568.5
Expenditures:						
Budgetary expenditures:						
Current year	9,269.2	13,019.5	10,356.1	9,813.8	10,236.2	12,208.2
Preceding year	596.9	708.6	537.7	483.6	606.1	539.2
Earlier years	1,206.1	79.4	56.0	77.5	9.6	5.5
Net expenditures on suspense accounts^a	−93.2	−222.6	−7.6	100.6	33.0	23.5
Payments of assigned revenue	100.2	101.5	99.5	99.3	142.6	168.7
Nonbudgetary expenditures:						
Roosevelt Highway	....	....	....	....	....	....
Other	....	....	7.6	....	....	....
Nonbudgetary investment of funds	....	....	....	....	....	....
Net disbursements from custody accounts	7.2	....	....	8.4	7.4	0.6
Other nonbudgetary disbursements (net)	37.0	....	....	....	....	319.5
Increase in Treasury balances	1,328.8	....	1,187.9	1,125.4	1,162.2	303.3
Total	12,452.2	13,686.4	12,237.2	11,708.6	12,197.1	13,568.5

	1943/44	1944/45	1945/46	1946/47	1947/48	1948/49
Receipts:						
Budgetary receipts	16,818.0	16,879.6	29,393.4	40,536.1	39,631.6	44,452.5ᵈ
Receipts of assigned revenue	87.3	230.2	422.2	389.4	1,431.7	1,555.9
Net change in tax and other receivablesᵃ	−81.1	−109.7	+12.3	−450.0	−418.3	−44.5
Nonbudgetary loan receipts	.....	.....	.....	121.7	1,178.7	1,736.8
United States contribution to Roosevelt Highwayᵇ	.....	.....	308.4	226.4	95.0	340.5
Net receipts on custody accounts	54.1	.....	190.4	1,258.7	2,958.2	.....
Other nonbudgetary receipts (net)	933.3	149.7	.....	372.7	159.9	.....
Decrease in Treasury balances	.....	5,988.5	.....	.....	2,635.4	2,834.0
Total	17,811.6	23,138.3	30,326.7	42,455.0	47,671.6	50,875.2
Expenditures:						
Budgetary expenditures:						
Current year	13,666.8ᵉ	21,308.8	26,388.2	29,629.0	39,567.2	42,931.9
Preceding year	914.9	549.7	2,442.1	1,721.5	1,813.1	3,986 1
Earlier years	4.7	25.9	50.6	25.3	68.7	111.1
Net expenditures on suspense accounts	55.8	824.6	−716.6	3,459.4	1,697.0	−3,191.5
Payments of assigned revenue	134.4	183.7	448.4	512.7	912.1	696.3
Nonbudgetary expenditures:						
Roosevelt Highway	.....	221.7	780.3	1,280.0	2,451.0	1,500.0
Other	.....	.....	.....	.....	703.3	1,686.3
Nonbudgetary investment of funds	.....	13.4	.....	.....	359.2	.....
Net disbursements from custody accounts	.....	10.5	.....	.....	.....	2,667.5
Other nonbudgetary disbursements (net)	.....	.....	884.8	.....	.....	487.5ᶠ
Increase in Treasury balances	3,035.0	.....	48.9	5,715.7	.....	.....
Total	17,811.6	23,138.3	30,326.7	42,455.0	47,671.6	50,875.2

ᵃ Increase —; decrease +.
ᵇ On basis of an agreement between Guatemala and the United States.
ᶜ Documentos pendientes (minus sign indicates net deduction from budgetary expenditures).
ᵈ Includes sale of United States government bond of $1 million.
ᵉ Includes purchase of United States government bond of $1 million.
ᶠ Including nonbudgetary interest and amortization payments of Q380,000.

debits of suspense accounts (*documentos pendientes*), which are shown under expenditures; permanent funds; transitory accounts (*cuentas de orden*), and refunds and corrections (*erario nacional*). "Net receipts on custody accounts" and "Other nonbudgetary receipts (net)" have, of course, not been included in cash receipts. In years in which credits of these items exceed debits, they are shown as net expenditures.

Tables 15 and 16 are based on collected-revenue data. But since the original classification (in seven or eight groups of receipts) is primarily of historical and administrative significance, receipts have been regrouped into the four classes shown in Table 15. The classification of tax receipts likewise has been adjusted to conform to the new headings shown in Table 16.

Municipalities.—The data on municipalities were obtained from the General Statistical Office. Figures pertaining to years prior to 1945/46 are partly estimated since the available data did not include all municipalities. Funds received by the municipalities from the government have been deducted since they have already appeared under government receipts.

San Carlos University.—Receipts from the government have been excluded, so that the figures include only tuition payments, examination and laboratory fees, donations, etc.

Social Security Institute.—The receipts figures do not include the contributions of the government and of other autonomous entities. Since the fiscal year of the Social Security Institute does not coincide with that of the government, the amounts pertaining to each fiscal year have been partly estimated.

Production Development Institute. — The small amount shown in Table 13 represents interest receipts from private borrowers. The initial contributions of the government to the Institute are not included.

IV

GOVERNMENT EXPENDITURES
AND THE PUBLIC DEBT

THE PRECEDING chapter has presented a survey of the sources of public revenues in Guatemala and a brief discussion of their most significant features. The present chapter examines the opposite side of the public ledgers and presents a survey of public expenditures, together with a comparison of receipts and expenditures. In later chapters, with this chapter's exposition as a background, government receipts and outlays will be considered in relation to their impact on the various sectors of the economy. A discussion of the composition of government expenditures, however, is in itself of interest because it gives a first direct indication as to how the government spends its funds.

EXPENDITURES OF NATIONAL GOVERNMENT, MUNICIPALITIES, AND ENTITIES

Table 21 presents a comprehensive picture of the expenditure of public funds in Guatemala. Perhaps the most important fact revealed in the table is the expansion of total public expenditures, from 12.7 million quetzales in 1937/38 to 53.8 million in 1948/49. The major proportion of this expansion was, of course, a result of the increase of prices, which began in 1943 and continued uninterruptedly until the end of 1949. In the same period, but particularly in the years since the end of the war, the expansion of government expenditures has resulted also from the assumption of additional functions by the national government, particularly in the field of economic and financial development. The expansion of government activities is in part also reflected in the establishment of new autonomous entities, such as the Social Security Institute, the National Olympic Committee, and the Pro-

TABLE 21

Expenditures of National Government, Municipalities, and Autonomous Entities, 1937/38 to 1948/49

Fiscal Year	Total		National Government [a]		Municipalities		San Carlos University		Social Security Institute		National Olympic Committee		Production Development Institute	
	Q1,000	Per cent of Total	Q1,000	Per cent of Total	Q1,000	Per cent of Total	Q1,000	Per cent of Total	Q1,000	Per cent of Total	Q1,000	Per cent of Total	Q1,000	Per cent of Total
1937/38	12,718.5	100.0	10,979.0	86.3	1,739.5	13.7	.....	...	.....	...	.....	...	.....	...
1938/39	15,289.0	100.0	13,584.9	88.9	1,704.1	11.1	.....	...	.....	...	.....	...	.....	...
1939/40	13,014.9	100.0	10,950.8	84.1	2,064.1	15.9	.....	...	.....	...	.....	...	.....	...
1940/41	12,580.8	100.0	10,475.5	83.3	2,105.3	16.7	.....	...	.....	...	.....	...	.....	...
1941/42	12,936.9	100.0	10,884.9	84.1	2,052.0	15.9	.....	...	.....	...	.....	...	.....	...
1942/43	15,279.5	100.0	12,776.4	83.6	2,503.1	16.4	.....	...	.....	...	.....	...	.....	...
1943/44	16,874.9	100.0	13,642.2	80.8	3,232.7	19.1	.....	...	.....	...	.....	...	.....	...
1944/45	25,838.7	100.0	22,944.1	88.8	2,726.6	10.6	168.0	0.6	.....	...	.....	...	.....	...
1945/46	32,430.5	100.0	28,944.6	89.3	3,149.9	9.7	336.0	1.0	.....	...	.....	...	.....	...
1946/47	40,016.0	100.0	36,226.6	90.5	3,387.4	8.5	336.0	0.8	66.0	0.2	.....	...	.....	...
1947/48	51,113.3	100.0	46,759.5	91.5	3,244.3	6.3	434.3	0.8	392.0	0.8	283.2	0.6	.....	...
1948/49	53,797.5	100.0	47,403.9[b]	88.1	3,894.0	7.3	500.0	0.9	1,183.9	2.2	498.2	0.9	317.5	0.6

[a] Excluding payments of assigned revenues made to autonomous entities and other institutions.
[b] Including nonbudgetary debt payments of Q380,000.

duction Development Institute; until 1943/44, expenditures of San Carlos University were included in the expenditures of the national government, but the university also is now autonomous. Expenditures of municipalities also increased substantially during this period, but declined in relative importance as other government outlays rose more rapidly. In recent years they have accounted for considerably less than 10 percent of total public expenditures, while prior to 1944/45 they accounted for up to 19 percent of the total.

EXPENDITURES OF THE NATIONAL GOVERNMENT

The analysis of government expenditures which follows differs somewhat from that of government receipts in the preceding chapter. In the face of the rapid changes which occurred in the last few years in the size and composition of government expenditures, it seems more appropriate to focus primary attention upon the extent of these changes rather than on the composition which prevailed in the last year under consideration. The analysis is supplemented by a discussion of appropriation procedures and the control and administration of public expenditures, and by a brief account of government receipts and expenditures in relation to the public debt. Finally, expenditures of the Guatemalan government are compared with those of other countries, particularly in Latin America.

Expenditures of the national government are shown in Table 22. Liquidated expenditures are the figures shown in the accounts of the Court and Control Office of Accounts. They include all expenditures that were approved for disbursement in a given year in accordance with budget appropriations; nonbudgetary expenditures and transfers of assigned revenues to autonomous entities and other institutions are excluded. They include, however, funds whose disbursement has been approved but which had not yet been paid out when the annual accounts were closed.

The cash expenditures data represent actual disbursements in each fiscal year. They include disbursements of appropriated funds not only for the current fiscal year, but also for preceding years. In addition, transfers of assigned revenues and certain nonbudgetary disbursements, particularly payments on suspense accounts, are included.[1] A comparison of liquidated expenditures with cash expenditures shows that until 1943/44 the latter were usually somewhat smaller than the former. Between 1944/45 and 1945/46 the growth of extrabudgetary expenditures and credit operations are reflected in an excess of cash disbursements over liquidation figures. Cash disbursements in 1948/49 understate the sum of actual Treasury outlays by more than one million quetzales because certain extrabudgetary credit operations and the establishment of permanent funds for the various ministries were not included.

TABLE 22

EXPENDITURES OF NATIONAL GOVERNMENT, 1937/38 TO 1948/49

(*In thousands of quetzales*)

Fiscal Year	Liquidated Expenditures	Cash Expenditures
1937/38	11,141.6	11,079.2
1938/39	14,014.7	13,686.4
1939/40	11,035.5	11,050.3
1940/41	10,632.6	10,574.8
1941/42	10,962.8	11,027.5
1942/43	13,381.9	12,945.1
1943/44	18,347.7[a]	13,776.6[a]
1944/45	19,954.3	23,127.8
1945/46	29,234.4	29,393.0
1946/47	32,380.4	36,739.3
1947/48	45,941.0	47,671.6
1948/49	49,442.0	47,720.2

[a] Excluding $1 million for purchase of United States government bond.

Functional Purposes of Expenditures

For the purpose of this study government expenditures have been grouped into the following five categories: (1) general administration, (2) national defense, (3) cultural and social serv-

[1] See page 84.

ices, (4) economic and financial development, and (5) public debt service.

Government expenditures are also classified in the next section as outlays for wages and salaries, pensions, purchases of materials, and transfer payments to autonomous agencies, municipalities, and other institutions. These various categories differ considerably from those customarily employed in Guatemalan budget and accounting statements, which are based—like those of other countries—on the organizational pattern of the government in ministries and their subdivisions.

The five functional categories are believed to reflect adequately the principal functions of government. The distinction of government expenditures by types of payments (salaries and wages, purchases of materials, public debt payments, and transfer payments) is, as will be seen in later chapters, useful as an indication of shifts of the direction of government expenditures and, indirectly, of the objectives of the government's financial operations.

Tables 23 and 24, in which estimates of the composition of the liquidated expenditures by their various purposes are presented, reveal that the increase in the total was largely, aside from price rises, the result of an expansion of social and cultural expenditures and expenditures for the country's economic and financial development. Between 1937/38 and 1948/49, expenditures for economic and financial development, which consisted primarily of expenditures for public works, increased about tenfold; social and cultural expenditures increased eightfold. Conversely, administrative expenditures increased not quite four times and expenditures for national defense rose only by approximately 180 percent. Expenditures on the public debt shown in these tables include payments on the funded foreign and domestic debt, as well as payments of debts incurred through the purchase of goods and services. With the virtual retirement of the foreign debt in 1944/45, expenditures in this category declined in the last years to relatively insignificant proportions.

TABLE 23

EXPENDITURES OF NATIONAL GOVERNMENT, BY PURPOSES, 1937/38 TO 1948/49[a]

(In thousands of quetzales)

	1937/38	1938/39	1939/40	1940/41	1941/42	1942/43
Administrative expenditures	4,057.7	4,231.6	4,301.3	4,124.9	4,475.5	5,668.5
Ordinary	3,589.2	3,649.5	3,660.5	3,725.5	3,873.6	3,781.6
Extraordinary	468.5	582.1	640.8	399.4	601.9	1,886.9
Social and cultural expenditures	2,044.5	2,171.5	2,055.6	2,156.9	2,138.5	2,403.4
Ordinary	1,472.7	1,508.1	1,546.8	1,530.5	1,556.0	1,703.3
Extraordinary	571.8	663.4	508.8	626.4	582.5	700.1
Expenditures for economic and financial development	1,258.9	1,454.8	1,441.9	1,654.6	1,812.5	2,511.2
Ordinary	215.5	210.5	228.9	241.2	251.5	240.2
Extraordinary	1,043.4	1,244.3	1,213.0	1,413.4	1,561.0	2,271.0
National defense expenditures	1,908.1	1,891.4	1,827.1	1,959.0	1,870.7	2,147.5
Ordinary	1,680.0	1,700.1	1,732.3	1,761.5	1,765.4	1,786.6
Extraordinary	228.1	191.3	94.8	197.5	105.3	360.9
Public debt service (ordinary)	1,872.4	4,265.4	1,409.5	737.2	665.6	651.3
Total	11,141.6	14,014.7	11,035.5	10,632.6	10,962.8	13,381.9
Total ordinary expenditures	8,829.8	11,333.6	8,578.0	7,995.9	8,112.1	8,163.0
Total extraordinary expenditures	2,311.8	2,681.1	2,457.4	2,636.7	2,850.7	5,218.0

[a] Liquidated budgetary expenditures.

	1943/44	1944/45	1945/46	1946/47	1947/48	1948/49
Administrative expenditures	6,847.1	6,041.8	11,047.6	11,222.0	12,487.6	15,450.8
Ordinary	4,001.1	5,184.1	9,998.7	9,722.3	11,005.9	13,828.5
Extraordinary	2,846.0	857.7	1,048.9	1,499.7	1,481.7	1,622.3
Social and cultural expenditures	2,524.1	3,942.2	7,248.0	8,636.9	12,579.1	16,506.6
Ordinary	1,738.0	2,210.9	4,403.1	5,441.7	6,366.9	7,910.4
Extraordinary	786.1	1,731.3	2,844.9	3,195.2	6,212.2	8,596.2
Expenditures for economic and financial development	1,848.3	3,153.6	6,496.0	8,035.7	16,080.5	11,526.1
Ordinary	291.5	285.6	3,044.8	4,474.5	4,464.4	4,812.5
Extraordinary	1,556.8	2,868.0	3,451.2	3,561.2	11,616.4	6,713.6
National defense expenditures	2,398.9	3,802.5	3,336.9	3,806.2	4,206.5	5,286.8
Ordinary	1,856.2	2,060.5	2,039.2	2,147.3	2,147.0	2,556.6
Extraordinary	542.7	1,742.0	1,297.7	1,658.9	2,059.0	2,730.2
Public debt service (ordinary)	4,729.3	3,014.2	1,105.9	679.6	587.3	671.7
Total	18,347.7	19,954.3	29,234.4	32,380.4	45,941.0	49,442.0
Total ordinary expenditures	12,616.1	12,755.3	20,591.7	22,465.4	24,571.5	29,779.7
Total extraordinary expenditures	5,731.6	7,199.0	8,642.7	9,915.0	21,369.5	19,662.3

TABLE 24

DISTRIBUTION OF EXPENDITURES OF NATIONAL GOVERNMENT, BY PURPOSES, 1937/38 TO 1948/49

(In percent of total expenditures)

Year	Administrative Expenditures	Social and Cultural Expenditures	Economic and Financial Development	National Defense Expenditures	Public Debt Service (ordinary)	Total
1937/38	36.2	18.5	11.3	17.2	16.8	100.0
1938/39	30.2	15.5	10.4	13.5	30.4	100.0
1939/40	39.0	18.6	13.1	16.6	12.8	100.0
1940/41	38.8	20.3	15.6	18.4	6.9	100.0
1941/42	40.8	19.5	16.5	17.1	6.1	100.0
1942/43	42.4	18.0	18.7	16.0	4.9	100.0
1943/44	37.2	13.8	10.1	13.1	25.8	100.0
1944/45	30.3	19.8	15.8	19.0	15.1	100.0
1945/46	37.8	24.8	22.2	11.4	3.8	100.0
1946/47	34.7	26.7	24.8	11.8	2.0	100.0
1947/48	27.2	27.4	35.0	9.2	1.2	100.0
1948/49	31.3	33.3	23.3	10.7	1.4	100.0

Another aspect of the composition of government expenditures is significant in this connection. In the period under consideration, those proportions of expenditures for social and cultural purposes which are termed "extraordinary" in the government accounts and which consist largely of expenditures for the construction of school buildings, hospitals, etc., rose even more than ordinary expenditures which are made up largely of salary and wage payments. In other words, the figures reflect substantial additions to the "plant" providing social and cultural services for the country.

These changes are reflected also in the percentage composition of total expenditures. As shown in Table 24, in the prewar years administrative expenditures represented by far the largest single item, while social and cultural expenditures and expenditures for economic and financial development together absorbed less than one-third of the total. National defense expenditures were larger than outlays for economic development. In the first postwar years (1945/46 and 1946/47), administrative expenditures still absorbed more than one-third of the total; in 1947/48, however, they fell for the first time below the 30 percent mark but rose again in the subsequent year. Development expenditures, on the other hand, exceeded 20 percent in every postwar year, reached 35 percent in 1947/48, and then receded to 23 percent in the following year. Social and cultural expenditures likewise inched upward, though at a rather slower pace; between 1945/46 and 1947/48 they accounted for approximately one-fourth of total expenditures. In 1948/49, as a result of large expenditures for hospital construction and the building of the Olympic Stadium, they accounted for one-third of total expenditures. National defense expenditures, on the other hand, declined in relative importance. They amounted to approximately 10 percent in the postwar years, compared with 16 to 19 percent before and during the war under the regime of General Ubico.[2]

[2] A further analysis of changes in government expenditures, including a distinction between changes in "real" and money terms, will be found in chapter vii.

Composition of Expenditures

The tendencies indicated in the breakdown of government expenditures by purpose are borne out by the analysis of expenditures by type of payments (Tables 25 and 26). The most significant development reflected in the tables is the disproportionately large increase of expenditures for the purchase of equipment and other materials. This indicates that investment activities of the government have increased relatively more than expenditures in connection with its other functions. Expenditures on wages and salaries remained more stable throughout the entire period, with the exception of the last four years when they increased rapidly, partly as a result of salary and wage increases and partly because of an expansion of government activities, particularly through the operation of the nationalized farms. The total figure, however, conceals the fact that in connection with increased investment activities a substantially larger proportion of these income payments went to labor employed on public construction projects, while expenditures for salaries in government offices increased relatively less.

Expenditure data on interest and amortization payments pertain to the funded debt only; payments of short-term debts are included under material purchases and income payments. These figures reflect the retirement of the major proportion of the foreign debt in 1945/46 and the decline of the external debt burden thereafter.

Of lesser importance is the increase in transfer payments. In the last two years, these expenditures included substantial amounts of payments into sinking funds for the retirement of certain parts of the internal debt. These funds are maintained in the Banco de Guatemala.

APPROPRIATION PROCEDURES AND EXPENDITURES CONTROL

The Budgetary Process

The budgetary process of the Guatemalan government is regulated by constitutional provisions,[3] the budget law, amended by Legislative Decree Number 397[4] and by the administrative regulation (*Reglamento*) of November 27, 1947.

Preparation of the budget.—The law provides that before December 31, every government agency must present an estimate of its expenditures for the following fiscal year (beginning July 1) to the Budget Office.

The estimates of expenditures are to be made on the basis of the experience of previous years, allowance being made for the cost of new projects and the elimination of functions. The Budget Office revises the estimates of receipts and expenditures to determine their legality and their consistency with current price conditions. The annual budget distinguishes expenditures for the following seven branches (*ramos*): (1) Congress (*Organismo Legislativo*); (2) Presidency (*Presidencia de la República*); (3) Judiciary Power (*Organismo Judicial*); (4) Ministries of State (*Ministerios de Estado*); (5) Public Debt (*Deuda Pública*); (6) Pensions (*Clases Pasivas*); and, in the last four years, (7) Extraordinary Investments (*Inversiones Extraordinarias*). Each branch is divided into sections (*secciones*), chapters (*capítulos*), and items (*partidas*).

Expenditures are classified as ordinary fixed, ordinary variable, extraordinary, and extraordinary investment expenditures. Ordinary fixed expenditures include salaries, wages, and rents, i.e., those of foreseeable and recurrent character. Ordinary variable expenditures include such items as office supplies, food, and transportation, the amounts of which cannot be determined in advance with certainty. Extraordinary expenditures cover outlays that cannot be itemized, such as repairs, purchases of equipment, etc. Extraordinary investments include investment expenditures such as construction of roads and buildings and contributions to

---

[3] Title V (Article 119) determines the fiscal prerogatives of Congress; Title VIII (Articles 177 to 187) deals with budgetary procedures; and Title IX (Articles 188 to 198) with the Court and Control Office of Accounts.

[4] Of June 9, 1947.

TABLE 25

GOVERNMENT CASH EXPENDITURES, BY TYPES OF PAYMENT, 1937/38 TO 1948/49

(In thousands of quetzales)

	1937/38	1938/39	1939/40	1940/41	1941/42	1942/43
Total	11,079.2	13,686.4	11,050.3	10,574.8	11,027.5	12,945.1
Income payments	7,665.1	7,899.8	7,352.1	7,266.7	7,662.3	7,691.8
Wages and salaries	6,746.1	6,927.1	6,474.5	6,397.1	6,807.5	6,765.8
Wages in kind	646.3	684.1	604.6	589.7	552.5	617.3
Pensions	272.7	288.6	273.0	279.9	302.3	308.7
Material purchases	2,433.9	2,790.1	2,398.7	2,728.8	2,762.6	4,654.6
Public debt payments	880.0	2,895.0	1,200.0	480.0	460.0	430.0
External	670.0	460.0	530.0	480.0	460.0	430.0
Internal	210.0	2,435.0	670.0	.....	.....	.....
Payments to autonomous entities	100.2	101.5	99.5	99.3	142.6	168.7

	1943/44	1944/45	1945/46	1946/47	1947/48	1948/49
Total	14,776.6	23,127.8	29,393.0	36,739.3	47,671.6	48,100.2
Income payments	8,718.3	9,720.9	18,751.8	23,498.9	30,368.8	31,600.0
Wages and salaries	7,632.1	8,169.5	16,937.1	21,224.8	27,429.9	28,590.5
Wages in kind	738.6	1,056.3	748.9	938.5	1,212.9	1,410.7
Pensions	347.6	495.1	1,065.8	1,335.6	1,726.0	1,598.8
Material purchases	5,763.9	6,783.2	10,052.8	12,597.7	16,280.7	15,423.9
Public debt payments	160.0	6,440.0	140.0	130.0	110.0	380.0
External	160.0	6,440.0	140.0	130.0	110.0	.....
Internal	.....	.....	.....	.....	.....	380.0
Payments to autonomous entities	134.4	183.7	448.4	512.7	912.1	696.3

TABLE 26

DISTRIBUTION OF GOVERNMENT CASH EXPENDITURES, BY TYPES OF PAYMENT, 1937/38 TO 1948/49

(In percent of total expenditures)

	1937/38	1938/39	1939/40	1940/41	1941/42	1942/43	1943/44	1944/45	1945/46	1946/47	1947/48	1948/49
Total	100.0	100.0	100.0	100.0	100.0	100.0	100.0	100.0	100.0	100.0	100.0	100.0
Income payments	69.2	57.7	66.5	68.7	69.5	59.4	59.0	42.0	63.8	64.0	63.7	65.7
Salaries and wages	60.9	50.6	58.5	60.5	61.7	52.2	51.7	35.3	57.6	57.8	57.5	59.5
Wages in kind	5.8	5.0	5.5	5.6	5.0	4.8	5.0	4.6	2.6	2.6	2.6	2.9
Pensions	2.5	2.1	2.5	2.6	2.8	2.4	2.3	2.1	3.6	3.6	3.6	3.3
Material purchases	22.0	20.4	21.7	25.8	25.0	36.0	39.0	29.3	34.2	34.3	34.2	32.1
Public debt payments	7.9	21.2	10.9	4.6	4.2	3.3	1.1	27.9	0.5	0.3	0.2	0.8
External	6.0	3.4	4.8	4.6	4.2	3.3	1.1	27.9	0.5	0.3	0.2	...
Internal	1.9	17.8	6.1	...	...	...	...	...	...	...	...	0.8
Payments to autonomous entities	0.9	0.7	0.9	0.9	1.3	1.3	0.9	0.8	1.5	1.4	1.9	1.4

municipal governments and autonomous agencies, not included in assigned revenues.

Article 177 of the constitution establishes the principle of budgetary unity according to which all expenditures and receipts of the state must be included in one budget. However, Congress approves separately the budgets of certain autonomous agencies,[5] such as the Production Development Institute, the National Mortgage Institute, and the Social Security Institute, since their receipts do not form part of Treasury receipts. The budget norms (*normas presupuestales*) of the budget for the fiscal year 1949/50 provide that the sales proceeds of goods and services produced by government enterprises can be reserved (*disponibilidades privativas*) for the purposes of the enterprise in question if the Ministry of Finance and the Court and Control Office of Accounts approve.

The law provides that every budget must be balanced, in the sense that expenditures must not exceed, in a given year, the amount of estimated receipts, including loans and Treasury balances. After the budget has been prepared and approved by the Minister of Finance, it is presented to the Cabinet for discussion and approval. In order to curb attempts by individual government departments to have appropriations adjusted after the Cabinet has approved them, the above-mentioned government regulation of November 27, 1947, explicitly prohibits such revisions. It further stipulates that only the Minister of Finance can deal directly with Congress regarding budget matters. No other member of the Cabinet can request Congress to modify the budget bill submitted by the Cabinet.

Legislative enactment.—Article 178 of the constitution stipulates that the budget must be presented to Congress by the Minister of Finance within the first fifteen days of the first period of the ordinary session that opens on March 1. Congress is required to discuss and approve the budget before May 30. If the budget is

[5] Prior to the fiscal year 1949/50, the budgets of some autonomous agencies were not subject to congressional approval.

not approved before the beginning of the fiscal year, the President has the right to apply the appropriations of the preceding year until the new budget is approved.

Receipts and expenditures are discussed and approved article by article. The 1948/49 budget contained more than 3,500 items, listing every single appropriation for salary payments, scholarships, etc. This detailed consideration of the budget is required under the provisions of the budget law which stipulate that credits for ordinary expenditures must be listed individually for each item. Extraordinary investment expenditures, however, are listed and appropriated in lump sums.

Modifications after enactment.—After the budget is approved and signed by the President, appropriations can be increased only by Congress. If Congress is not in session, the administration can authorize additional expenditures, but such additional administrative appropriations must be reported to Congress within the first fifteen days of its ordinary session.

Requests for increased appropriations must be made by the individual government departments to the Ministry of Finance. The Ministry in turn must obtain the consent of the Court of Accounts before submitting the request to Congress or to the President.[6]

In view of the legal stipulation that the budget must be technically in balance, requests for additional appropriations are always combined with a revision of estimates of receipts. Estimates of budget receipts can be changed only by Congress at the request of the administration if the Court and Control Office of Accounts submits a favorable opinion in writing. The budget law provides that receipts estimates can be changed only under the following conditions: (*a*) receipts during the first four months of the fiscal year must differ significantly from the budget estimates, (*b*) estimated increases of receipts from one source must not be offset by a reduction of receipts from other sources, and (*c*) if the esti-

[6] See, however, pp. 83–84.

mate of total receipts is revised downward, appropriations likewise must be reduced.

In recent years, the accumulation of Treasury balances and
receipts in excess of original estimates has almost invariably resulted in an increase of appropriations in the course of the fiscal
year. As Table 27 indicates, the increases were relatively small
until 1943/44. In that year additional appropriations exceeded

TABLE 27

COMPARISON OF APPROPRIATIONS AND LIQUIDATED GOVERN-
MENT EXPENDITURES, 1937/38 TO 1948/49

(*In thousands of quetzales*)

| Fiscal Year | Appropriations | | Liquidated Expenditures | Liquidated Expenditures as Percent of | |
	Original	Final		Original Appropriations	Final Appropriations
1937/38	9,788.5	11,836.2	11,141.5	113.8	94.1
1938/39	10,332.6	14,767.4	14,014.6	135.6	94.9
1939/40	10,555.2	12,012.5	11,035.5	104.6	91.9
1940/41	10,258.4	11,716.1	10,632.5	103.6	90.7
1941/42	10,223.1	11,632.6	10,962.8	107.2	94.2
1942/43	10,033.2	14,135.2	13,381.9	133.4	94.6
1943/44	10,575.7	22,689.1ᵃ	17,347.7ᵃ	164.0	76.4
1944/45	15,257.4	21,425.1	19,954.3	130.8	93.1
1945/46	25,412.2	30,626.3	29,234.4	115.0	95.4
1946/47	28,125.1	33,782.2	32,380.3	115.1	95.8
1947/48	34,479.0	47,368.7	45,941.0	133.2	97.0
1948/49	44,646.0	52,611.8	49,442.0	110.7	94.0

ᵃ Excluding appropriation for, and purchase of, a United States government bond
of $1 million.

the original budget by more than 100 percent. In later years, the
discrepancies between original and final appropriations were
somewhat smaller, but they still were large enough to detract
from the significance of the original budget. The large amounts
of additional appropriations were in part necessitated by the
rising price level, but in part they must be ascribed to a major
weakness in budget practices: the fiscal accounts for the preceding year are usually closed several months after the budget is
approved. The budget liquidation data—which in recent years

showed substantial Treasury balances — have been taken as a justification for requesting additional appropriations and expanding government operations, with complete disregard of the fact that a drawing down of Treasury balances has essentially the same expansionary impact on the economy as a government deficit. In consequence of the large amounts of additional appropriations, the comparison between liquidated and authorized expenditures invariably shows an excess of final appropriations over liquidated expenditures. The latter were, however, always larger than the original appropriations.

The budget law reserves for Congress the authority to transfer appropriated funds from one branch (*ramo*) of the government to another. (Only when Congress is not in session can the administration authorize such transfers, but it must report them to the next session of Congress.) The administration has, however, the right to transfer funds within each branch. Since the largest expenditures of the government are concentrated in the ministries of state which form one branch, and in the branch, "extraordinary investment," the administration has wide latitude in the use of appropriated funds. In a certain sense, this latitude defeats the budgetary control functions exercised by Congress.

Administration and Control of Expenditures

Disbursements.—All disbursements of government funds are made by the Treasury or its agencies. Ordinary expenditures can be disbursed on the basis of the budgetary appropriations. However, extraordinary expenditures (including extraordinary investment expenditures) require a special authorization (*acuerdo de erogación*) by the President. The process of obtaining an *erogación* involves the approval of the Minister under whose jurisdiction and budget the particular expenditure falls, the Budget Office, the Court and Control Office of Accounts, the Minister of Finance, and the President. The authorization is published in the *Diario Oficial* (Official Gazette). The procedure of securing a payments authorization frequently takes several weeks. For this reason, authorizations for payments on suspense account (*documentos pendientes*) frequently have been resorted to. As the annual reports of the Court and Control Office of Accounts have pointed out, the extensive use of this *documentos pendientes* procedure has resulted in a circumvention of budget limitations and made budgetary controls largely ineffective. As Table 28 shows, payments

TABLE 28

PAYMENTS ON SUSPENSE ACCOUNT (DOCUMENTOS PENDIENTES),
1937/38 TO 1948/49

(*In thousands of quetzales*)

Fiscal Year	Payments on Suspense Account	Budgetary Cash Expenditures	Suspense Account Payments as Percent of Budgetary Cash Expenditures
1937/38	2,999.9	11,072.2	27.1
1938/39	2,512.3	13,807.5	18.2
1939/40	2,060.5	10,949.8	18.8
1940/41	2,340.1	10,374.9	22.6
1941/42	2,423.7	10,851.9	22.4
1942/43	3,249.7	12,752.9	25.5
1943/44	4,148.2	13,586.4[a]	30.5
1944/45	6,165.0	21,884.4	28.2
1945/46	7,067.9	28,880.9	24.5
1946/47	9,861.6	28,375.8	34.1
1947/48	14,786.4	41,549.0	35.6
1948/49	6,929.9	48,029.1	14.4

[a] Excluding purchase of United States government bond of $1 million.

on suspense account have amounted in some years to one-third of total budgetary cash expenditures. In order to eliminate the use of this device, the Court and Control Office of Accounts established in 1948 permanent funds (*fondos permanentes*) for nine ministries. The purpose of the establishment of the permanent funds is to keep suspense-account payments outstanding at any time within the limits of the permanent funds. These funds amounted at the end of 1948/49 to 957,000 quetzales, of which amount 620,000 quetzales were allocated to the Ministry of Communications and Public Works. The relatively low volume of payments on suspense accounts in 1948/49 indicates that the new procedure has been quite successful so far.

Budget controls.—The controls over the financial operations of the government are exercised by the Court and Control Office of Accounts, an independent government agency. The Court of Accounts consists of five members. Two of them are appointed by the Supreme Court, two by Congress, and one by the President. Each member is appointed for a term of four years. In addition to the government accounts proper, the Court and Control Office of Accounts controls the financial transactions of the City of Guatemala, of San Carlos University and of certain other autonomous institutions. Within four months after the end of each fiscal year, the Ministry of Finance is required to send a report to the Control Office. The report must provide information on the assets and liabilities of the government and on the Treasury position, a comparison between appropriated and liquidated expenditures, and a general statement on the financial conditions of the country.

Within three months after receiving this report, the Court and Control Office of Accounts reports to the President and to Congress on the "state and management of the Treasury, the public debt, the budget and its execution." In recent years the reports of the Court of Accounts have been openly critical of the expenditure practices of some ministries. The attention of the President and of Congress was called to the use of confidential funds for the payment of salaries in excess of appropriations, to the practice of evading public bidding procedures by splitting up purchases into amounts below Q1,000 and to various circumventions of budgetary limitations on expenditures.[7]

THE PUBLIC DEBT AND CREDIT OPERATIONS

Year-to-year changes in the size of the direct obligations of the national government since June 30, 1937, are shown in Table 29.[8] As may be seen, the recent public-debt history of Guatemala may

---

[7] See chapter v, p. 126.

[8] Contingent liabilities of the national government, in the form of guaranties of bonds issued by the municipalities and the National Mortgage Credit Institute, are not shown. These obligations are discussed in chapter x.

TABLE 29

COMPOSITION OF PUBLIC DEBT

(In millions of quetzales; end of June)

Item[a]	1937	1938	1939	1940	1941	1942	1943	1944	1945	1946	1947	1948	1949
Internal debt:													
Northern Railway Bonds (6%)[b]	0.10	0.10	0.10	....	....	....	....	....	....	....	....	....	....
Internal Debt Bonds 1887 (6%)[b]	0.21	0.21	0.21	....	....	....	....	....	....	....	....	....	....
Loans from banks[c]	2.57	2.58	0.09	0.04	0.01	....	....	....	....	0.40	0.40	2.20	4.24
Treasury letters and notes	....	....	....	....	....	....	....	....	....	....	....	1.39	7.10[f]
Bond for the consolidation of the coinage system	....	....	....	....	....	....	....	....	....	2.60	2.60	2.60	2.60
Other internal obligations[c]	0.09	0.09	0.73	....	....	....	....	....	....	....	....	....	....
Total internal debt	2.97	2.98	1.13	0.04	0.01	....	....	....	....	3.00	3.00	6.19	13.94
External debt:													
Los Altos Railway Readjustment Bonds, 1936 (3%)[d]	1.74	1.64	1.54	1.43	1.31	1.24	1.13	1.08	0.93	0.83	0.73	0.63	0.63
Guatemalan External Sterling Debt Bonds, 1895–1913, 1928 (4%)	7.44	7.47	7.07	5.37	6.12	6.12	6.12	6.12	1.83	....	....	....	....
Bonds of Republic of Guatemala of 1947, 1928 (8%)	1.33	1.33	1.33	1.32	1.32	1.32	1.32	1.30	....	....	....	....	....
Guatemalan External Gold Loan, 1930 (7%)	2.46	2.46	....	....	....	....	....	....	....	....	....	....	....
Other external debt obligations[e]	0.94	1.01	0.81	0.76	0.80	0.81	0.88	0.92	0.25	0.17	0.18	0.02	0.04
Total external debt	13.92	13.91	10.75	8.88	9.55	9.49	9.45	9.42	3.01	1.00	0.91	0.65	0.67
Total debt	16.89	16.89	11.88	8.92	9.56	9.49·	9.45	9.42	3.01	4.00	3.91	6.84	14.61

[a] Individual items are not shown when less than Q5,000.

[b] Includes accumulated interest.

[c] Floating debt except in 1940, which also includes a loan from the Compañía Agrícola in prepayment of taxes.

[d] Changes from 1938 to 1941 are partly due to changes in the value of the pound sterling.

[e] Includes deferred-interest certificates and obligations to Anglo-California National Bank and to Allgemeine Elektrizitaets Gesellschaft, Berlin, for telephone installations.

[f] Includes letters and notes of Social Security Institute amounting to Q50,000.

be roughly divided into two periods. From 1937 to 1946, debt policy was presumably determined by a desire to extinguish a burdensome, high-interest debt. The period since 1946 has been characterized by an increase in domestic borrowing, induced in part by the new government's announced policy of promoting a higher rate of economic development, but primarily associated with expenditures for the Sixth Olympic Games of the Caribbean Area which were held in Guatemala City during the spring of 1950.

Historical Survey

As of June 30, 1937, the total debt of the Guatemalan government amounted to 16.9 million quetzales. Of this, 13.9 million was in the form of external sterling and dollar obligations, and 3.0 million represented internal debt, most of which was owed the Anglo-South American Bank. Service charges were relatively heavy, the interest on the external debt alone amounting to more than Q500,000.

During the fiscal year 1938/39, the government commenced the task of reducing this burden. Utilizing cash balances accumulated during previous years and the proceeds from a tax-anticipation loan of one million quetzales from the Compañía Agricola,[9] the authorities retired 4.1 million quetzales of obligations through cash payments, and succeeded in reducing the debt by an additional 2.0 millions through agreements with various creditors. As a result, the 7 percent dollar loan of 1930 was completely liquidated, as were the obligation to the Anglo-South American Bank and the outstanding internal bonded debt.[10]

The tax-anticipation loan from the Compañía Agricola was the only new net borrowing of significant size which occurred during the 1937–46 period. This transaction did not represent a break with the general policy of debt reduction, since it was only carried out in order to facilitate the retirement of other, more

---

[9] A subsidiary of the United Fruit Company.

[10] Most of the payments on the internal bonded debt were effected during 1938/39, although they are not shown on the books until the following year.

burdensome obligations and was extinguished through tax offsets within two years. From that date until 1946/47, there was no internal debt to speak of. What was carried under this heading on the books of the Court and Control Office of Accounts were commercial liabilities which were not paid during the fiscal year in which they were incurred.

In the case of the external debt, the government continued to amortize the Los Altos Railway bonds during the period, setting aside on the average Q100,000 per year and sometimes taking advantage of market conditions to purchase bonds below par. But no further substantial reductions in external obligations were made until 1944/45.[11] During that year, the Bonds of the Republic of 1927 were retired completely. At the same time, the 4 percent sterling debt was called for redemption at full face value. Only Q4.29 million of bonds were exchanged for cash before the offer was closed on January 15, 1945, and the remaining 1.83 million of these bonds were declared canceled under the assumption that they were held by enemy aliens.

Since the beginning of 1945, the external debt has been of negligible size; on June 30, 1949, it amounted to only some Q670,000.

Postwar Credit Operations

In the case of the internal debt, the retirement policy was reversed after the end of the war, and the government commenced borrowing again. During 1945/46, the authorities incurred a liability of 0.4 million quetzales to the Banco de Guatemala in connection with the latter's contribution to the International Monetary Fund; they also issued a special bond of 2.6 millions to compensate the new central bank for assuming the liability of the outstanding Treasury coin issue. Both of these transactions were obviously intragovernment bookkeeping arrangements, and al-

---

[11] The decline in the quetzal value of the 4 percent sterling debt from 7.44 million on June 30, 1937, to 6.12 million on June 30, 1941, was entirely due to the depreciation of the pound sterling during the period. No cash payments were made, and the sterling value of the outstanding bonds remained unchanged.

though they represent legal liabilities of the government, they had no monetary or economic impact on the country.

Really important borrowing started in 1947/48 when the government obtained a loan of 1.8 million quetzales from the National Mortgage Credit Institute. Of these funds, 1.5 million were used for the construction of the Olympic Stadium, and the remainder was spent for low-cost housing. Although interest payments have been maintained, no repayment of the principal has so far taken place. On the contrary, during the following year (1948/49), the loan from the National Mortgage Credit Institute was increased to 3.84 million, the stadium expenses having by that time risen to 3.3 million and the housing costs to 0.54 million.

These credit operations of the government were partly reflected in another set of transactions with the National Mortgage Credit Institute, for the government actually reborrowed funds which it had given to this agency in the form of letters and notes for 1.39 million (October 1947) and 1.00 million (October 1948).[12] The combined result of both sets of transactions was to increase the government debt by 6.23 million, although the addition to national income through government expenditures amounted to only 3.84 million. However, both the letters and notes given to the National Mortgage Credit Institute and the funds reborrowed from it represent separate legal liabilities of the government.

The only other major debt operation which took place during the period covered by this study (through June 30, 1949) was the issuance of 5 million in bonds to the production Development Institute (INFOP) as a partial contribution to its capital.[13] INFOP had not disposed of any of these securities by the end of fiscal 1948/49, but sold 2.5 million to the Banco de Guatemala during the first six months of 1949/50.[14]

[12] The National Mortgage Credit Institute repaid 0.34 million of the first issue during 1948/49.

[13] Between June 30, 1949, and December 31, 1949, the government borrowed 4.4 million in new funds and repaid 1.2 million on outstanding loans. The public debt thus increased by 3.2 million during this six-month period.

[14] The activities of the Production Development Institute are analyzed in some detail in chapter xi.

INTERNATIONAL COMPARISON

Introduction

Thus far, the discussion of government expenditures has been confined to an account of the experience of the Guatemalan government in recent years. In order to provide a broader basis for appraising the relative importance of various classes of government expenditures, this section presents a comparison of Guatemalan expenditures with those of other countries. The countries chosen for this comparison are the same as those selected for the international comparison of receipts in chapter iii. The categories of expenditures are those presented in preceding sections of this chapter with the exception of a sixth category required for certain classes of payments which did not seem to fit the other classifications.

The comparison shows that although considerable differences exist from country to country in the relative importance of the various categories of government expenditures, it is possible to discern a broad but fairly well-defined pattern. In most of the countries shown, two-thirds to three-fourths of the total budgetary outlays were allocated in more or less equal proportions to administrative, social and cultural, and development purposes. With few exceptions, considerably smaller amounts were devoted to national defense and public debt service. The expenditure distribution of the Guatemalan government conformed quite closely to this general pattern.

Administrative Expenditures

A major part of government outlays in almost all of the countries under consideration was for administrative purposes, as is shown in Table 30. In Guatemala these expenditures amounted to approximately 27 percent. El Salvador, Peru, Venezuela, and Denmark expended a larger part (40 to 45 percent) of their total outlays for such activities than any of the other countries shown in the table. The smallest share of expenditures for administrative purposes, 6 to 8 percent, was recorded for the United States. This percentage is probably due to a large extent to a higher

TABLE 30

COMPOSITION OF GOVERNMENT EXPENDITURES OF SELECTED COUNTRIES[a]

(Fiscal year ended with month indicated)

	Total Expenditures (*Millions of national currency*)	Percentage Composition of Expenditures by Function					
		Administrative	National Defense	Cultural and Social	Economic Development	Public Debt Service	Other Expenditures
Guatemala (June 1948)	45.9 quetzales	27.2	9.2	27.4	35.0	1.3	....
Chile (December 1946)	6,726.2[b] pesos	27.0	34.2	25.1	13.3	0.4	....
El Salvador (December 1949)	52.4 colones	39.5	11.2	21.4	23.1	4.8	....
Haiti (September 1948)	83.6 gourdes	25.6	17.0	21.2	23.4	12.8	....
Mexico (December 1946)	1,770.4 pesos	25.2	14.3	14.6	29.2	16.7	....
Peru (December 1946)	617.2 soles	41.5	25.4	20.9	7.5	4.7	....
Venezuela (June 1946)	754.7 bolivares	40.6	7.4	10.9	40.9	0.2	....
United Kingdom (March 1947)	3,910.3 pounds	37.3	11.6	34.7	3.7	12.7	....
United States (June 1948)							
Federal only	34,179.1 dollars	5.5	33.4	25.4	6.5	15.2	14.0[c]
Federal and state	46,140.6 dollars	8.5	24.7	32.9	11.4	12.2	10.3[c]
Denmark (March 1947)	2,494.8[d] kroner	45.4	8.4	27.3	1.0	17.9	....[c]
New Zealand (March 1947)	182.8 NZ pounds	17.2	14.1	32.2	11.9	14.2	10.4[c]

[a] The data shown refer in each case to budgetary expenditures of national government only. Because outlays for education, highway construction, etc., which in other countries are borne by the national government, are to a large extent made by state governments in the United States, state as well as federal expenditures have been included for the United States.

[b] Ordinary and supplementary budgets only; excludes nonbudgetary expenditures estimated at 23 percent of the reported ordinary and supplementary budgets.

[c] Comprises foreign relief, international reconstruction and rehabilitation (UNRRA), monetary stabilization (contributions to the International Monetary Fund and International Bank), and payments for Philippine war damages and rehabilitation.

[d] Wherever data were available, gross expenditures have been substituted for the net figures reported in the closed budget.

[e] Consists mainly of gifts to the United Kingdom as contributions to war costs.

degree of administrative efficiency in that country, although it may also reflect to relatively large part of total expenditures devoted to national defense purposes.

Expenditures for National Defense

Because of the generally unsettled conditions which have prevailed throughout the world since the end of the war, defense expenditures in several of the countries account for a fairly large part of total government expenditures. The United States and Chile allocated more than 33 percent of their outlays to this purpose, while most of the remaining countries kept defense expenditures within 11 to 25 percent of their total outlays; only Guatemala, Venezuela, and Denmark devoted less than 10 percent of government expenditures to this purpose.

Social and Cultural Expenditures

The proportion of total outlays spent for social and cultural purposes varied widely from country to country, according to prevailing social attitudes and institutions. The United Kingdom, New Zealand, and the United States, whose pension, insurance, and other social programs are among the most extensive and advanced of any in the world, devoted approximately a third of their expenditures to social and cultural purposes. Guatemala, with 27 percent of its expenditures allocated to such purposes, equaled the experience of Denmark and approached fairly closely the proportion allocated in the first three countries. The importance of such outlays in the United States, however, is somewhat understated because the expenditures of subordinate governmental bodies, which include large outlays for education, public health, recreation, and unemployment compensation, do not appear in the federal and state data shown. Social and cultural expenditures in the other countries compared ranged from 11 percent in Venezuela to 25 percent in Chile.

Economic Development Expenditures

Budgetary outlays for economic development formed a relatively large proportion of total government expenditures in most of the Latin-American countries shown. Guatemala, with 35 percent, was second only to Venezuela where 40 percent of government expenditures were devoted to development purposes. El Salvador, Haiti, and Mexico followed with 20 to 30 percent, and Chile and Peru allocated smaller proportions of their budgets for this type of expenditure. As might be expected, budgetary outlays for development purposes in the economically more advanced countries, where private capital investment is larger, were relatively unimportant.[15]

A comparison of development expenditures for a single year, of course, does not provide an adequate basis for judging the relative development effort of the various countries. In some instances the expenditures made in the years shown represent only initial phases of major development plans which may take many years to complete and may require disbursements many times larger than those expended at the beginning. Nor is the full extent of governmental participation always revealed by budgetary expenditures of the national government, since development projects financed through financial institutions especially created for this purpose may not appear in the budget statistics of government expenditures.

Public Debt Service

The comparison of expenditures for public debt service are subject to limitations similar to those noted in the preceding discussion of development outlays. Because debt retirement is accomplished in some instances through institutions whose operations are outside the ordinary budget, actual changes in the public debt may not be revealed by budget liquidation records. The comparison also fails to specify those amortization payments which are offset by borrowings and thus represent only refunding operations.

[15] The small percentage shown for the United Kingdom is due to the fact that most of the investment expenditures of the national government are not included in the budget and to the fact that a large proportion of public investment, such as highway construction and public housing, is undertaken by local governmental bodies whose expenditures are not included in the table. The latter also applies, with some modification, to the United States.

The virtual liquidation of the Guatemalan foreign debt and the minor amount of domestic debt outstanding in 1947/48 reduced the service burden on the Guatemalan budget to negligible proportions. In the case of Chile, the even lower percentage shown was a result of the fact that the amortization of the public debt in Chile is largely entrusted to the Caja de Amortización, which applies earmarked, nonbudgetary tax revenues, as well as revenues from other agencies, to the servicing of the public debt and of obligations issued by certain agencies. Among the Latin-American countries shown, Mexico, with 17 percent, and Haiti, with 13 percent, devoted the largest budgetary shares to public debt service. Expenditures for this purpose claimed a similar portion of the budgets of New Zealand, Denmark, the United Kingdom, and the United States.

STATISTICAL NOTE

Expenditures of the national government.—The expenditure figures shown in Table 21 purport to represent cash expenditures. They were computed from Treasury movement data presented in Table 20. They include all budgetary expenditures, irrespective of the year for which they were budgeted, as well as nonbudgetary expenditures and net expenditures on suspense account. Nonbudgetary expenditures appear in Table 20 under three headings: "Expenditures for Roosevelt Highway"; "Other," which comprise expenditures on the housing construction program in 1947/48; and "Other nonbudgetary disbursements (net)." The last group corresponds to the item "Other nonbudgetary receipts (net)," shown under receipts and explained in the Statistical Note to chapter iii. "Other nonbudgetary disbursements (net)" appear only in those years in which the gross credit entries of all types of expenditures included in this group exceeded the gross debit under the same headings.

Disbursements of assigned revenues are not included in expenditures of the national government as shown in Table 21 since the amounts involved appear as expenditures of the autonomous institutions and municipalities to which they are assigned. They are included, however, in the cash expenditure figures shown in Table 22.

Expenditures on suspense account are shown "net." That is to say, those amounts which are offset by debit entries have been deducted from the *total* credit entries on suspense account because the debit offset indicates that the expenditures in question have been charged against a budgetary appropriation, the disbursement of which is included in budgetary expenditures, while those disbursements on suspense account, which at the annual closing of the Treasury accounts had not been charged as yet against appropriations, represent an addition to budgetary expenditures. In those fiscal years, however, in which the debit offsets of suspense accounts exceed gross disbursements on suspense account (thus resulting in a nominal increase of budgetary expenditures), the difference between debit and credit entries had to be deducted in order to arrive at the correct amount of cash expenditures. Therefore, net expenditures on suspense account appear in Table 20 in some years with a minus sign.

Liquidated expenditures of the national government shown in Tables 23 and 24 were taken from official government accounts prepared by the Court and Control Office of Accounts. The classification of expenditures by purpose presented in Tables 23 and 24 was especially prepared for this study by the Research Department of the Banco de Guatemala. These tables were based on an analysis of payrolls and special authorizations (*acuerdos de erogación*), since the breakdown of the official liquidation data proved to be insufficiently detailed for this purpose. In certain instances, the data obtained from the analysis of payrolls and authorizations were supplemented by a comparison with budget data which are, as indicated above, more detailed than liquidation data. A reconciliation of the classification of expenditures by purpose with the original liquidation data would be too voluminous and too cumbersome to warrant presentation here.

The data shown in Tables 25 and 26 (expenditures by types of payment) were derived from an extensive sampling of the disbursement accounts of the Court and Control Office of Accounts. For a limited number of years all disbursements were analyzed; in intervening years the same percentage distribution of the various types of expenditures applicable to subtotals (of branches [*ramos*] and ministries) was used as those in fully analyzed years.

Municipalities.—Expenditure data were taken from the same sources as municipal receipts; for years prior to 1946/47, the same adjustments were made as in the receipts accounts.

San Carlos University and Social Security Institute.—Expenditures include disbursements of funds received from the national government.

Production Development Institute.—Expenditure data include administrative disbursements as well as disbursements of loans made to private enterprises.

V

THE IMPACT OF THE FISCAL SYSTEM ON BUSINESS

By PRESENTING a description of the Guatemalan fiscal system and of the economy within which it operates, the preceding chapters have laid the groundwork for an analysis of the effects of the government budget on various aspects of the country's economic life. This and the following three chapters consider the impact of the fiscal system upon the business community, the individual household, and the operations of the government itself, while the final three chapters explore the influence of budgetary operations on the national income, the monetary system, the balance of payments, and the economic development of the country.

The purpose of the present chapter is to investigate the effects of the fiscal system on various forms of industrial, commercial, and agricultural activity, i.e., on the business community in the widest sense of the term. Since the most obvious and most immediate impact of the government's fiscal operations on business is the impact of taxation, most of the discussion will be concerned with an analysis of the effects of taxation on the profitability, size, and conduct of business operations, the structure of production, the form of business organization, and the size and direction of business investment. The government in its role as a buyer and seller of goods and services, including the hiring of personnel, also affects business in various ways; this aspect of the effects of fiscal operations will be discussed in the final section of the chapter.

TAX SHIFTING IN GUATEMALA

In Guatemala, as in many other countries, business firms *pay* most of the nation's taxes. But this obviously does not mean that businesses *bear* all or even most of the taxes collected from them. Quite the contrary: almost all taxes paid by business firms may be presumed to be shifted either forward in the form of higher prices on goods that are bought by their customers, or backward in the form of lower returns to those supplying services, particularly labor, to business firms.

Before we investigate the process and the effects of tax shifting in Guatemala, a few general remarks about the concept of tax shifting and its specific application to this study seem necessary. The concept of tax shifting is fairly ambiguous and implies different things to different people. Tax shifting is usually discussed in connection with the analysis of the reaction of individuals or individual business firms to the imposition or abolition of a particular tax or to the raising or lowering of the rates of particular taxes. Conceptual difficulties often arise because attempts are made to separate the incidence or direct money burden of a tax from its indirect effects. In this study the analysis of tax incidence serves primarily as a prelude to the analysis, in later chapters, of such aggregative effects of the Guatemalan tax system as its influence on the distribution of income, the level of consumption and income, and the balance of payments. For this reason the present section is concerned primarily with the more *limited* incidence concept of tax shifting; the *wider* incidence and the indirect effects of the Guatemalan tax system are the subject of other parts of the study.[1]

The shiftability of taxes varies, of course, with the economic structure and fiscal system of individual countries, and it is extremely difficult to obtain definite quantitative results from a

---

[1] In other words, an attempt is made to apply to the Guatemalan tax structure methods of tax shifting analysis similar to those developed in the classic studies of Colm and Tarasov for the United States, and Shirras and Rostas, and Barna for the United Kingdom: Helen Tarasov (under the supervision of Gerhard Colm), "Who Pays the Taxes?" *TNEC Monograph No. 3* (Washington, D.C.: U.S. Government Printing Office, 1941); Helen Tarasov, "Who Does Pay the Taxes?" *Social Research*, Supplement IV (New York, 1942); G. Findlay Shirras and L. Rostas, *The Burden of British Taxation* (New York: The Macmillan Company, 1943); Tibor Barna, *Redistribution of Incomes Through the Fiscal System in 1937* (Oxford: Clarendon Press, 1945).

statistical inquiry. In order to make an exhaustive study, detailed information would be required on the market conditions of individual industries, the responsiveness of supply and demand for different products to price and income changes, the ability or desire of consumers to substitute one product for another, and a number of other equally complex factors. The collection and analysis of such information would in itself be a separate time-consuming task, and although the findings with respect to tax shifting would then be more exact, they would not necessarily enhance the validity of the broader findings of the study. For this purpose, all that is needed is a knowledge of the probable range in which tax shifting takes place in Guatemala.

Some of the factors which determine the extent of tax shifting, like the nature of the tax liability and the degree of competition and market structure of individual industries, may remain basically unchanged for fairly long periods of time, but others, like the general state of economic and business activity and the degree of government interference with the free movements of prices and wages, may change radically from year to year. A detailed analysis that is based on the conditions prevailing in Guatemala in the fiscal year 1947/48 follows.

Tax Shifting and the Nature of Individual Taxes

From the point of view of tax shifting, Guatemalan taxes fall into two major groups: those which fall on all competing firms in an industry and regularly account for part of the tax costs of business enterprises, and those which do not. The greatest part of collections belong to the first of these categories. Alcoholic beverages and tobacco production taxes, import and export taxes, business license and transaction taxes, and those motor vehicle and property taxes that are imposed on businesses[2] are all paid regularly by enterprises in particular industries, and tend to add equally to the average cost of the competing firms. Entrepreneurs

---

[2] Motor vehicle, property, and property transfer taxes are paid by both business units and individuals. An examination of the motor vehicle registry and mortgage records indicate that business pays approximately two-thirds of these.

generally treat such taxes like any other type of business cost and attempt to pass them on to the consumer in the form of higher prices, a process which, other things being equal, is made easier by the fact that the tax liability of every firm in the industry is proportionate to the amounts of its inputs.

The second group of taxes comprises the business profits tax, the property transfer taxes paid by business, fees, fines, and certain minor miscellaneous taxes. These duties do not regularly form part of the costs of all enterprises in an industry but affect particular firms only. As in the preceding case, the entrepreneur affected by these taxes will attempt to shift his tax liability forward to the consumer, but since his competitors probably do not have to pay them, he may, under conditions approximating perfect competition, be able to raise prices only at the risk of losing part of his market.

The business profits tax is probably less fully shifted than other taxes on Guatemalan businesses. Because of the Q500 exemption and the fact that only firms with a capital of Q2,500 are subject to it, the tax is paid only by some firms in an industry and, in view of its progressiveness, the companies which pay it are taxed at different rates. Nevertheless, interviews with Guatemalan accountants, government officials, and businessmen themselves indicate that businessmen consider the business profits tax as part of their total business cost, and—depending on conditions in individual industries—pass a substantial proportion of it on to their customers.

Tax Shifting and the Market Structure of Individual Industries

These considerations with respect to the shiftability of different types of taxes must be modified to take account of the degree of competition and market structure prevailing in individual industries. Although a detailed analysis of business conditions and the market structure in Guatemala is beyond the scope of this study, even a brief investigation indicates that, in general, market conditions are conducive to a high degree of tax shifting. In most important areas of business activity, there are comparatively few competing firms. Protected by the relatively high costs of inland transportation and, in some instances, by tariff walls and import controls, many Guatemalan businessmen encounter little competition from abroad. Moreover, because of the smallness of the domestic market, traditional high-profit margins, and the relatively slow responsiveness of production to price changes, the degree of price competition, except in certain lines and on certain occasions, is limited.[3] With these qualifications, businessmen can pass on their taxes in the form of higher prices without fear of losing sales, because their competitors will follow suit.

There are certain important Guatemalan industries in which taxes cannot be shifted forward to the consumer. Chief among these is the coffee industry, the country's major foreign-exchange earner. The coffee export tax does, of course, add equally to the costs of all exporters, but since the Guatemalan product accounts for only slightly more than 2 percent of world coffee exports, it is doubtful that even the combined efforts of all Guatemalan coffee exporters can influence the world price. Much the same conclusion can be drawn with respect to the banana industry, notwithstanding the fact that the United Fruit Company, the country's leading producer and exporter, probably acts as a price leader in the United States market, setting sales prices that are accepted as the prevailing market price by other banana importers. Since only a portion of the company's total production is grown in Guatemala, its managers would probably not risk curbing total sales in the American market by raising prices in an effort to pass on the tax liabilities incurred in that country.

With respect to the export of chicle, the situation was somewhat different in earlier years, for the companies were probably able to shift the exploitation and export taxes to the foreign consumer. However, with the growth of competition from synthetic products in the United States, shifting has most likely been negli-

---

[3] Interindustry competition, as contrasted with intraindustry competition, is discussed on p. 118.

gible in the last few years. This appears to be in part borne out by the falling of production and exports that has recently occurred, although a large part of this decline might have taken place in the absence of the chicle taxes.

In the case of the coffee export tax, there are special reasons to believe that it is shifted backward, not to wages, but rather to the entrepreneurial income of the producer. In view of the great weight of the tax relative to the profit margins of exporters, it is quite clear that the government does not intend to have the exporter actually bear the coffee export tax. Because it is less costly to collect and more difficult to evade a duty imposed at a convenient shipping point than one levied at the place of production, it seems clear that the government uses the exporter as an intermediary in the collection of the tax from the grower. Some support for this view is contained in the prevailing form of sales contracts between growers and exporters; these stipulate the purchase price, f.o.b., minus inland transportation costs and export taxes.

It is not believed that the plantation owner can pass the tax backward to his employees to any significant extent. In most sectors of the Guatemalan coffee industry, the wage structure is conventional, nonmonetary, and even paternalistic in character. The money wage, which at present averages about thirty-five centavos per day, is usually supplemented by additional income in the form of food and housing, and—in the case of permanent laborers—by the use of a small, rent-free plot of ground. In view of the closeness of the average coffee worker's income to the subsistence level, the opportunity for shifting the coffee export tax backward is severely limited. Although the coffee industry is a major employer of labor, its workers, particularly those who are hired seasonally, are not necessarily tied to it. Many have the alternative of cultivating their own lands more intensively, and some have the opportunity of moving to urban areas. Moreover, on account of the relative scarcity of labor during the boom of the last few years, it is very unlikely that *finca* owners would have lowered wages, for fear of having their crops go unharvested. The possibility is not precluded, however, that some sort of slow shifting process takes place and that wages have not risen as they might have in the absence of the tax. But the result, by and large, has been that the coffee export tax, which is paid by the exporter, has been borne to a very large extent by the coffee grower.[4]

Tax Shifting in 1947/48

The state of general economic and business activity and the degree of government interference in the free functioning of various markets also exercise an influence on the extent to which taxes are shifted during any period. Since these factors may vary significantly from year to year, it must be borne in mind that the conclusions given in this section apply primarily to the year under consideration, namely 1947/48, although they are valid for other years in which the tax structure and economic conditions were similar.

The year 1947/48 was characterized in Guatemala, as in the rest of the world economy, by a shortage of goods and services in terms of money purchasing power and a consequent inflationary increase in prices. Under such circumstances, all taxes, and particularly the business profits tax, tend to become more highly shiftable for two important reasons. In the first place, consumer expenditures for goods and services become less responsive to price increases than under more normal conditions, and businessmen find it easier to pass on taxes in the form of higher prices. Second, each individual firm in an industry will feel more confident in raising its prices to the full extent of a tax because the manager will expect his competitors—when faced with the same seller's market—to do the same.[5]

Although there was no general price-control law in effect in

---

[4] The same conclusion applies, of course, to other taxes paid by or shifted to the coffee producer.

[5] In a seller's market, of course, businessmen may charge as high a price in the absence of a tax as they would with it. This indicates the conceptual difficulty of distinguishing in actual practice between tax incidence and other factors affecting price.

Guatemala during 1947/48, controls did exist on selected items like housing, medicines, milk, sugar, cotton, alcoholic beverages, and a few imported metal products. For the most part, these did not interfere with the shifting of the taxes applicable to the items. The legislation stipulated that major taxes (e.g., import duties in the case of the metal products and production taxes in the case of alcoholic beverages) were to be counted as part of the allowable cost of the business. Other taxes were not explicitly provided for, but since these were generally taxes that had been in effect for a period of years, they had already become incorporated in the normal cost structure of business and were consequently included in allowable cost by implication.

In two instances, however, the controls seem to have limited the ability of business to shift taxes. A special sugar sales tax of Q1.50 per quintal was imposed only on the sugar that was produced on plantations belonging to persons who were on the wartime black list and for this reason was not taken into account when the legal sugar price was established. The existence of rent controls, moreover, checked the freedom of landlords to pass on the property tax to their tenants, but since some evidence exists that the controls were not strictly or uniformly enforced, it would appear that this interference was quite small.

A statistical estimate showing the probable order of magnitude of the taxes paid and shifted by business during 1947/48 is presented in Table 31. Four groups of taxes may be distinguished: (1) those which fall equally on all firms in industries whose market structures are conducive to shifting and are thus fully passed on to the consumer,[6] (2) those which are imposed on some firms only or on a net income base and which are estimated to have been shifted 50 percent because of the seller's market that existed during that year, (3) those which are par-

---

[6] In technical terms, complete shifting of an individual tax may, of course, occur only in the limiting case of the price elasticity of demand being equal to zero and the price elasticity of supply being infinite. In the case of these taxes, however, actual shifting so closely approximates this theoretical case that a more defensible approximation of the true situation is given by shifting them completely than by arbitrarily selecting some figures below 100 percent.

tially unshifted because of the market structure in particular industries, and (4) those which are completely unshifted due to market conditions or the existence of price controls.

TABLE 31

ESTIMATE OF TAXES PAID AND SHIFTED BY BUSINESS IN 1947/48

(In thousands of quetzales)

Type of Tax	Taxes Paid by Business	Taxes Shifted by Business to the Consumer	Unshifted Portion of Business Taxes
Consumption taxes[a]	8,196	8,196	....
Import duties on consumers' goods	6,628	6,628	....
Air and rail transportation taxes	165	165	....
Business license taxes	415	415	....
Business profits tax	3,048	1,524	1,524
Property transfer taxes[b]	73	36	37
Fees and Fines[c]	146	73	73
Property taxes[b]	325	293	32
Motor vehicle taxes[b]	145	131	14
Import duties on business goods	6,445	5,314	1,131
Business transaction taxes	1,980	1,782	198
Miscellaneous taxes[c]	74	67	7
Export taxes	2,664	....	2,664
Sugar taxes	49	....	49
Special taxes[d]	81	....	81
Total taxes paid by business	30,434	24,624	5,810
Total as percent of total tax collections	97%	—	—
Total as percent of total taxes paid by business	100%	81%	19%

[a] Includes entertainment, alcoholic beverage, and tobacco taxes.
[b] Two-thirds of these taxes estimated as being paid by business.
[c] One-half of these taxes estimated as being paid by business.
[d] Includes absentee ownership and special income taxes on the Guatemalan Electric Company and central bank.

To an important extent, taxes which lower consumption through the shifting process imply a substitution of the production of government goods and services for private goods and services[7] and this decline in the demand for total private production affects the business community adversely. Despite the presence of these wider, indirect effects, however, the narrow concept of shifting employed in this section is useful for it facilitates the

[7] These aggregative effects on production are discussed in connection with the analysis of the influence of the fiscal system on national income in chapter ix.

analysis of tax incidence from the point of view of changes in the composition rather than the level of tax receipts. The business community is probably adversely affected by all types of taxes, but it is undoubtedly better off under the present system which is characterized by a high proportion of shiftable taxes than it would be under a system that permitted less extensive shifting.

During 1947/48, the business community paid approximately 97 percent of all taxes collected by the government.[8] Of this total, about 80 percent was shifted forward to the consumer, and the remainder was borne by the business firms themselves. The burden of this unshifted portion varied as between individual industries; an analysis of the incidence of taxes on selected business enterprises is presented next.

The Burden of Taxes on Selected Business Enterprises

Table 32 shows the impact of taxation on eight types of enterprises, which are believed to be representative of a large section of the Guatemalan business community. Since all firms are assumed to have the same net income before taxation, differences in income do not affect the results,[9] which are related only to the different types of business and the different taxes imposed on them by the Guatemalan fiscal system, as it was constituted in 1947/48.[10] Of course, different types of business of the same net-income size have different amounts of invested capital and different sales volumes. Estimates, based on information collected by the Research Department of the Banco de Guatemala, have accordingly been made of the capital and sales volumes that on the average would apply to the different types of businesses with annual profits of Q20,000.

[8] Except the assigned taxes, which are not taken into account in this and subsequent tables on the tax burden. During 1947/48, collections of these taxes amounted to 1,085.5 thousand quetzales, and consisted of 910.1 thousand quetzales of consumption taxes on alcoholic beverages and cigarettes, 68.3 thousand quetzales in additional import duties on consumers' goods, and 107.1 thousand quetzales in coffee export tax surcharges. All but the last are probably fully shifted to the consumer.

[9] The relationship between taxation and the size of business firms is discussed in a subsequent section. See p. 114.

[10] The present tax system does not differ in any important respects from the one prevailing in 1947/48.

TABLE 32

IMPACT OF TAX SYSTEM UPON SELECTED BUSINESS FIRMS IN 1947/48[a]

(In quetzales)

	Cotton Grower	Sugar-Cane Grower	Coffee Grower	Coffee Exporter	Importer	Retailer	Textile Manufacturer	Liquor Manufacturer
Business income accounts in the absence of a tax system								
Business property:								
Real estate	18,000	45,000	50,000	80,000	25,000	.....	32,000	25,000
Other property	20,000	46,000	20,000	18,000	57,000	32,000	65,000	30,000
Total business property ...	38,000	91,000	70,000	98,000	82,000	32,000	97,000	55,000
Total receipts	35,289	61,651	44,715	283,271	101,629	77,097	91,693	120,096
Total costs	15,289	41,651	24,715	263,271	81,629	57,097	71,693	100,096
Net business income	20,000	20,000	20,000	20,000	20,000	20,000	20,000	20,000
Business income accounts under the 1947/48 tax system								
Total receipts:								
Receipts from goods and services[b] ..	35,480	61,994	42,000	283,271	101,855	86,620	94,058	241,717
Receipts from shifted taxes	520	1,636	......	......	18,145	1,380	1,942	4,168
Total receipts	36,000	63,630	42,000	283,271	120,000	88,000	96,000	245,885
Total costs:								
Cost of goods and services[b]	15,480	41,994	25,065	245,005	81,855	66,620	74,058	221,717
Tax costs	520	1,636	373	19,196	17,191	426	988	3,214
Total costs	16,000	43,630	25,438	264,201	99,046	67,046	75,046	224,931

Net income before business profits tax[a]	20,000	20,000	16,562	19,070	20,954	20,954	20,954	20,954
Business profits tax liability[b]	.....	.....	.....	1,773	2,051	2,051	2,051	2,051
Net income after business profits tax[c]	20,000	20,000	16,562	18,297	18,903	18,903	18,903	18,903
Loss of business income as a result of tax system[d]	.....	.....	3,438	1,703	1,097	1,097	1,097	1,097
Loss as percent of original net business income[e]	.....	.....	17%	9%	6%	6%	6%	6%

[a] The figures, as is indicated in the text, are examples only, and their seeming exactness should be interpreted accordingly.

[b] Includes taxes that are shifted to the firm by enterprises from which it purchases goods and services.

[c] In those enterprises subject to the business profits tax, net income before business profits tax is higher than net business income in the absence of a tax system because the shifting of this tax increases net profits; in the cases of other types of taxes on business, shifting doesn't raise net taxable income because the government considers these taxes as deductible costs for business profits tax accounting purposes.

[d] Net business income in the absence of a tax system, less net income after business profits tax.

[e] I.e., in the absence of a tax system.

Estimates of the total sales, total costs, and net income which the various firms would have had if there had been no tax system in Guatemala during 1947/48 are shown in the upper part of the table, while estimates of their actual business income accounts under that year's tax system are given in the lower section. Under this form of presentation, both the shifted and unshifted portions of the taxes imposed on the different businesses are illustrated.

Notwithstanding the seeming accuracy of the results shown in Table 32, they do, of course, contain a wide margin of error. But the final figure is low enough in every case to indicate that the incidence of taxation on business is relatively small. Significant variations exist among the various enterprises. The burden is highest (17 percent) in the case of the coffee grower,[11] who, as has been seen, can probably pass on only a limited part of his tax costs. It is next highest for those enterprises which are subject to the only partially shiftable business profits tax, and lowest in the cases of the sugar-cane and cotton growers, who are not subject to this tax. In the latter two cases, however, the apparent absence of any tax burden should not be considered as an indication that the tax has had no effect on these enterprises. Even if the demand for the products of these enterprises was completely irresponsive to price changes, their high tax payments would necessitate the investment of additional working capital to finance production.

It should be borne in mind that this analysis has been concerned with the statutory tax liabilities of the various firms rather than with their actual tax payments during 1947/48. Considering the absence of modern accounting standards and weaknesses in the administration of some of the taxes,[12] some tax evasion undoubtedly did occur, and the effective tax burdens of business are probably smaller than those indicated above. However, even if this factor is disregarded, it is evident that despite some range of

[11] The percentage burden of the coffee export tax varies, of course, with the price of coffee because it is levied on a specific basis. Since 1947/48, the price of coffee has risen much more than costs of production, and the tax burden on the coffee grower has declined commensurately. In 1949/50, it amounted to only 10 percent instead of 17 percent in the earlier year.

[12] The administration of taxes is discussed in chapter vii.

uncertainty surrounding the entire concept of shiftability, the burden of taxation on business is not very high.

The great shiftability of taxes upon business firms appears to indicate that attempts by the government to increase the tax burden of business relative to that of the consumer are likely to prove unsuccessful. Through the shifting process, a large part of the additional revenue would undoubtedly come out of the pockets of consumers. There is, however, one important, practical reason for continuing the prevailing practice of *collecting* the bulk of tax receipts from business: the task of revenue administration is thereby greatly simplified.

THE EFFECTS OF TAXATION ON BUSINESS

Although the direct incidence of the tax system on business is relatively small, the taxes which business firms pay and bear do have some fairly important indirect effects. The present section traces these effects on profit incentives, the form of business organization, the size of business firms, and the composition of production.

On Profit Incentives

The effects of taxes on profit incentives depend almost as much on the economic psychology of the business community as on the size of the prevailing tax burden. Because of the smallness of the domestic market and traditional ways of doing business, Guatemalan entrepreneurs in general exhibit a high-unit-profit mentality—i.e., a desire to make a large profit per unit on a small total volume of sales. According to businessmen who were interviewed, the most common method of pricing in Guatemala is to set a price which is equal to average cost, plus a standard percentage markup; therefore, prices are very often raised to a greater extent than the tax—i.e., to the extent of the tax plus the normal percentage markup. The average businessman presumably does not make too great an effort to discover the new price at which profits (after the imposition of a tax) will be maximized, and this would appear to indicate that the influence of taxation on his profit incentives is limited.

This conclusion appears to be supported by the fact that in many areas of economic activity there exists a belief that conditions external to the individual firm (e.g., price movements on the world market, government deficits or surpluses) exercise a much greater influence on the size of profits than do the policies and efforts of the managers of the firm. During the last decade, the high price of coffee and general world-wide prosperity has had a buoyant effect on the Guatemalan economy. Under these conditions, the level of taxes is of little significance to over-all business planning when compared with important dynamic considerations like rising consumer demand and the increased opportunity to make inventory profits and other forms of capital gains. In most of the postwar years, a large part of Guatemalan business profits were in the nature of windfall returns, the taxing of which has little effect on the incentives of businessmen.

On the Form of Business Organization

The effects of the tax system on the form of business organization is of interest for the future economic development of the country. The experience of other nations reveals that the corporate form of enterprise has greatly accelerated their economic progress. Incorporation has considerable advantages in attracting equity capital and bank credit both at home and abroad, and tends to encourage the reinvestment of business earnings. Rational and modern accounting methods are much more characteristic of corporations than of other forms of business organization; and the spread of these methods can carry benefits to the economy in general and the tax authorities in particular.

Prior to the introduction of the business profits tax in 1938, there was definite discrimination against corporations in Guatemala, for they were required to pay a tax of 5 percent on their net incomes whether distributed or not; profits of unincorporated businesses were tax-free. As the coverage of the business profits tax has expanded, this discrimination has been reduced in most instances. At the present time, all domestic corporations pay a special tax of Q50 per annum, but this sum is negligible and probably covers only the special cost of regulating corporations. Only in one important instance does serious discrimination still exist: incorporated agricultural enterprises are subject to the business profits tax, whereas unincorporated ones are not.

The extent of this discrimination is shown in Table 33, which compares the business income and tax accounts of two firms of sugar-cane growers and coffee producers (in different income brackets) that are similar in all respects except that one is incorporated and the other is not. In each of the four comparisons, as may be seen, the tax burden of the incorporated firm is substantially higher than that of the unincorporated one. The incorporated sugar grower is unable to shift any of the business profits tax because most sugar growers are unincorporated, while the coffee grower, as previous analysis has indicated, probably cannot shift any of his tax liabilities. The difference is greater in the case of the sugar grower and increases as business income becomes larger. The significance of this discrimination is partly offset by the fact that the advantages of the corporate form of organization are probably less important for agricultural than for industrial and commercial enterprises; thus, the prevailing discrimination in this area of economic activity is primarily significant from the standpoint of equity.

However, the very fact that some discrimination against corporations now exists in Guatemala's fiscal system indicates that full recognition is not accorded to the role which corporate enterprise could conceivably play in the future development, and particularly the industrialization, of the country. In this connection, it is important to point out that the proposed income tax law which is now before the Congress provides for a twofold progressive taxation of corporate earnings (once as business profits, once as dividends), the most serious type of discrimination which can be imposed against corporations.

TABLE 33

IMPACT OF TAX SYSTEM UPON FORM OF BUSINESS ORGANIZATION IN 1947/48[a]

(*In quetzales*)

	Unincorporated Sugar Grower	Incorporated Sugar Grower	Unincorporated Coffee Grower	Incorporated Coffee Grower	Unincorporated Sugar Grower	Incorporated Sugar Grower	Unincorporated Coffee Grower	Incorporated Coffee Grower
Business income accounts in the absence of a tax system								
Business property:								
Real estate	45,000	45,000	50,000	50,000	90,000	90,000	100,000	100,000
Other property	46,000	46,000	20,000	20,000	92,000	92,000	40,000	40,000
Total business property	91,000	91,000	70,000	70,000	182,000	182,000	140,000	140,000
Total receipts	61,651	61,651	44,715	44,715	123,302	123,302	89,430	89,430
Total costs	41,651	41,651	24,715	24,715	83,302	83,302	49,430	49,430
Net business income	20,000	20,000	20,000	20,000	40,000	40,000	40,000	40,000
Business income accounts under the 1947/48 tax system								
Total receipts:								
Receipts from goods and services	61,994	61,994	42,000	42,000	123,988	123,988	84,000	84,000
Receipts from shifted taxes	1,636	1,636	.....	.....	3,272	3,272	.....	.....
Total receipts	63,630	63,630	42,000	42,000	127,260	127,260	84,000	84,000

Total costs:								
Cost of goods and services	41,994	41,994	25,065	25,065	83,988	83,988	50,130	50,130
Tax costs	.....	1,636	373	373	3,272	3,272	746	746
Total costs	43,630	43,630	25,438	25,438	87,260	87,260	50,876	50,876
Net income before business profits tax	20,000	20,000	16,562	16,562	40,000	40,000	33,124	33,124
Business profits tax liability	.....	1,908	.....	1,431	.....	5,733	.....	4,263
Net income after business profits tax	20,000	18,092	16,562	15,131	40,000	34,267	33,124	28,861
Loss of business income as a result of tax system	.....	1,908	3,438	4,869	.....	5,733	6,876	11,139
Loss as percent of original net business income	.....	10%	17%	24%	.....	14%	17%	28%

[a] For explanation, see notes to Table 32.

On the Size of Business Firms

The analysis thus far has primarily been concerned with the impact of taxation on business firms of equal size, but the impact of the fiscal system varies also according to the size of the enterprise. One such instance is the increasing differential in the tax burden on incorporated and unincorporated agricultural units as they grow larger. (This has already been illustrated in Table 33.) Another somewhat similar case arises because the coffee producer bears the coffee export tax, while many other types of business enterprises are subject to the business profits tax.

Table 34 presents comparisons of textile manufacturers and coffee growers with different degrees of entrepreneurial efficiency[13] at three different levels of net business income. Because of the specific nature of the coffee export tax, the percentage burden of taxes tends to remain the same regardless of the size of the coffee plantation, while the burden on the textile manufacturer rises progressively as the size of the business unit increases. As a result, at the Q10,000 income level the weight of taxes on the coffee producer is five times as large as on the textile manufacturer, but it is only three times as large at the Q20,000 level, and twice at the Q40,000 level. The size of these differentials depends, of course, on the price of coffee[14] and the degree to which the textile manufacturer is able to pass on his profits tax liability. But the important conclusion is that no matter what the size of the differential, either the smaller or the larger coffee producers will be taxed at a different rate from textile manufacturers of corresponding size.

The situation is complicated by the fact that not all coffee growers are equally efficient. Table 34 also compares an efficient and an inefficient coffee producer, both of whom have the same income of Q20,000 before taxes. As would be expected from the

---

[13] An efficient entrepreneur is assumed to be one who earns normal returns on his invested capital. The inefficient grower is assumed to make 20 percent less and the very efficient grower the same amount more than the efficient producer.

[14] See pp. vii and 197.

specific nature of the export tax, it penalizes inefficiency because the inefficient coffee grower is taxed at a rate of 21.5 percent, while the tax liability of the efficient grower amounts to only 17.2 percent of income. If large coffee farms tend to be more efficiently operated than small ones, the effect of the coffee tax is to encourage a growth in the size of farms;[15] this concentration may have socially undesirable effects, however.

The influence of the business profits tax on the size of enterprises is somewhat different. It is generally believed that a graduated tax on net business income penalizes more efficient producers and deters firms from expanding in size, although other factors such as the economies of large-scale production may counteract this influence. In Guatemala, the size-penalizing effect of the progressive business profits tax is probably somewhat strengthened by the fact that a small enterprise probably shifts a larger portion of this tax than a large one. However, in the absence of a personal income tax, considerations of equity probably override this purely technical consideration, and on balance a strong case can be made for a progressive business income tax.

On the Structure of Production

One of the most complex of the indirect effects of the Guatemalan tax system is its influence on the structure of production. When the responsiveness of the demand for a product to price changes is limited, forward shifting of a tax by sellers increases consumers' money expenditures for the product, although their consumption of it may decline. The affected consumers obviously have to obtain the additional funds from some source, and since the largest part of the population of Guatemala lives at or close to the subsistence level, they would probably be forced to reduce expenditures for other goods and services. From available information, it is impossible to say definitely which sectors of the Guatemalan economy would be affected by these indirect effects of

---

[15] The very efficient coffee grower with an income of Q40,000 is taxed at a rate of only 12.9 percent.

TABLE 34

IMPACT OF TAX SYSTEM UPON SIZE OF BUSINESS FIRMS IN 1947/48[a]

(In quetzales)

	Efficient Coffee Grower	Textile Manufacturer	Efficient Coffee Grower	Inefficient Coffee Grower	Textile Manufacturer	Efficient Coffee Grower	Very Efficient Coffee Grower	Textile Manufacturer
Business income accounts in the absence of a tax system								
Business property:								
Real estate	25,000	16,000	50,000	62,500	32,000	100,000	75,000	64,000
Other property	10,000	32,500	20,000	25,000	65,000	40,000	30,000	130,000
Total business property	35,000	48,500	70,000	87,500	97,000	140,000	105,000	194,000
Total receipts	22,357	45,847	44,715	55,894	91,693	89,430	67,072	183,386
Total costs	12,357	35,847	24,715	35,894	71,693	49,430	27,072	143,386
Net business income	10,000	10,000	20,000	20,000	20,000	40,000	40,000	40,000
Business income accounts under the 1947/48 tax system								
Total receipts:								
Receipts from goods and services	21,000	47,029	42,000	52,500	94,058	84,000	63,000	188,116
Receipts from shifted taxes	.....	838	.....	.....	1,942	.....	.....	4,842
Total receipts	21,000	47,867	42,000	52,500	96,000	84,000	63,000	192,958

Total costs:								
Costs of goods and services	12,532	37,029	25,065	36,332	74,058	50,130	27,597	148,116
Tax costs	186	494	373	466	988	746	559	1,976
Total costs	12,718	37,523	25,438	36,798	75,046	50,876	28,156	150,092
Net income before business profits tax	8,282	10,344	16,562	15,702	20,954	33,124	34,844	42,866
Business profits tax liability	.....	722	.....	.....	2,051	.....	.....	6,382
Net income after business profits tax	8,282	9,622	16,562	15,702	18,903	33,124	34,844	36,484
Loss of business income as a result of tax system	1,718	378	3,438	4,298	1,097	6,876	5,156	3,516
Loss as percent of original net business income	17%	3%	17%	22%	6%	17%	13%	9%

* For explanation, see notes to Table 32.

tax shifting, but on a priori grounds, it seems clear that the indirect effects would be most pronounced in the case of those business enterprises which produce unessential items, the demand for which is highly responsive to a decline in income.

In assessing the influence of variations in the burden of unshifted tax liabilities (see Table 32) on the composition of production, account must be taken of the different rates of return on invested capital that prevail in various lines of economic activity. The case of the coffee export tax is indicative of the difficulties involved; although the coffee grower has the highest tax burden in almost all income brackets, there has been no shift away from coffee production in recent years, and investment in coffee property still is considered the most desirable and profitable outlet for private capital.

Agricultural activity[16] has been encouraged since the introduction of the business profits tax on industrial and commercial enterprises in 1938, and this tax advantage increased commensurably when the rates of this tax were raised in 1943, 1944, and again in 1946. Similarly, the tax system has favored investment in real estate. Until the introduction of the tax on income from capital (*impuesto sobre beneficios de capital*) in 1944, there was no tax on income from this source, and even since that date sporadic and ineffective enforcement of the tax has tended to favor the field of real estate activity.

Import duties have probably had more influence on the structure of production. Although the protective effects of tariffs lie outside the scope of tax policy per se and form part of commercial policy, it seems appropriate to discuss them briefly, especially since it is not always possible to separate the protective and fiscal aspects of import taxes. Originally, the Guatemalan tariff was introduced primarily for fiscal purposes, but with the increase in the ad valorem equivalents of the specific duties during the prolonged period of low prices of the 'thirties, protective features became important. Scarcities of certain types of foreign goods during the

---

[16] Excepting incorporated agricultural enterprises.

war and postwar years strengthened the protective effects of the tariff, and recently there have been instances of tariff increases for purely protective purposes.

At the present time, import duties afford protection mainly to textile and clothing manufacturers, agricultural producers, and food processors like flour millers. Because of the insufficiency of domestic production in the case of textiles and flour, the duties on these products are still important revenue producers. There is little evidence that unduly large profits are earned in the protected industries, but the tariff has in effect subsidized inefficient and obsolete production techniques in some areas, particularly textiles.

The government has recently embarked on a limited program of directly fostering domestic production through tariff protection. Fortunately, however, the authorities have attempted to avoid long-run subsidization of inefficiency. In the case of a tariff recently introduced on matches, the law stipulates a reduction in the duty rate each year so that, at the end of four years, the tariff will be the same as it was before protection was introduced. If the law is strictly enforced and further protection is not granted, this device does indeed represent a definite advance over the old-fashioned types of protective tariffs that have been employed elsewhere.

THE EFFECTS OF TAXATION ON BUSINESS INVESTMENT

In view of the government's definite policy and intention of fostering the economic growth of the country, the effects of the tax system on business investment are of particular interest. There is little evidence that taxes interfere with the volume of investment by domestic business firms, although it does appear that certain elements of the system are unfavorable to the investment of foreign capital in Guatemala. Let it be noted at once, however, that at the present time tax policy is the least important of the principal factors influencing foreign investment in Guatemala; the general political and economic climate is of much greater significance.

Investment of Domestic Business Enterprises

The relatively low incidence of taxes on business firms offers conclusive evidence that taxes do not appreciably reduce the volume of business profits which are available for reinvestment, while the limited adverse effect of business taxes on incentives, as well as the absence of an individual income tax, indicates that the influence of the tax system on the desire to invest is likewise not significant. Nevertheless, there are certain other aspects of the government's tax policy which merit attention in this connection.

Through the industrial development law (Ley de Fomento Industrial),[17] the government has attempted to encourage business investment by a policy of granting tax exemptions for limited periods of time. For the purposes of the law, industries are classified according to their essentiality to the economy, their utilization of national or imported raw materials, whether they are already in existence or are to be newly established, and the participation of foreign or domestic investors in their capital structure. The type and duration of exemptions, which include elimination of customs duties on capital equipment and raw materials, suspension of the property tax, and reduction of the business profits tax, vary with the category into which the firm or industry in question falls.

According to the records of the Ministry of Economy, fifty-nine enterprises, some of them with foreign participation, have availed themselves of the law's privileges during the first two and one-half years of its operation. The government's tax-exemption policy thus appears to have been moderately successful in encouraging the development of industry, although one cannot determine how many of the new firms would have been founded even if the exemptions had not been granted.

Exemptions are of particular value to a new firm in an established industry when this firm has only a limited share of the market. Under this condition the older firms would presumably continue to charge a price high enough to cover most of their tax

17 Congressional Decree Number 459. of November 21, 1947.

costs, and the profits of the new firm would be larger than in the absence of the exemptions, thereby encouraging its growth and expansion. In the case of new industries, the exemptions enable firms to compete with imports from abroad and also reduce the amount of original investment needed in these projects.[18] Moreover, the policy of periodically lowering the exemption from the business profits tax so that new enterprises are required to pay the full tax after five years encourages them to become gradually competitive within this period and tends to prevent the long-run subsidization of inefficiency.

In certain instances, the business profits tax impedes capital investment in industrial enterprises. Only firms with a capital in excess of Q2,500 are subject to it, and in the case of small firms this provision may deter them from increasing their invested capital. The base of the business profits tax, moreover, does not directly take account of differences in the technical capital requirements of firms. Less progressive firms with a low capital-to-labor ratio are favored by the graduated rates, and this tends to discourage further investment by capital-intensive firms. Of course, the depreciation allowance of 10 percent per annum permitted under the law does much to mitigate this effect, but in some instances it is still probably of importance.

The most serious weakness of the tax system with respect to investment is that it favors speculative rather than productive ventures, for the absence of a tax on capital gains definitely offers incentive to persons who wish to indulge in real estate, land, or inventory speculation. The real estate transfer tax (*impuesto sobre venta y permuta de inmueblas*) and the capital stock transfer tax (*impuesto sobre traspasos de acciones*) do, of course, substitute for the capital gains tax to some extent, but their low rates greatly limit their usefulness as a deterrent to speculative ventures. Moreover, the property transfer tax may become a serious impediment to otherwise productive transfers during periods of

[18] During the construction stage of an industry and before operations begin, a firm can obviously not shift taxes forward to consumers, and taxes on equipment and property thus necessitate a larger initial investment.

low or falling prices, for the seller may have to assume its burden in addition to a capital loss.

Investment of Foreign Capital

The tax treatment of foreign capital is of obvious interest because of the significant part which these companies have played in the past development of the country and the likelihood that their role will continue to be important in the future.

Foreign corporations now pay a flat yearly tax (*cuota*) of Q300, as contrasted with one of Q50 that is paid by domestic corporations, but the principal special tax which affects foreign capital is the one levied on the returns on investment in Guatemala, which are received by persons residing abroad (*impuesto sobre beneficios de ausentes*). The rates of this tax correspond to those of the business profits tax, except that there is a Q10,000 exemption. Until recently, the law pertaining to this tax has been interpreted so as to avoid the double taxation of earnings. That is to say, the transfer of dividends by companies subject to the business profits tax were not subject to the *ausente* tax, while interest payments abroad were taxed.[19]

There are, however, several cases pending before the courts, which involve a new interpretation of the *ausente* tax law. The new view being advanced by the Guatemalan tax authorities would make the transfer of dividends as well as interest payments abroad subject to the *ausente* tax. If this interpretation prevails, it would amount to double taxation at progressive rates of foreign capital for dividend payments in excess of Q10,000.

The effects of the tax system on foreign capital are more complex than those on domestically owned businesses, for they are influenced by the economic conditions and tax policies of other countries. A prospective foreign investor is less concerned with the absolute level of Guatemalan taxes than with the net addition

---

[19] In effect, this interpretation favors foreign lenders as compared to domestic lenders to Guatemalan businesses, for the latter are subject to a tax on the return from capital (*impuesto sobre beneficios de capital*) which has an exemption of only Q500.

that these taxes make to his total international tax liability. After making proper allowances for the differences in risks and profit expectations of investment alternatives in other coutries, he will tend to invest in Guatemala only when his total international tax liability is more favorable there than elsewhere. Local discrimination between foreign and native capital will, of course, affect his decision, but such discrimination will tend to be of secondary importance unless it is indicative of a general attitude of a government toward foreign investment.

In the past, foreign capital has been attracted to Guatemala by safeguards which assured immunity from the imposition of future taxes. In the contracts which the three most important foreign companies (United Fruit, International Railways of Central America, and Guatemalan Electric Company) signed with the government, all taxes for which they would be liable during the life of the contracts were explicitly stipulated. Originally, these contracts had little or no tax exemption value, but as the country's tax system has expanded over the years, the fiscal value of the contracts has increased commensurately. At the present time, the companies are exempt from paying the business profits tax on income from their normal operations and import duties on some of the capital equipment which they use, but they are required to pay the profits tax on income derived from the commissaries which they operate for their employees and the import duties on the products which are sold in these stores. All three companies pay social security taxes, but only United Fruit is required to pay the full property tax, the railroad equipment of IRCA and the electrical installations of the Electric Company being exempt from this liability. In addition, the companies are subject to certain special taxes which were imposed in the original contracts in return for privileges granted. United Fruit, for example, pays a banana export tax,[20] and Guatemalan Electric Company is liable

---

[20] As the output of independent banana producers increased over the years, the coverage of the banana export tax has been expanded, and the tax has now lost all, or nearly all, of its original special character.

for taxes on gross and net sales of electric energy and on funds which its consumers have on deposit with it.

Because data on net profits attributable to the Guatemalan operations of these companies were not available, it was not possible to determine the exact value of the tax exemptions granted to these foreign-owned companies. But a careful estimate indicates that in all three cases the tax liability is in the neighborhood of one-half of what it would be in the absence of the contracts. These tax exemptions were at one time an effective method of encouraging investment, for the three companies are not able to shift their tax liabilities to so great an extent as most other Guatemalan business firms. This inability to shift does not reflect on the foreign ownership of the companies but is the result of the particular market situations of the three firms. As was stated earlier in the chapter, United Fruit, although in the position of price leader in the world market, probably finds it unprofitable to shift the banana export tax to the foreign consumer,[21] and the same arguments can be used to explain the low shiftability of the company's other tax liabilities. The position of the railroad and electric companies is, of course, somewhat different, for almost all their business is transacted in the domestic market. Both these enterprises are public utilities, however, and, as such, are not able to alter their prices with every change in market conditions.

The government's tax exemption policy has proved to be a successful method of encouraging foreign investment in the past, but it appears questionable whether it is suitable under present conditions, except in so far as foreign capital participates in the benefits of the industrial development law. During the immediate future, as in the past, the United States is likely to be the principal source of foreign funds for the Guatemalan economy. For this reason, two provisions of the American tax system exercise an important influence on the effects which Guatemalan taxes have

---

[21] To the extent that the company's Guatemalan taxes are higher than those it pays in other countries where it conducts operations, United Fruit may, of course, tend to shift production to these other areas by failing to maintain its Guatemalan investment.

on American-owned corporations. In order to avoid international double taxation, the United States allows these corporations a credit for the taxes levied on their net income which they pay to other countries, and, as a result, foreign income taxes do not add to the aggregate international tax burden as long as they are not in excess of the American tax. Moreover, in order to encourage the investment of American capital in the other countries of North and South America, the United States taxes so-called Western Hemisphere corporations at a special rate of 24 percent instead of the standard rate.[22]

Neither of these provisions is taken into account in the existing contracts which the government has with United Fruit, IRCA, and the Guatemalan Electric Company, for they have been concluded before the changes in the American laws were introduced. Because of the existing United States corporate income tax, the exemptions from the business profits tax do not reduce the aggregate tax burden of the companies and thus do not offer any incentive to further foreign investment. Under the contracts, moreover, the Guatemalan economy fails to derive benefits from the fact that all three companies are Western Hemisphere corporations and enjoy special low tax rates in the United States. For the most part, the taxes which the companies pay at the present time are not included in the credit allowable against payment of the United States tax because they are imposed on sales or property rather than net income.[23] Taxes of this type, which, as was shown earlier, are not readily shiftable in the case of the three companies, add to their total international tax burden and thus tend to deter any increase in their investment.

[22] Under the Western Hemisphere Trade Act of October 21, 1942, United States corporations whose business is carried on wholly in the Western Hemisphere are exempt from the income surtax if, during the last three years, 95 percent or more of their gross income was drawn from sources outside of the United States, and if, at the same time, 90 percent of such income was derived from the active conduct of a trade or business.

[23] To the extent that noncreditable taxes paid to the Guatemalan government reduce the net income of a company, they reduce its United States tax liability.

THE GOVERNMENT AS A COMPETITOR, CUSTOMER, AND SUPPLIER OF BUSINESS

The influence of the budget on the business community extends beyond the effects of the government's power to tax, for the government is itself a large business unit which engages in buying and selling activities. Through its purchases, the government serves as a customer for the goods and services produced by business firms; it competes with these firms for the services of wage earners and salaried employees and for goods produced within the Guatemalan economy or imported from abroad. Through its selling activities, the government supplies important services to agricultural, industrial, and commercial enterprises. Moreover, since it became an owner of many plantations and other enterprises, it also competes with private business in the sale of certain raw materials and finished products.

Effects of Government Purchases

The government's purchases of materials have risen strikingly in the past decade. Having ranged between 2.4 and 2.7 million quetzales annually during the late 'thirties and early 'forties, government expenditures for this purpose had risen to 16.3 million quetzales by 1947/48.[24] Since 4.1 million of this sum were spent directly on purchases from abroad, sales by domestic business amounted to 12.2 million quetzales during that year. Although this figure represented only 3.2 percent of the country's gross national product, the government was an important customer of several industries, importers and the producers of foodstuffs, cattle, and construction materials particularly benefiting from its purchases.

The public purchase law[25] (Ley de Licitaciones) attempts to protect the government from paying unduly large profits to the businessmen from whom it buys goods and services. The law pro-

---

[24] See chapter iv, Table 24.
[25] Decree Number 3021, of December 5, 1942.

vides for competitive bidding on all purchases in excess of Q1,000, but leaves public officials much leeway in determining which is the best bid. The bidding procedure may be suspended by executive decree, and the annual reports of the Court and Control Office of Accounts indicate that it is occasionally circumvented by splitting up purchases. There is no readily available evidence which indicates that business makes unduly high profits on its sales to the government, but there are indications that a more rigid application of the law—and particularly the publication of the various bids submitted—would help to cut down waste. Reports from the business community, moreover, indicate that there are occasionally inordinate delays in government payments for purchases.

Through its purchases, the government has sometimes competed with private business for scarce products. In recent years, this has been particularly evident in the case of construction materials. During 1947 and 1948, when a world-wide scarcity of these materials existed, the large share that the Guatemalan government took of the export quota allocated by United States licensing authorities to this country undoubtedly drove up the price of imported construction goods for private industry. Although the United States prices of construction materials rose only 28 percent during this period,[26] their prices in Guatemala increased by 85.8 percent,[27] notwithstanding the fact that the ad valorem equivalent of import duties declined. With the abatement of the world-wide scarcity in 1949, government purchases have primarily influenced the prices of domestically produced construction materials. The prices of these increased 3.2 percent during 1949,[28] even though the prices of imported materials declined by 3.3 percent.

Government also competes with private industry in the purchase of the services of labor. In the case of white-collar em-

---

[26] United States Bureau of Labor Statistics, *Monthly Index of Wholesale Prices.*

[27] General Statistical Office, *Monthly Index of Prices of Imported Construction Materials.*

[28] General Statistical Office, *Monthly Index of Prices of Domestically Produced Construction Materials.*

ployees, government salaries are at present smaller than salaries for comparable jobs in private industry and commerce, and government competition for this class of worker is not too strong salary-wise. Working conditions in the public service are generally reported to be better than those in private industry, however. In some instances, this has caused an improvement of working conditions in the private sector, thereby resulting in higher business-operating costs.

The situation is somewhat different in the case of nonagricultural day laborers (*jornaleros*), especially those who are employed on public works and other construction projects. For such workers, the government pays a higher wage than that obtainable in private industry. This policy tends to induce wage increases in the construction industry, and has contributed to the inflationary building boom of recent years, when large-scale public works were undertaken with private construction activity at a high level.

The Influence of the Government's Selling Activities

Government sales of goods and services also affect the profitability of private business operations. In analyzing these selling activities, which are similar to transactions between two private individuals or business firms, it is useful to distinguish between the government's public service enterprises and commercial operations.

Through its public service enterprises, the Guatemalan government produces various services which cannot be purchased elsewhere in the economy and sells them to private business firms. These activities are of a noncompetitive nature and fall within the scope of government functions in most other countries. Although income from this source has grown steadily during the past decade, its relative importance as a producer of government revenue has declined. As shown in Table 13, receipts from public service enterprises increased from 670.3 to 1,384.2 thousand quetzales between 1937/38 and 1947/48, but amounted to only 3.5 percent of total government revenues in 1947/48 as contrasted with 5.4 percent in the earlier year. Sales of postal and electric communications services account for the bulk of this source of income, and during 1947/48 provided 38.1 and 37.7 percent respectively. The remainder is obtained from the sale of diverse services, among the most important of which are custom's warehouse and unloading facilities, public health, and the issuance of publications of a technical nature.

The government's commercial enterprises differ from these public service enterprises in one major respect. They compete directly with private business, and the various buying units in the private sector are faced with a choice of buying from the government or from other business firms. Income from this source, which accounted for only 417.3 thousand quetzales or 3.3 percent of total revenue in 1937/38, has grown spectacularly in recent years. It reached a peak of 9,611.1 thousand quetzales in 1946/47 and then declined to 6,393.4 thousand quetzales, or 16.1 percent of the total, in 1947/48. The profits of the National Lottery produced 26.5 percent of the government's commercial income during that year, and the sale of goods made in government hospitals and prisons, the National Printing Office, and rents from public lands accounted for another 10.1 percent. By far the largest share (63.4 percent) was provided from the sale of products grown on the nationalized farms, but this figure understates the importance of the government's agricultural activities, since it does not include income from "intervened" properties which in recent years has amounted to approximately half of that of the national farms. In 1948/49, the national and intervened farms together produced 21.7 percent of the country's coffee crop, as well as a large variety of other products.

These activities of the government are clearly of a commercial nature, and they give rise to special problems of operation and administration. In the preamble of a recent law establishing the Department of National Farms (Departamento de Fincas Rústicas Nacionales e Intervenidas)[29] as an autonomous entity, the Guate-

29 Legislative Decree 573, of February 15, 1949.

malan Congress has referred to these difficulties in the following explicit terms: On the one hand, "government is naturally slow in adapting itself to the needs of an institution which is engaged in the production and sale of agricultural products," for such activities "require a commercial organization which can make rapid decisions to meet changing market conditions." On the other hand, the public interest requires that these activities "should always be subject to the strict control and supervision of the state."[30]

In an attempt to resolve this basic dilemma, the Congress has placed most of the commercial activities of the government under the jurisdiction of the Department of National Farms. This organization, which is under the control of a five-man board of directors, employs 25,000 workers and in addition to managing the national and intervened farms, now operates one tannery, one flour mill, three white-sugar mills, ten sugar-loaf (*panela*) mills, and 165 coffee depulping and processing mills. Flexibility of sales and production policy is provided for by the autonomy of the organization and separate accounting arrangements, but the public interest is protected by having the books of the department audited by the Court and Control Office of Accounts. Moreover, in an attempt to ensure adequate internal accounting procedures, the revenues of individual farms are deposited in separate accounts in the National Mortgage Bank, and costs of operation are charged against these individual accounts.

All sales of products by the department which are in excess of Q3,000 must be made at public auction. Buyers are required to make a deposit of 25 percent at the time of purchase, the rest being payable against receipt of the shipping documents. All sales are final, except that the department reserves the right to refuse bids which it considers unsatisfactory. According to the law, products

[30] A sharp criticism of the administrative and financial practices of the nationalized farms is contained in the annual report of the Court and Control Office of Accounts for the fiscal year 1947/48. Speaking of the farms before they became an autonomous entity, the court charged that they "constitute a serious burden on the public treasury" and that "their administration has been defective."

may be exported directly if this is more profitable, and, wherever practicable, exportable farm products are to be sold directly to foreign consumers, eliminating all middlemen if possible. In practice, however, the vast majority of the sales are made through the auction system, an arrangement which minimizes the impact of government competition on other business firms.

An appraisal of managerial efficiency on the government-operated farms should give due weight to the fact that the government is a relatively new and inexperienced entrepreneur. Since the Department of National Farms has been operating in its present form for only one year, it would not be fair to compare the relative efficiency of government and private farm management at the present time, even if the data for such comparison existed. The evidence which is available does indicate that government management has been steadily improving: during the 1948/49 crop year, coffee production on the government farms reached 334,215 quintals[31] and exceeded that of any previous year, even though 32 of the intervened farms had already been returned to private hands; net profits for the fourteen months ending June 30, 1949, amounted to 32 percent of gross sales.

These over-all figures conceal differences in the efficiency with which individual units are operated. During the period under review, 51 of the 117 government farms were run at a loss. Although variations in soil fertility and type of product provide a partial explanation of this great diversity in the experience of individual farms, a large part of it is undoubtedly due to differences in the capabilities of individual managers. By taking steps to improve the management of the unprofitable units, the government and the Department of National Farms will not only be providing additional revenues for the government, but will also, because of the overwhelming importance of coffee in the total output of the farms, be acting to increase the foreign-exchange earnings of the economy.

[31] Of 100 Spanish pounds (equal to 101.41 pounds avoirdupois).

VI

THE TAX SYSTEM AND
PRIVATE INCOME

THE PRECEDING chapter discussed the effects of the fiscal system on the business community; although the evidence is not so conclusive as the absolute data of the chapter would indicate, it seems reasonably clear that business firms, or, more specifically, the owners of business firms in their entrepreneurial capacity, bear only a small portion of the total tax burden. The purpose of the present chapter is to analyze the impact of the Guatemalan tax system on individuals and individual households in their dual capacity as income recipients and consumers.

THE CLASSIFICATION OF TAXES BORNE BY
INDIVIDUAL FAMILIES

The taxes which families bear reflect the diverse role that households play in the economic and social life of the country. Three major groups of taxes may be distinguished: (1) those which families pay directly to the government in their capacity as income recipients, property owners, or merely members of the community, (2) those which are borne by them in their role as owners or part owners of business enterprises, and (3) those which they pay indirectly in the form of higher prices on the goods and services which they purchase from business.[1]

The first group consists of property, property transfer, and motor vehicle taxes paid by individuals,[2] the inheritance and gift tax, a radio-use tax of twenty-five centavos a month, a 0.4 percent

---

[1] Under certain circumstances, particular classes of families do, of course, also pay some taxes indirectly in the form of lower wages received by the head of the household. However, as the analysis of the preceding chapter has shown, this type of tax burden seems to have been of little quantitative significance in Guatemala in recent years.

[2] It will be recalled that it was estimated that business firms pay two-thirds of these taxes. See Table 31.

tax on salaries, and a few other miscellaneous taxes, fees, and fines. This group is by far the least important quantitatively, and in 1947/48 accounted for only about 3 percent of all taxes borne by Guatemalan families (see Table 31).

The second and third groups correspond to the unshifted and shifted portions of the taxes paid by business, the composition of which was analyzed in the last chapter. In 1947/48, they made up approximately 18 and 79 percent, respectively, of taxes falling on households.

This classification serves the purpose of showing that the great part of Guatemalan taxes are hidden in the prices of goods and services that people buy. It is also a necessary step in determining whether the incidence of individual taxes is proportional, progressive, or regressive—i.e., whether the proportion of a tax to household income remains constant, rises, or declines as the level of family income grows larger. Normally, one would expect that, with the exception of capitation taxes, direct taxes and unshifted business taxes would be either proportional or progressive, depending on whether or not the tax rates are graduated. Most shifted taxes, on the other hand, tend to be regressive because low-income families generally consume a higher proportion of their incomes than high-income families. In certain instances, however, the incidence of shifted taxes may be progressive. This is probably true, for example, of taxes on air travel and entertainment, for rich households spend a proportionately larger share of their incomes for these services than poor families.

The incidence of Guatemalan taxes in 1947/48 is analyzed in Table 35. In addition to showing progressive, proportional, and regressive groups, the table also includes a mixed group of taxes which are progressive over one range of incomes and regressive over another. As may be seen, the progressive taxes make up the smallest (about 5 percent) part of the total, for only four taxes fall into this category. The case for including the unshifted portion of the business profits tax, the inheritance and gift tax, and the *ausente* tax is clear, for they all have significant basic exemptions and a graduated rate structure. The property tax, it is true, imposes proportional rates, but its incidence is, nevertheless, progressive because the distribution of property in Guatemala,

TABLE 35

ESTIMATES OF PROGRESSIVE, PROPORTIONAL, REGRESSIVE, AND MIXED
TAXES IN 1947/48

(*In thousands of quetzales*)

Tax Groups	
Progressive:	
Unshifted business profits tax	1,524
Inheritance and gift tax	87
Absentee tax	23
Consumers' property tax	163
Total progressive taxes	1,797
Progressive taxes as percent of total taxes	6%
Proportional:	
Export taxes	2,664
Other unshifted business taxes[a]	1,599
Stamp tax on salaries	180
Consumers' miscellaneous taxes, fees, and fines	221
Total proportional taxes	4,664
Proportional taxes as percent of total taxes	16%
Regressive:	
Consumption taxes	8,004
Import duties on business goods	5,314
Shifted business profits tax	1,524
Other shifted business taxes[a]	2,776
Total regressive taxes	17,618
Regressive taxes as percent of total taxes	56%
Mixed:	
Import duties on consumers' goods	6,628
Air and rail transportation taxes	165
Consumers' motor vehicle taxes	73
Radio tax	41
Consumers' property transfer taxes	36
Life insurance premium tax	21
Entertainment taxes	192
Total mixed taxes	7,156
Mixed taxes as percent of total taxes	22%
Total taxes, fees, and fines	31,235

[a] For explanation, see Table 31.

as in most other countries, is more unequal than the distribution of income.[3]

Proportional taxes are more important than progressive taxes, making up about one-sixth of the total. Although the stamp tax on salaries is the most obviously proportionate of all Guatemalan taxes, the group consists primarily of export duties and other unshifted business taxes. These, as was seen in chapter v, are imposed on the production or sales of individual industries, and presumably fall proportionately on firms of different size (and hence on business owners with different incomes). Also included in the group are certain miscellaneous taxes, fees, and fines which are paid directly by households, for there are no factors that appear to make these either regressive or progressive.

The largest category of taxes includes those with a regressive impact, as might be expected from the high shiftability of most Guatemalan taxes. Making up more than one-half of the total, they consist of consumption taxes levied on specific products like tobacco, alcoholic beverages, salt, and matches, and of the business profits tax, import duties on business goods, and other taxes which business firms shift forward in the form of higher prices. The proportionate share which families spend on the individual taxed commodities and on consumption as a whole is believed to vary by and large inversely with household income.

The mixed group also consists predominantly of taxes which are shifted to the consumer, although it does include some directly paid taxes (i.e., the radio tax and those property transfer taxes which are paid by households). In this instance, however, the share of income which consumers spend for the taxed goods and services varies directly rather than inversely with income— at least up to very high levels of income where savings become important. In the case of import duties on consumers' goods, which are quantitatively the most significant member of this group of taxes, this is true for two reasons: as the income level rises, families (1) tend to substitute imported products for domestic

[3] This factor also increases the progressiveness of the inheritance and gift tax.

goods, even though they may, at the same time, consume a smaller proportion of their incomes, and (2) tend to devote a higher percentage of their expenditures for imports to high-tariff luxury items.

The burden of this class of taxes falls particularly heavily on the middle-income groups; in the lower-income brackets, the proportionately small share of income spent on items subject to these taxes keeps the incidence low, while the increasing importance of savings limits the burden on the upper-income groups. Thus, the mixed taxes, which comprise an estimated one-fifth of all taxes, counteract to some extent the fact that Guatemalan tax revenues include only a very small proportion of progressive taxes. It should be emphasized, however, that, from the point of view of tax equity, they are not a substitute for a progressive personal income tax.

THE INCIDENCE OF TAXES ON INDIVIDUAL HOUSEHOLDS

The fact that more than one-half of Guatemalan tax receipts are the yields of regressive taxes does not necessarily imply that the incidence of the entire tax system is regressive. In every instance the composite incidence of all taxes taken together is a function of the relative degrees of progressiveness or regressiveness of individual taxes, and depends on the source of income, size of income, and savings habits of particular households.[4]

Most of the variations in tax incidence which result from differences in the source of income occur in the case of households which derive their income from entrepreneurial activity, and for this reason they were explored in the preceding chapter.[5] It will be recalled that the major instances of variations in business tax burdens arise because the shiftability of taxes varies from industry to industry, and because only industrial and commercial

---

[4] Differences in the expenditure patterns of individual families obviously also influence tax incidence, but since these primarily cause variations in the tax burden among households in the same income group (rather than among families in different income groups), they are considered in a subsequent section.

[5] See particularly Tables 32 and 34.

enterprises are subject to the business profits tax. Further complexities in the incidence pattern are introduced when the tax burden of profit income is compared with the burden on other sources of income; since there is no general income tax in Guatemala, salaries, wages, and professional earnings are not subject to income taxation.

In view of this great variation in family tax burden with respect to source of income, it might be argued that no conclusion can be reached with regard to the over-all incidence of the Guatemalan tax system, particularly since no tax on individual incomes exists in the country. This is not the case, however, for there appears to be a broad correlation between the source and size of the incomes of Guatemalan households. The heads of families in the lower brackets are mainly small farmers and agricultural and urban workers; those in the middle brackets consist primarily of salaried employees, independent professional people, and small shopkeepers; and the income recipients in the higher brackets derive income primarily from industrial and commercial enterprises and coffee and sugar plantations.

Table 36 compares the estimated tax burdens of a number of these typical families in various income groups.[6] Each family is assumed to be of average size for the country—i.e., to have five members.[7] As may be seen, total taxes borne vary greatly, and range from 5 percent of household income in the case of a small indigenous farmer to 28 percent for the family of a coffee grower with an income of Q20,000. The incidence of the entire system appears to be progressive up to the upper-middle-income brackets. Beyond this point it continues to be progressive for those who pay the business profits tax but becomes decidedly regressive for the families which are not subject to this tax. The case of the coffee-grower's family is somewhat unique, for he bears the special coffee export tax. The incidence of taxes on the

---

[6] For an explanation of the methods used in making these estimates, see the Statistical Note at the end of this chapter.

[7] Needless to say, this is only a simplification of the exposition; the variation in the size of family obviously affects the results.

TABLE 36

BURDEN OF TAX SYSTEM ON TYPICAL FAMILIES IN 1947/48

(In quetzales)

	Indigenous Farmer	Indigenous Farmer	Skilled Urban Worker	Government Employee	Retailer	Private Employee	Physician	Engineer	Importer	Sugar-Cane Grower	Coffee Grower	Coffee Exporter	Textile Manufacturer	Liquor Manufacturer
Family income	250	600	1,200	1,200	3,600	3,600	6,000	8,000	10,000	10,000	20,000	20,000	40,000	40,000
Real personal property .	200	600	...	...	3,000	5,000	16,000	20,000	30,000	65,000	200,000	70,000	145,000	120,000
Direct taxes:														
Municipal improvement assessment ..	1	1	2	2	2	2	2	2	2	2	2	2	2	2
Salary taxes[a]	...	...	17	19	...	50	...	...	...	...	...	...	...	...
Property tax	1	2	...	...	9	15	48	60	90	195	600	210	435	360
Inheritance and gift tax[b]	...	...	...	...	1	2	8	10	15	39	223	45	141	103
Unshifted business profits tax	...	...	...	...	93	...	...	...	378	...	...	1,772	3,155	3,155
Other unshifted business taxes[c]	...	...	...	...	...	...	...	...	...	...	3,438	930	...	...
Miscellaneous taxes, fees, and fines	*	*	1	1	2	2	4	5	6	6	12	12	24	24
Total direct taxes	2	3	20	22	107	71	62	77	491	242	4,275	2,971	3,757	3,645
Direct taxes as percent of total tax burden	16%	7%	14%	16%	23%	17%	10%	10%	38%	24%	77%	68%	60%	58%
Consumption taxes:														
Excise taxes[d]	4	12	32	24	79	79	129	164	193	198	298	325	633	649
Import duties on consumers' goods	1	6	29	32	108	109	187	255	299	301	548	559	967	986
Total consumption taxes	5	18	61	56	187	188	316	419	492	499	846	884	1,600	1,635
Consumption taxes as percent of total tax burden	42%	42%	44%	42%	41%	45%	52%	53%	38%	47%	15%	20%	25%	26%

Shifted taxes:													
Import duties on business goods	2	11	27	27	75	75	109	137	141	145	216	235	448	462
Shifted business profits tax	1	3	8	8	22	22	31	39	41	42	62	67	129	132
Other shifted national business taxes	1	5	12	12	34	34	50	62	64	65	97	106	203	209
Shifted municipal business taxes	1	4	11	11	30	30	44	55	57	59	87	95	182	187
Total shifted taxes	5	23	58	58	161	161	234	293	303	311	462	503	962	991
Shifted taxes as percent of total tax burden	42%	51%	42%	42%	36%	38%	38%	37%	24%	29%	8%	12%	15%	16%
Total tax burden	12	44	139	136	455	420	612	789	1,286	1,052	5,583	4,358	6,319	6,271
Total tax burden as percent of income	5%	7%	12%	11%	13%	12%	10%	10%	13%	10%	28%	22%	16%	16%

a Includes stamp tax on salaries and social security tax.
b Assuming that taxpayer makes provision for tax over a period of twenty years.
c See Table 32.
d Includes tobacco and liquor excises, air and rail transportation taxes, and taxes on entertainment.
* Less than fifty centavos.

high-income family shown is definitely progressive, relative to lower-income families which derive income from other sources, but is probably regressive with respect to less well-to-do coffee families.

By breaking up the total tax burden into: (1) taxes which are directly paid or shifted back to families who own businesses (direct taxes), (2) those which are paid in the form of high prices on definite types of goods and services (consumption taxes), and (3) those which add to the prices of almost all goods and services (shifted taxes), the table throws some light on the causes of the particular incidence structure. Direct taxes, which, as we have seen, are either progressive or proportional, account for a much higher share of the total burden on rich households than poor households. Consumption taxes, which include import duties and taxes on entertainment and personal transportation, are relatively most important in the case of middle-income families, but since they also include tobacco and liquor excises, they take a larger proportion of the income of poor families than rich families. It is primarily this group of taxes which causes the progressiveness of the system in the lower and middle brackets. Shifted taxes, on the other hand, are definitely regressive throughout the entire range of incomes, and amount to a constantly declining proportion of the total tax burden of the families.

It is necessary to point out several qualifications which must be made with respect to the reliability and completeness of the results embodied in Table 36. In the first place, the tax burdens of the various families include only the directly measurable incidence of certain taxes. Protective import duties, for example, give rise to an important indirect burden, which may or may not be regressive, for consumers generally pay a higher price for the domestic goods which they purchase in protected markets. Second, the figures, as in the preceding chapter, refer to statutory, not effective, tax liabilities, and, as a consequence, the extent to which the business profits tax is evaded reduces its progressiveness commensurately. Finally, as emphasized in the previous chapter, the estimates of the shiftability of taxes, particularly the business profits tax, are at best approximations, for even when all necessary market data were available, conceptual difficulties would remain and permit only tentative answers to the questions of tax shifting.

As a partial check on the influence of these shiftability assumptions on our results, the tax burdens for the same group of families were recomputed on the alternative assumption that the business profits tax is completely unshifted. The results under this alternate assumption are shown in Table 37. As might be expected, the

TABLE 37

Tax Incidence Under Modified Assumption in 1947/48

(*In quetzales*)

Occupation of Head of Family	Family Income	Business Profits Tax			
		Partly Shifted[a]		Not Shifted	
		Total Tax Burden		Total Tax Burden	
		Amount	Percent of Family Income	Amount	Percent of Family Income
Indigenous farmer	250	12	5	11	5
Indigenous farmer	600	44	7	41	7
Skilled urban worker	1,200	139	12	131	11
Government employee	1,200	136	11	128	11
Retailer	3,600	455	13	516	14
Private employee	3,600	420	12	398	11
Physician	6,000	612	10	581	10
Engineer	8,000	789	10	750	9
Importer	10,000	1,286	13	1,556	16
Sugar cane grower...........	10,000	1,052	10	1,010	10
Coffee grower	20,000	5,583	28	5,521	28
Coffee exporter	20,000	4,358	22	4,291	21
Textile manufacturer	40,000	6,319	16	8,767	22
Liquor manufacturer	40,000	6,271	16	8,715	22

[a] See Table 36.

"new" tax burden is lower in the case of households who do not pay the business profits tax and higher in the case of those who do. It is readily apparent, however, that the modified assumption does not change the basic character of the results obtained in Table 36.

The tax system is definitely progressive up to the upper-middle-income brackets and continues to be that way in the case of households who pay the business profits tax.

THE IMPACT OF THE PROPOSED INCOME TAX

The preceding section examined the impact of the existing tax system on families with different sizes and sources of income. The purpose of the present section is to consider how an important proposed modification of the tax system will affect these results.

Under the general income tax bill which has been before Congress for some time, the present progressive rate structure of the business profits tax will be extended to *all* sources of income with three important modifications: (1) partners in business enterprises will be taxed on their individual shares of the profits rather than on the income of the business as a whole, (2) for taxpayers with incomes of Q10,000 or less, the present minimum exemption of Q500 for each business enterprise will be replaced by individual exemptions of Q900 for a single person, Q1,400 for a married couple, and Q250 for each additional dependent, and (3) incomes of Q10,000 or less which are derived solely from work will be taxed at a rate of 80 percent of that applying to incomes derived entirely from capital.[8]

The principal effects of the proposed law will be to increase the over-all progressiveness of the tax system and to eliminate the present discrimination which exists between industrial and commercial income on the one hand, and agricultural, salary, and professional income on the other. One new and important form of discrimination will be introduced—i.e., that between the owners of unincorporated and incorporated businesses.[9] The difficulty of fitting coffee income into the total tax picture will remain.[10] The tax liabilities of small businessmen (i.e., those with incomes of Q10,000 or less) who are now subject to the business profits tax

---

[8] Mixed incomes—i.e., those derived partly from work and partly from capital—will be taxed at 90 percent of the full rate.
[9] See p. 110.
[10] See p. 114.

will decline, as will those of the owners of all unincorporated industrial and commercial firms which are not individual proprie-
torships.

The effects of the proposed law on tax burdens are less certain
than those on tax liabilities. It is generally agreed that a tax on
individual incomes is one of the least shiftable of all major taxes.
In the case of salary earners, it appears quite certain that their
bargaining position is, in most instances, not strong enough to
enable them to shift the proposed tax to their employers. But the
situation is more complex in the case of businessmen. On the one
hand, they will probably be able to shift a portion of the tax because the present practice of shifting part of the business profits
tax has to a certain extent become incorporated in the cost structures of their firms and industries. The shiftability of the proposed tax, on the other hand, will probably be smaller than that
of the business profits tax since its base is one degree further
removed from the costs of the business enterprise itself.

All of these changes are shown in Table 38, which compares
the tax burdens of various households (previously considered in
Table 36) before and after the enactment of the proposed income
tax law. The increase in the incidence in the case of the importer,
textile manufacturer, sugar cane grower, and liquor producer is
probably somewhat overstated[11] because the table compares two
limiting cases of 50 percent shifting in the case of the business
profits tax and no shifting in the case of the individual income
tax. In actuality, if and when the law is finally enacted, the burden of taxes on these business owners will probably lie somewhere
between the two limits shown, depending on the extent to which
they will be able to continue to shift their personal tax liabilities.

The previously drawn distinction between statutory tax liabilities and actual tax payments is especially important with respect
to the proposed income tax. The experience of many other countries has shown that the administration of an individual income
tax—particularly as it applies to independent professional people

---

[11] Similarly, the decline of the retailer's tax burden is probably somewhat understated.

TABLE 38
Effect of Proposed Income Tax Law on Family Tax Burdens
(In quetzales)

Occupation of Head of Family	Retailer	Private Employee	Physician	Engineer	Importer	Sugar-Cane Grower	Coffee Grower	Coffee Exporter	Textile Manufacturer	Liquor Manufacturer
Family income	3,600	3,600	6,000	8,000	10,000	10,000	20,000	20,000	40,000	40,000
Real personal property	3,600	5,000	16,000	20,000	30,000	65,000	200,000	70,000	145,000	120,000
Total tax burden before										
passage of law[a]	455	420	612	789	1,286	1,052	5,583	4,358	6,319	6,271
Less taxes repealed by law	93	...	...	...	378	...	...	1,772	3,155	3,155
Plus taxes added by law[b]	78	67	182	297	478	470	1,276	1,746	5,656	5,672
Total tax burden after										
passage of law	440	487	793	1,086	1,386	1,522	6,859	4,332	8,820	8,788
Difference in tax burden	−15	+67	+182	+297	+100	+470	+1,276	−26	+2,501	+2,517
Total tax burden as percent of income:										
Before passage of law	13%	12%	10%	10%	13%	10%	28%	22%	16%	16%
After passage of law	12%	13%	13%	14%	14%	15%	34%	22%	22%	22%

a See Table 36.
b Assuming that each family has two dependent children.

and farmers—is far more difficult than that of a business income tax. In this connection, it should be pointed out that Guatemalan experience with the tax on the returns from capital (*impuesto sobre beneficios de capital*) indicates that tax consciousness and administration will have to improve considerably before a personal income tax will become a successful fiscal instrument.[12]

Notwithstanding this fact, however, the law—if enacted—should yield, during the early years of its existence, between two million and three million quetzales annually in additional revenue; this yield should increase appreciably as administration of the tax improves with experience. The figure of two to three million quetzales must, of course, not be taken as too accurate an estimate. But if one takes account of such pertinent factors as the distribution of income, the level of proposed exemptions, the prevalence of business profits as a source of income in the higher brackets, and the initial difficulties of administration, the estimate appears to be a reasonable appraisal of the order of magnitude of the initial additional yield of the proposed tax.

TAX DISCRIMINATION BETWEEN GROUPS OF CONSUMERS

In the preceding sections, the family tax burden was analyzed from the point of view of differences in the size and source of household income. In this section, attention is focused on the tax differences which exist between families with similar incomes but with different income-disposal patterns. In Guatemala, these differences are particularly important in the cases of (1) indigenous and nonindigenous families, and (2) heavy and light consumers of taxed commodities.

Discrimination Between Indigenous and Nonindigenous Families

The tax discrimination which prevails between indigenous and nonindigenous families is one reflection of the more basic cleavages existing between the two major sectors of the economy.

---

[12] See pp. 160–66.

As was pointed out in chapter ii,[18] indigenous and *ladino* families come from two socially and culturally distinct groups and normally engage in different types of economic activities. Unlike the typical low-income urban family, the average indigenous household is a business as well as a consumer unit, and an important part of its business output is produced not for commercial sale but for consumption within the household itself. Even when the family does go outside of the household economy in order to dispose of its surplus produce and to purchase other goods and services, it buys and sells in local village markets, where transactions in goods produced within the indigenous sector far exceed purchases of goods which are produced in the commercial sector of the economy.

Since the largest part of the country's taxes are borne by consumers in the form of higher prices, these differences are reflected in variations in the tax burdens of the two groups of families. It is, of course, true that the indigenous household, in its capacity as a small agricultural producer, pays and bears import duties on certain agricultural implements which its urban counterpart does not pay, but this factor is more than offset by differences in consumption habits. Because 30 percent of the consumption by indigenous families, according to the Goubaud Carrera study, consists of self-produced food, they do not bear the shifted transaction, business profits, and transportation taxes that have become incorporated into the cost structures of commercial retailers and wholesalers of food. Moreover, since most of the transactions in the local village markets could probably just as easily take place without the use of money—i.e., through barter—they are almost as difficult for the national government to tax as if they were actually effected through this medium.

The only items in the indigenous economy which are readily susceptible to effective excise taxation are those which are imported from other parts of the economy. These consist almost entirely of tools, shoes, textiles, needles, drugs, liquor, and to-

---

[18] See p. 24.

bacco products, and account for only a small part of the total consumption of most indigenous families.[14] In the case of liquor and tobacco products, moreover, many families frequently evade taxes by substituting corn silk and home-brew (*chicha*) for the products of legally licensed manufacturers. Municipal market taxes of one to five centavos per seller, which are imposed in nearly all villages, also add to the indigenous tax burden.[15]

The degree of tax discrimination which exists between indigenous and nonindigenous households is shown in Table 39, which compares three pairs of urban and indigenous families who have the same total income. In every case, the tax burden on the indigenous household is smaller than that on its urban counterpart, but the degree of discrimination narrows as the incomes become larger. Within both sectors, the incidence of taxes is progressive over the range of incomes studied, but the rate of progression among the indigenous families is greater. This higher rate of progression is explained by the fact that, with an increase in family income, the ratio of home-produced to total income declines and the participation in the tax-burdened market economy increases.

Discrimination Between Heavy and Light Consumers of
Taxed Commodities

A second major type of tax discrimination prevails between families who have the same incomes but are heavy or light consumers of taxed commodities. Since individual families have considerable freedom of choice in determining in what manner they wish to dispose of their incomes, differences in taste may cause significant variations of the tax burden within the same income group—variations which are particularly important in the lower brackets where, as was shown in Table 36, consumption and shifted business taxes account for almost all of the family's tax burden. The extent to which variation can exist within a partic-

---

[14] Although clothing consumption is important, a large part of the production takes place within the indigenous sector itself.

[15] In the statistical analysis which follows, the burden of these taxes on the indigenous families is probably somewhat underestimated.

TABLE 39

Tax Burden Differences Between Indigenous and Nonindigenous Families in 1947/48[a]

(In quetzales)

Occupation of Head of Family	Indigenous Farmer	Unskilled Urban Worker	Indigenous Farmer	Semiskilled Urban Worker	Indigenous Farmer	Skilled Urban Worker
Family income	250	250	600	600	1,200	1,200
Real personal property	200	...	600	...	1,500	...
Direct taxes:						
Municipal improvement assessment	1	1	1	1	2	2
Salary taxes	...	4	...	10	...	17
Property tax	1	...	2	...	5	...
Inheritance and gift taxes	...	...	...	...	*	...
Miscellaneous taxes, fees, and fines	*	*	*	*	1	1
Total direct taxes	2	5	3	11	8	20
Direct taxes as percent of total tax burden	16%	20%	7%	17%	8%	14%
Consumption taxes:						
Excise taxes	4	5	12	12	23	32
Import duties on consumers' goods	1	3	6	12	25	29
Total consumption taxes	5	8	18	24	48	61
Consumption taxes as percent of total tax burden	42%	31%	42%	37%	42%	44%
Shifted taxes:						
Import duties on business goods	2	6	11	14	23	27
Shifted business profits tax	1	2	3	4	6	8
Other shifted national business taxes	1	2	5	6	10	12
Shifted municipal business taxes	1	2	4	5	9	11
Total shifted taxes	5	12	23	29	48	58
Shifted taxes as percent of total tax burden	42%	49%	51%	46%	42%	42%
Total tax burden	12	25	44	64	104	139
Total tax burden as percent of income	5%	10%	7%	11%	9%	12%

[a] For explanation, see footnotes to Table 36.
* Less than fifty centavos.

ular income group is, of course, limited by the fact that all types of consumption are not equally avoidable. But it appears quite reasonable to assume that Guatemalan households can readily avoid heavy taxes on liquor and tobacco products, entertainment, imported textiles, and luxury imports, without suffering any significant decline in their objective well-being.

Table 40 shows the tax burdens of two indigenous and two urban families who have the same income but spend different

TABLE 40

VARIATIONS OF TAX BURDEN WITHIN AN INCOME GROUP IN 1947/48[a]

(In quetzales)

| | Indigenous Farmer | | Skilled Urban Worker | |
	Heavy Consumption	Light Consumption	Light Consumption	Heavy Consumption
Family income	1,200	1,200	1,200	1,200
Taxes on alcoholic beverages	23	8	27	9
Taxes on cigarettes	12	4	15	5
Taxes on entertainment	...	...	6	2
Duties on imported textiles	11	4	28	9
Duties on luxury imports	11	4	12	4
Total avoidable taxes	57	20	88	29
Other taxes	69	69	80	80
Total tax liability	126	89	168	109
Total tax liability as percent of income	10%	7%	14%	9%
Tax liability of heavy consumer as percent of light consumer ...	142%		154%	

[a] For explanation, see footnotes to Table 36.

proportions of them for heavily taxed goods and services. The heavy consumer is in both instances assumed to spend 50 percent more for these avoidable items than the average consumer with the same income (see Table 39), while the light consumer correspondingly is assumed to spend 50 percent less. As may be seen, the difference in tax incidence resulting from this disparity is quite large. The indigenous household which consumes many avoidable goods and services bears nearly 50 percent more in taxes than its more frugal counterpart, and the differential is even larger in the case of urban families.

These comparisons bring out one of the major weaknesses of a tax system which relies primarily on consumption taxes, for their burden may inadvertently be distributed in an inequitable manner. Of course, heavy taxes on particular articles frequently serve nonfiscal purposes. The taxation of alcohol and tobacco products, for example, may have the sumptuary aim of curbing the consumption of these "socially undesirable" products, while import duties may have a balance-of-payments objective of protecting the country's foreign-exchange reserves. Moreover, as was brought out at the beginning of the chapter, the effect of the duties on luxury imports on families of different incomes (as contrasted with those in the same income group) is to introduce an important element of progression into the Guatemalan tax system over a certain range of incomes.

CHANGES IN THE TAX BURDEN OVER TIME

The estimates of tax incidence presented in the preceding sections are based on the average level of prices which existed during the 1947/48 fiscal year and are applicable primarily to that period. Movements in the prices of individual commodities, and in the price level as a whole, cause variations in the real weight of taxes—i.e., in the actual quantity of goods and services which households could buy with the funds which go to the government. Since the extent of these variations differs for individual taxes, price movements also result in a change in the distribution of the tax burden among different income groups. The present section examines how the price changes of recent years have influenced the incidence of the Guatemalan tax system.

The steady rise in the price level since the late 'thirties has been most important in the case of import duties, the government's major source of revenue. Since almost all of these taxes are imposed on a specific or weight basis, increases in import prices have in most instances caused a commensurate decline in the ad valorem equivalent of the duties, i.e., in the percentage relationship of the duties to the cost of imports. This is clearly shown in Table 41, which compares the ad valorem rates for 1938, 1943, and 1948.

In some cases, however, notably gasoline and medicines, the government compensated for price increases by raising the specific taxes on the products, and in others, particularly cement and

TABLE 41

BURDEN OF IMPORT DUTIES IN SELECTED YEARS[a]

(As percent of value, F.O.B., of imports)

	1938	1943	1948
Gasoline	210.0	183.9	231.4
Lubricating oil	86.3	83.4	74.9
Agricultural machinery	8.2	8.2	0.4
Hoes	10.7	10.4	10.6
Gray cement	141.7	....	0.4
Iron and steel	23.6	20.9	12.2
Wheat flour	66.2	56.0	24.9
Newsprint	22.0	19.9	11.8
Sodium carbonate	70.7	39.0	33.7
Trucks	18.7	15.6	12.0
Automobiles	24.0	24.0	24.4
Automobile tires	32.0	25.0	22.1
Lightning rods	30.2	23.0	16.1
Electric light bulbs	19.0	16.3	11.8
Typewriters	17.7	14.6	10.5
Woolen cloth	59.9	37.0	24.4
Cotton cloth	70.0	46.5	29.0
Rayon cloth	277.8	86.7	52.9
Cotton thread	22.1	17.1	12.7
Cotton shirts	46.3	35.2	25.4
Olive oil	31.2	12.5	11.5
Vegetable fats	36.5	16.9	12.3
Drugs and medicines	32.0	34.6	31.3
Perfumes	25.8	21.3	17.6
Evaporated milk	100.5	65.3	1.7
All imports[b]	31.6	29.5	19.8

[a] Computed rates, including tariffs, consular fees, and all other taxes on imports.
[b] Ad valorem equivalent of actual collections during fiscal year ending six months before end of calendar year.

agricultural machinery, the decline in ad valorem rates was intensified by a lowering of the import duties. On balance, however, it appears quite clear that the major effect of the rise in import prices was to lower the real weight of import duties. The percentage rate on all imports was only 19.8 percent in 1948, as compared with 31.6 percent in 1938.

The conclusion with respect to the consumption taxes on alcoholic beverages and tobacco products is somewhat different. These taxes, to be sure, are also levied on a specific basis, but in this case the effects of price increases were more or less evenly offset by increases in the tax rates. In the case of the business profits tax, on the other hand, the war and postwar inflation acted to increase the real weight of the tax. Because of the progressiveness of this tax, an increase in money income places the taxpayer in a higher bracket, and if this rise in money income is not accompanied by a commensurate increase in real income, his real rate of tax will be higher.

Table 42 shows the real weight of the business profits tax on five business owners whose real incomes remained unchanged during the past decade. Since the rates of the tax were periodically changed during the period, the tax burden for each year is shown under three different assumptions: what it would have been if the original 1938 rates had been effective throughout the period; what it actually was under the rates that existed in each of the selected years; and what it would have been if the 1947/48 rate structure had been in use throughout. As may be seen, the effect of the inflation was to raise the real weight of the tax in all instances where the larger money income pushed the taxpayer into a bracket with a higher marginal rate, and, with the very narrow brackets of the present rate structure, this would have occurred in every case.[16]

The higher level of prices has produced diverse changes in

---

[16] Price increases will, of course, have this same effect on the real weight of the personal income tax, if and when it is enacted. Their effect would be even more pronounced in the case of the proposed tax, for inflation would also lower the real value of the basic exemptions to the taxpayer.

the impact of other types of taxes. In the case of the stamp tax on salaries and transactions, the effects have probably been neutral, for this tax is imposed proportionately to money amounts. The coffee export tax, on the other hand, has become progressively less burdensome, because the profits of the producers have increased tremendously since the later 'thirties. The same thing is

TABLE 42

EFFECTS OF PRICE LEVEL CHANGES ON BURDEN OF BUSINESS PROFITS TAX

	Average Rate of Business Profits Tax[a]				
	1939/40	1943/44	1944/45	1946/47	1947/48
Real income: Q5,000:					
At original tax rates	5.0	5.0	5.0	5.0	6.0
At actual tax rates	5.0	5.0	6.0	6.7	7.1
At 1947/48 tax rates	5.4	6.0	6.4	6.7	7.1
Real income: Q15,000:					
At original tax rates	6.0	7.0	7.0	7.0	7.0
At actual tax rates	6.0	7.0	10.0	11.5	12.6
At 1947/48 tax rates	8.2	9.7	10.8	11.5	12.6
Real income: Q50,000:					
At original tax rates	8.0	8.0	10.0	10.0	12.0
At actual tax rates	8.0	10.0	18.0	21.4	22.8
At 1947/48 tax rates	16.2	19.0	20.6	21.4	22.8
Real income: Q100,000:					
At original tax rates	12.0	12.0	12.0	12.0	12.0
At actual tax rates	12.0	20.0	30.0	29.3	30.6
At 1947/48 tax rates	23.9	26.7	28.3	29.3	30.6
Real income: Q200,000:					
At original tax rates	12.0	12.0	12.0	12.0	12.0
At actual tax rates	12.0	20.0	40.0	34.1	35.3
At 1947/48 tax rates	28.4	31.4	33.2	34.1	35.3

[a] Real income at 1939/40 prices. The G.N.P. deflator was used to compute the money income that corresponded in each year to the real income shown. The average tax rate was then computed on the basis of the money-income data thus derived.

true of the proporty tax to an even greater extent. Real estate assessments for the most part have not been changed during the period under review, and rising market prices have tended to lower the effective rate of the tax significantly. Assuming that a piece of property was assessed at its true market value in 1937, the price increases which have occurred since that year would, as is shown in Table 43, have reduced the real burden of the tax from 0.3 percent at the time of assessment to only 0.111 percent in 1949.

On balance, it would appear that the price changes of the last ten or twelve years have decreased the real burden of taxes on the lower-income groups and, at the same time, increased their real weight on those households in the upper groups which are subject to the business profits tax. If rate changes are considered, the result is still the same, for higher liquor and tobacco tax rates were accompanied by a more progressive business profits tax rate structure. As a result, the tax incidence in Guatemala today is slightly more progressive than it was ten years ago.

TABLE 43

INFLUENCE OF REAL ESTATE PRICE CHANGES ON EFFECTIVE
PROPERTY TAX RATE BETWEEN 1937 AND 1949

(*Tax rate per Q1,000 of real estate value, in quetzales*)

Year	Assessed Value of Real Estate in Quetzales	Market Value of Real Estate[a] in Quetzales	Effective Property Tax per Thousand
1937	1,000	1,000	3.00[b]
1938	1,000	981	3.06
1939	1,000	976	3.07
1940	1,000	974	3.08
1941	1,000	976	3.06
1942	1,000	1,138	2.64
1943	1,000	1,360	2.21
1944	1,000	1,600	1.88
1945	1,000	1,900	1.58
1946	1,000	2,426	1.24
1947	1,000	2,596	1.16
1948	1,000	2,618	1.15
1949	1,000	2,693	1.11

[a] Index of domestically produced construction materials is taken as an approximation of the change of the market value of real estate.
[b] Assuming that in 1937 the assessed value was equal to the market value.

STATISTICAL NOTE

The estimates of tax liabilities of individual households presented in Tables 36 and 39 are based on information provided by the Goubaud Carrera study, the Arias study, the official revenue statistics, and the various tax laws in effect during the 1947/48 fiscal year. To a very large extent, the methods used in making these estimates are the same as those subsequently employed in chapter ix to obtain the distribution of the tax burden by family-income groups, and are described in detail in the Statistical Note to that chapter.[17] The principal differences between the two sets of estimates are as follows:

Direct taxes.—With the exception of the miscellaneous taxes, the estimates in Tables 36 and 39 represent computed tax liabilities, and were obtained by applying actual tax rates to family income and capital. (It should be noted that the estimates in Table 39 represent actual tax payments, and were adjusted to take account of actual collections and the fact that each family in a particular income bracket is not subject to the same types of direct taxes.)

Consumption taxes.—The estimates for the lower- and middle-income groups were derived in the same way as in chapter ix, and then adjusted by interpolation to conform to disposable income[18] rather than total income. Figures for the upper-income households were obtained by extrapolating these estimates on the basis of the consumption figures of the Arias study; the results were then adjusted to conform to actual collection data.

Shifted taxes.—The same types of adjustments were made in the estimates of chapter ix as in the case of the consumption taxes.

[17] See pp. 225–28.
[18] Total income minus direct taxes.

VII

THE GOVERNMENT AND
THE BUDGET

THE TWO PREVIOUS chapters dealt with the effects of the tax system on business enterprises and individuals. The purpose of this and the following chapter is to determine how the government fared under the present fiscal system.

The relations between the government and the fiscal system are twofold. It is the government on the one hand which develops the fiscal system and modifies and amends it (through legislation and administration) if changes are deemed necessary. On the other hand, the fiscal system, once established, provides revenues for the government to enable it to discharge its various functions. It sets definite limits to the alternatives of fiscal and, indirectly, general economic policies which the government can pursue. It is the latter relation between the fiscal system and the government which is described and analyzed in this chapter.

EFFICIENCY OF TAX ADMINISTRATION

In order to appraise the efficiency of the Guatemalan tax administration, the amounts of revenues collected from each major group of taxes are first compared with the cost of collection associated with each group. Following that, some comments on the administration of certain major taxes are presented.

The Cost of Tax Collection

Estimates of the costs of collecting the various taxes are presented in Table 44. The cost data are based on the budgetary expenditures of the administrative agencies charged with the collection of specific taxes or groups of taxes. To the extent to which salaries and other expenditures could be allocated to a particular group of taxes, they are shown as direct costs. Expenditure associated with the administration of more than one group of taxes are shown as indirect costs; because of the lack of more precise information, they have been allocated proportionately to the amounts of the various groups or subgroups of taxes to which they pertain.[1]

TABLE 44

COST OF TAX COLLECTION BY MAJOR GROUPS OF TAXES IN 1947/48

(In thousands of quetzales)

Tax Group	Amount Collected	Cost of Collection			Cost as Per- cent of Revenue[a]
		Direct	Indirect	Total	
Direct taxes	3,215.5	135.6	42.4	178.0	5.5
Business income tax	*3,045.5*	*93.8*	*40.1*	*133.9*	*4.4*
Other	*170.0*	*41.8*	*2.3*	*44.1*	*25.9*
Property and property transfer taxes	597.1	76.4	7.9	84.3	14.1
Consumption taxes	8,286.2	262.1	109.3	371.4	4.5
Alcoholic beverages	*6,184.5*	*247.9*	*81.6*	*329.5*	*5.3*
Tobacco	*1,798.0*	*14.2*	*23.7*	*37.9*	*2.1*
Other	*303.7*	.....	*4.0*	*4.0*	*1.3*
Import taxes	13,072.5	479.3	316.8	796.1	6.1
Export taxes	2,664.0	42.7	40.1	82.8	3.1
Business licenses and transaction taxes	2,957.7	46.4	52.9	99.3	3.4
Other taxes	148.4	7.4	63.2	70.6	47.6
Fees and fines	293.1	6.4	7.4	13.8	4.7
Total tax revenue[b]	31,234.5	1,082.2	664.2	1,746.4	5.6

[a] Centavos per quetzal.
[b] Excluding assigned taxes.

Before commenting on the cost of tax collections, it must be pointed out that the percentage figures shown give only a very rough indication of the efficacy of the various taxes, since the nature of each tax determines the relative ease or difficulty of administration and collection. Thus, it is clear that export taxes, assessed as they are on a specific basis (per bag, per stem) at convenient assembly points (i.e., the ports of embarkation), are

[1] For example, the salaries in local tax administrations have been allocated proportionately to those internal revenues (as distinct from customs collections) that are locally administered and paid.

easier to collect than, for example, inheritance taxes, the assessment of which inevitably involves a complicated process of valuation.

Furthermore, the relation between costs of collection and the amounts collected provides an indication of only one measure of the cost of tax collection. It indicates to what extent the average cost of collection (of each individual tax or group of taxes) corresponds to the administrative objective of keeping such cost to a minimum. It does not, however, convey any indication regarding the maximization of net tax revenues (from collections minus cost of collections), which is achieved if a small increase in the cost of collection yields exactly the same amount of additional revenue. Or, to present the same proposition in its inverse form, additional expenditures on the collection of taxes are worth while from the point of view of the Treasury so long as any additions produce more than the same amount in additional revenues. A few remarks regarding the application of this principle will be found in the next section. But it might be pointed out at once that the addition of more tax-collection effort—which does not necessarily entail the employment of more personnel but would require better training and more efficient use of present personnel—is likely to yield just as much additional revenue as the addition of more personnel to the tax administration.

According to the data presented in Table 44, it appears that, on the average, it cost the government in the fiscal year 1947/48 the sum of 5.6 centavos to collect one quetzal of revenue. This figure compares with 6.7 centavos in 1937/38 and 7.5 centavos in 1942/43. The implied decline in the average cost between 1942/43 and 1947/48 was largely due, it appears, to an increase of tax rates of several taxes resulting in higher yields without a major increase in collection costs. But better administration and a fuller utilization of the staff of the collecting agencies, for instance, as a result of the increased volume of imports, have undoubtedly also contributed to bringing the average cost down.

But more significant than the average figure of 5.6 centavos

—which certainly does not seem to be excessive—is the wide range of the ratio of the cost of collection to the amounts collected through individual taxes. The cheapest cost of collection obtains in the case of the tobacco taxes, other consumption taxes, and export taxes. This is, as indicated above, not particularly surprising, since all these taxes are easy to collect, either at the place of production (tobacco) or at the port of shipment (exports). More remarkable is the fact that the costs of collection of the business profits tax, the yield of which is considerable, are very small, although the tax—like any other direct tax—is difficult to administer. The low costs involved can also be interpreted, however, as an indication that the administration of this tax is somewhat deficient and that an increase in administrative expenditures may produce an increase in revenue substantially in excess of cost.

As to the 6.1 centavos per quetzal involved in the collection of import duties, the cost ratio, though small in absolute terms, appears large if it is realized that import duties are generally considered easy to collect for reasons similar to those mentioned in the case of export taxes. It should be noted, however, that the expenditures involved in the maintenance of border guards, whose duty is the prevention of smuggling, is charged in the table as an indirect cost of duty collections. Since Guatemala has long open frontiers with three neighboring countries, these expenditures appear unavoidable. Indirectly, however, they point to another phenomenon which has some bearing in this connection: as a result of the price increases in Guatemala in recent years and of the high duty rates imposed on certain products of neighboring and other countries, the inducements to engage in smuggling, which have been particularly great in recent years, appear to have caused some increase in contraband traffic.

The high costs of collecting other taxes, the yields of which are decidedly minor, seem to indicate the essentially uneconomic nature of some of them. Although the original reasons for imposing them may have disappeared, they continue to be levied and yield a small amount of net revenue. But the high average cost of collection of this group of taxes and the apparent yield potential of others give the impression that it might be preferable to expend more administrative effort in the collection of more profitable taxes, if necessary, at the expense of eliminating some of the minor taxes. At any rate it seems advisable to investigate more closely the profitability of these minor taxes and to determine whether they should be continued or abolished, or whether their administration can be made less expensive.[2]

Another outstanding example of high collection costs is to be found in the group of other direct taxes which is made up primarily of the inheritance and gift tax. As mentioned before, this type of tax is difficult to administer; therefore, a higher collection cost relative to the yield seems unavoidable. There are indications, however, to be detailed below, that the main reason for the relative high cost of collection is the low valuation basis of the tax assessments. A similar situation apparently prevails in the case of property taxes, the net yield of which seems to be adversely affected also by an overly decentralized administration.

Administration of Major Taxes

Some further indication as to the efficacy of the Guatemalan tax administration is provided by a description of the assessment and collection procedures applied to certain major taxes. In the following paragraphs, some comments are also offered as to the appropriateness of prevailing methods of tax administration.

Business profits tax.—The business profits tax (*impuesto sobre utilidades de empresas lucrativas*) is assessed by a special administrative agency, the Contraloría del Impuesto sobre Utilidades, with which all business enterprises (excepting those engaged in agriculture, insurance, and mining) with a capital of Q2,500 or more must be registered.

In some sectors of the Guatemalan business community, the

---

[2] The latter applies also to those taxes and fees (e.g., motor vehicle licenses, special business licenses) that serve primarily nonfiscal control purposes.

opinion seems to prevail that there are many enterprises, especially in retail trade, that are not registered for the payment of the business income tax although their capital is larger than Q2,500. This opinion, however, does not seem to be borne out by statistical data that recently have become available. In 1949 there were 1,917 firms located in five departments which were registered with the Contraloría. For the same period 1,620 concerns, having five or more employees in the same departments, were registered at the Social Security Institute. Since there are reasons to believe that the coverage obtained by the Social Security Institute is more or less complete, and since it is not likely that the number of enterprises with an invested capital of Q2,500 and fewer than five employees exceeds 300, evasion of the profits tax through nonregistration appears to be less widespread than is frequently charged. This does not prove, however, that coverage is complete, and it still would appear advisable to canvass small shops periodically to determine whether or not their capital makes them subject to the business profits tax.

Firms registered with the Contraloría must submit at the end of each year a sworn declaration giving the amount of net earnings and other pertinent data. The Contraloría then prepares a preliminary assessment. A definite assessment is issued only after the books of the taxpayer have been audited. As a result of this practice, final assessments are issued after considerable delays, some of which are known to have been of several years' duration.

At the end of 1949, there were forty-six accountants employed at the Control Office. This number is considered sufficient for the current volume of declarations. Because of insufficient personnel in earlier years and occasional interruptions of the operations of the office, the agency is burdened, however, with a very large backlog of declarations for which final assessments have not as yet been issued. It has been estimated that some four years will be required to liquidate this backlog. The operations of the Control Office therefore will not be on a current basis until 1953.

The delays in preparing assessments obviously entail definite disadvantages for taxpayers who must wait for long periods to be advised of the amount of their tax liability. Moreover, the delays in the issue of final assessments are likely to cause losses of revenue to the government; such losses becoming more pronounced in periods of declining business activity and prices.

The slow pace of tax assessments seems even more deplorable because it appears that at present auditing consists largely of checking the figures in the taxpayers' books against those appearing on the tax declarations. Apparently, no attempts are being made to test the consistency of the tax declaration data with the volume of business, the markups of merchandise, the volume and value of inventories, etc. According to informed Guatemalan sources, tax evasion is particularly high among medium-sized and small enterprises. It is accomplished largely through an underreporting of inventories and of retail sales.

All persons familiar with the administration of the business income tax seem to agree that the major difficulties encountered in the administration of the tax are the prevalence of poor bookkeeping practices by business firms on the one hand, and the lack of well-trained personnel responsible for assessing taxes on the other. Although there is little that can be done immediately to improve bookkeeping practices, particularly since the overwhelming majority of firms are one-man, or one-family enterprises, better training of the accounting personnel—if necessary as a prerequisite for advancement—seems highly desirable and presumably could be undertaken without major costs to the government.

Real property tax.—The real property tax was originally based on an assessment of real estate made in 1921. The valuation was revised upward in 1931. In 1945, a special office, the Oficina Revisora de la Matrícula Fiscal, was established in the Bureau of Internal Revenue to reassess all properties. Up to the end of 1949, the office had reassessed 25,000 properties out of a total registration of 125,000. In 1948, the office reassessed 1,731 urban properties at 17.9 million quetzales. Prior to the reassessment, the assessed value of the same properties was 9.8 million quetzales. This suggests that properties not yet reassessed are undervalued by approximately 50 percent. However, well-informed persons have indicated on the basis of their own experience that the former assessed value of urban property is not more than 20 percent of the market value. In the case of rural property, it is said to amount to 50 percent of market value. The higher rate for rural properties is reportedly due to the provision in the banking law which requires that mortgage loans cannot exceed 50 percent of the assessed value of the property. This substantial difference between assessed and market values, together with the fact that the rate of three quetzales per thousand has not been changed since 1921 while the costs of collection have risen, has made the property tax one of the most expensive to administer. In some departments the property tax is collected by agents who are paid a commission of 20 percent of the sums they collect up to Q100 per month. It is reported that this procedure results in a slackening of collections as soon as the Q100 limit has been reached by the individual collector.

Statistical data indicate that the incidence of property tax delinquency is high. In a sample of 1,327 entries in the tax rolls, 879 items, or 66 percent, representing a total property value of Q830,213, were delinquent in August 1949.[3] As Table 45 shows, more than 60 percent of all delinquent tax payments were in arrears for over one year, almost 40 percent for more than three years, and 22 percent for more than ten years, which means that for all practical purposes the latter were no longer collectible.

A comparison of the values of all property included in the sample with the value of delinquent property indicates that 25 percent of assessed property was delinquent. The discrepancy between the numerical incidence of delinquency and the lower value percentage is explained by the high incidence of delinquency among owners of property assessed at Q100 to Q200,

[3] The sample is believed to be a close approximation to a random sample. The first entry on each sheet of the tax rolls was included in the sample.

whose annual tax liability is very small, ranging from thirty to sixty centavos.

TABLE 45

TAX DELINQUENCY IN REAL ESTATE TAXATION[a]

Periods in Arrears[b]	Number of Delinquent Taxpayers	Percent of Total Delinquency
1 to 4	333	37.8
5 to 8	133	15.1
9 to 12	66	7.5
13 to 16	36	4.0
17 to 20	41	4.6
21 to 24	23	2.6
25 to 28	17	1.9
29 to 32	12	1.3
33 to 36	10	1.1
37 to 40	15	1.7
41 to 44	10	1.1
45 to 48	9	1.0
49 to 52	12	1.3
53 to 56	11	1.2
57 to 60	8	0.9
61 and over	143	16.2
Total	879	100.0

[a] Based on sample taken from tax records in August 1949.
[b] The property tax is payable in quarterly installments; four periods correspond to one year.

According to the property tax law, delays in the payment of taxes of less than one year render the taxpayer subject to a penalty of 25 percent of the tax liability, and payments overdue for longer periods carry a penalty of 50 percent. Although these penalties would appear to be sufficient to stimulate timely payments, collections continue to be delayed because in recent years the administration has canceled the fines of all delinquent taxpayers who bring their tax liability up to date, and the taxpayers are aware of this. Delinquent property can be sold at auction, but this procedure is hardly ever resorted to.

The cost of the administration of the property tax has been estimated at approximately Q50,000 per year, or forty-eight centavos per owner of assessed property. Since the cost of collection of the tax appears to be more or less the same for large and small properties, the taxes paid on properties assessed at less than Q160 seem to be insufficient to cover the cost of collection and that the taxation of property valued up to Q300 is hardly worth while.

There is little doubt that substantial improvements can be, and should be, made in the administration of the property tax. Considerable advancement in this direction is to be expected from the reassessment now in progress. In view of the low yields of the tax at the old level of valuations, and of the discrimination inherent in the fact that some property is assessed at the old and some at the new valuation, it appears advisable to accelerate the present pace of the revaluation. It has been estimated that if the process of reassessment is continued at the present rate, completion of the task would require about sixteen years.

Inheritance and gift tax.—The inheritance and gift tax law stipulates that, for the purposes of the tax, the valuation of real estate property must not be lower than the assessed value for purposes of real estate taxation. In most instances the assessed value is accepted by the tax administration as the proper valuation. Since approximately 90 percent of all estates and donations subject to taxes consist of real estate and since, as indicated above, the majority of real property has not been reappraised since 1931, the yield of these taxes is adversely affected by the slowness of the reassessment of real property. At present, inheritance and gift taxes yield 9.1 percent of the value of taxable estates and gifts. But since real property is reported to be undervalued by at least 50 percent, the true average tax rate is presumably less than 5 percent.

Tax on alcoholic beverages.—For the purpose of controlling the production and wholesale distribution of alcoholic beverages and facilitating the collection of taxes, liquor factories can be operated and warehouses maintained only in locations approved by the government. Every shipment of liquor is recorded by a government official and reported to the Bureau of Internal Revenue where an account for every producer is kept. Every ten days each producer must discharge the tax liability shown in his account. This control system makes evasion among registered producers virtually impossible. It is estimated, however, that in addition to eight million liters produced annually by registered producers, four million liters are produced illegally for home consumption and illicit sale. The resulting tax evasion represents a loss to the government of about three million quetzales per year in gross revenues. One of the reasons advanced for the large-scale evasion of this tax is the high ad valorem equivalent of the tax rates. At present, the tax amounts to 65 percent of the whole-sale prices of cheaper qualities of *aguardiente*; to 62 percent in the case of other liquors; to 46 percent for whisky; and to 42 per-cent for beer. But since the cost of collection of this tax is rela-tively small, and since the imposition of the tax pursues in addi-tion to fiscal revenues also the social objective of discouraging the consumption of liquor, a lowering of the rates does not appear advisable. Rather, it would seem preferable to curtail the illegal production of liquor through a strengthening of the special police force in charge of enforcement of the prohibition against uncon-trolled production. The imposition of more drastic penalties against violators—who, it is reported, usually resume their ille-gal operations after payment of small fines—would also seem appropriate.

Import and export taxes.—The administration of import and export taxes is centralized in the customs service. At present, the customs administration is undergoing a reorganization which, it is expected, will result in substantial improvements of the service.

It is hardly necessary to say that a high degree of efficiency in the customs administration is of great importance from a fiscal point of view, since receipts of the customs service account for al-most one-half of all tax receipts. Moreover, speedy and efficient handling of imports and exports by the customs service would greatly benefit the business community and indirectly the Guate-malan economy as a whole.

One of the reasons for the occasional delays in customs processing and the accumulation of imported merchandise in customs warehouses seems to be the complicated duty schedule which contains an excessive number of individually listed items. Another reason for the delays is the fact that certain imports (e.g., gasoline) are subject to taxes that have not been consolidated with the tariff schedule and thereby make the levying of import taxes and accounting of customs collections unnecessarily complex. These deficiencies could be easily remedied.

THE COST OF GOVERNMENT

As has been shown in chapter iv, government expenditures rose between 1937/38 and 1948/49 from 10.8 million quetzales to 47.4 million. This increase of 320 percent, which if taken at face value might convey the impression of a vast expansion of the government apparatus, must now be analyzed to determine to what extent it was due to increased unit costs of government services and to what extent it was the result of an expansion of functions of the government.[4]

Unit Cost

In order to measure the changes in the unit cost of government services, a special index has been computed. The index consists of four components: (1) an index of government salaries, derived by dividing total appropriations for salary payments of the government by the number of salaried government employees provided for in the annual budget, (2) an index of wage rates paid by the government, derived from government payrolls, (3) the price index of construction materials, and,(4) the index of wholesale food prices in Guatemala City.[5]

Table 46 suggests that, of the total increase in expenditures shown there of 360 percent between 1937/38 and 1947/48,

[4] The related question of changes in the share of the government in the gross national product will be dealt with in chapter ix.

[5] The old wholesale food price index covering thirteen commodities was linked with the new (1946) index.

slightly less than four-tenths is accounted for by an increase in unit cost, so that approximately six-tenths of the increase must be attributed to an expansion in government activities which set in after the revolutionary changes in 1944/45.

TABLE 46

ANALYSIS OF CHANGES IN GOVERNMENT EXPENDITURES, 1937/38 TO 1947/48[a]

Fiscal Year	Government Expenditures, in Q1,000	Unit Cost of Government 1937/38=100	Government Expenditures at Constant (1937/38) Unit Cost, in Q1,000	Government Expenditures as Percentage of 1937/38	
				Actual	At Constant (1937/38) Unit Cost
1937/38	10,099.0	100.0	10,099.0	100.0	100.0
1938/39	10,689.9	96.2	11,228.9	105.9	111.2
1939/40	9,750.8	93.6	10,417.5	96.6	103.2
1940/41	9,995.5	94.1	10,622.2	99.0	105.2
1941/42	10,424.9	106.1	9,825.5	103.2	97.3
1942/43	12,346.4	108.2	11,410.7	122.3	113.0
1943/44	14,482.2	112.5	12,873.0	143.4	127.5
1944/45	16,504.1	133.7	12,344.1	163.4	122.2
1945/46	28,804.6	149.6	19,254.4	285.2	190.7
1946/47	36,096.6	173.4	20,817.0	357.4	206.1
1947/48	46,649.5	185.8	25,107.4	461.9	248.6

[a] Excluding transfers to autonomous entities and payments of interest and amortization on the public debt, since the cost of these payments obviously was not influenced by changes in unit cost.

If allowance is made, however, for expenditures connected with the administration and operation of the national farms, which affect the amount of expenditures in the last four years shown in the table, the remaining volume increase amounts to not quite 100 percent in the last year and to approximately 60 percent in the preceding two years. Conversely, if the government had maintained the same scope of operations as in 1937/38, expenditures would have amounted in 1947/48 to approximately 20.4 million quetzales. It may be of interest to note in this connection that (as shown in the next chapter) tax revenues at the 1936/37 rate structure would have amounted in 1947/48 to 23 million quetzales compared with actual collections of 31 million.

Government Salaries and Employment Policy

The relative smallness of the increase in the unit cost of government that took place between 1937/38 and 1947/48 has been largely a result of the slow rise of government salaries and wages. Approximately two-thirds of government expenditures are absorbed on the average by salary and wage payments. The index of average government salaries shown separately in Table 47 rose to 163 in 1947/48, and the index of government wage rates rose to 158. These increases compare with a rise to 197 in retail food prices in Guatemala City and a rise to about 190 in the price of imports. If the government had increased wages and salaries *pari passu* with the increase in the cost of living, the expansion of government activities that has taken place in the last ten years would not have been possible without either raising substantial additional tax revenues or incurring heavy deficits. If it is assumed that an expansion of government activities was in itself desirable—a more detailed discussion of this point will be found in subsequent chapters—the relatively small increase in the unit cost of government must be considered with satisfaction. One must not, however, lose sight of the fact that economy in the setting of salary and wage scales is likely to result in a gradual deterioration of the average efficiency of the government's labor force, particularly since the salaries paid to competent and well-trained white-collar workers by the business community are generally higher than those paid by the government.

Moreover, the salary data also indicate that the number of employees in the lower-salary brackets was increased disproportionately more than that of higher-paid employees. This indicates that in the course of the expansion of government activities an attempt has apparently been made to compensate for the unavailability of trained and experienced personnel by the employment of a large number of unskilled or partly trained employees. The result of this employment policy probably was a decline in over-all efficiency of the administration of the government's affairs. But since the expansion of government activities is almost certain to be permanent, the temporary disadvantage of limited training and experience may disappear in due course, provided the turnover of personnel is kept to a minimum.

TABLE 47

SALARY PAYMENTS OF THE GOVERNMENT AND CHANGES IN NUMBER OF GOVERNMENT EMPLOYEES, 1938/39 TO 1947/48ᵃ

Fiscal Year	Number of Government Employees	Salary Payments in Q1,000	Average Annual Salary in Quetzales	Index of Number of Employees, 1937/38=100	Index of Total Salary Payments, 1937/38=100	Index of Average Annual Salary, 1937/38=100
1938/39	18,599	5,257	282.6	100.0	100.0	100.0
1939/40	19,704	5,253	266.6	105.9	99.9	94.3
1940/41	20,928	5,318	254.1	112.5	101.2	89.9
1941/42	19,039	5,339	280.4	102.4	101.6	99.2
1942/43	19,142	5,033	262.9	102.9	95.7	93.0
1943/44	19,505	5,504	282.1	104.9	104.6	99.8
1944/45	20,211	6,856	339.2	108.7	130.4	120.0
1945/46	23,753	10,910	459.3	127.7	207.5	162.5
1946/47	27,594	12,714	461.0	148.4	241.8	163.1
1947/48	29,441	13,558	461.5	158.3	257.9	163.3

ᵃ Data based on annual budget figures. Actual salary payments and number of employees presumably were somewhat larger in the second half of the later years. This does not, however, affect the average salary index. Data pertain to permanent employees who hold an appointment (*nombramiento*) only. Employees of the national farms and salaries paid to them are not included in the figures, since the expenditures for the operation of the national farms are shown in the budget as a global figure only.

VIII

VARIATIONS IN GOVERNMENT RECEIPTS AND EXPENDITURES

THE PURPOSE of this chapter is to investigate the seasonal and cyclical variations of government receipts and expenditures. The analysis of seasonal movements of revenues and disbursements is obviously of practical operational significance, for it permits a distinction to be drawn between seasonal and other changes in the government's financial position. A discussion of cyclical changes of government receipts and expenditures is even more important since it raises several fundamental questions regarding the appropriateness of the Guatemalan tax structure and pattern of expenditures for the country's economic structure and institutions.

SEASONAL FLUCTUATIONS

Seasonal fluctuations of government receipts and expenditures are of importance for fiscal operations in three respects: (1) if they are too pronounced they may result in fortuitous expansions and contractions of the volume of money in circulation through the accumulation and decumulation of Treasury balances, (2) if Treasury balances are taken into consideration in the preparation of the annual budget, a surplus which is purely seasonal, or seasonally distorted upward or downward, may result in fallacious budget estimates, (3) substantial differences between seasonal fluctuations of government income and expenditures might require short-term financing, which in the absence of such differences would be unnecessary.

Table 48 shows indexes of seasonal variations of government receipts and expenditures. They are based on monthly income and expenditure data of the national government from 1939 to 1948. The indexes show that in the first six months of each calendar year receipts are, in the aggregate, 3 percent larger than in the second half of the year. This concentration of revenues is primarily due to the collection of coffee export taxes during the first three months of the year;[1] it is in itself of minor practical significance. The seasonal variations in receipts, however, must not be considered in isolation but rather in conjunction with expenditures. Expenditure data exhibit two distinct seasonal bulges. One appears at the end of the fiscal year when many government departments find large unspent balances to their credit in their budget accounts and either obligate, or actually disburse, them before they revert to the Treasury. This concentration of expenditures is offset by a pronounced decline in disbursements in July when payments are 30 percent below the monthly average. They stay below the average until October when a second temporary expansion occurs as the rainy season ends and various government departments begin to draw on their "extraordinary" appropriations to initiate or resume public works. If we assume a level of annual government receipts and expenditures of 48 million quetzales, the combined effect of the seasonal variations would be an accumulation of Treasury balances of 2 million quetzales in the course of the first three months of the year. If the cumulation is started at the beginning of the fiscal year, the Treasury surplus at the end of March amounts to 2.2 million quetzales.

Such seasonal accumulations may have important budgetary implications since Treasury balances are taken into consideration in the preparation of the annual budget which normally takes place in the early part of the year. In other words, in the preparation of the annual budget, account should be taken of the seasonal nature of the accumulation of such balances. At the present (1948/49) level of government receipts, approximately two million quetzales of the total Treasury balance should be allowed for as a purely seasonal phenomenon. The explicit recognition of seasonal changes in Treasury balances becomes the more important in view of the fact that, as a result of delays in coffee

[1] Coffee shipments begin in November, but the resulting tax collections in the last two months of the year are offset by a seasonal low in other revenues.

sales—particularly by nationalized and intervened farms—and large payments on the business profits tax in the early months of each year, the seasonal variations in receipts may have become more pronounced in recent years.

TABLE 48

SEASONAL FLUCTUATIONS OF GOVERNMENT RECEIPTS AND EXPENDITURES[a]

	Indexes of Seasonal Variations (*Monthly average* = 100)		Amounts in Millions of Quetzales			
	Government Receipts	Government Expenditures	Monthly Receipts	Monthly Expenditures	Changes in Treasury Balances[b]	
					Monthly	Cumulative
January	111	86	4.4	3.4	+1.0	+1.0
February	114	89	4.5	3.6	+0.9	+1.9
March	105	105	4.2	4.1	+0.1	+2.0
April	101	102	4.0	4.1	—0.1	+1.9
May	103	113	4.1	4.5	—0.4	+1.5
June	102	144	4.0	5.7	—1.7	—0.2
July	98	69	3.9	2.7	+1.2	+1.0
August	98	99	3.9	3.9	...	...
September	86	88	3.4	3.5	—0.1	+0.9
October	92	109	3.7	4.4	—0.7	+0.2
November	92	95	3.7	3.8	—0.1	+0.1
December	98	100	3.9	4.0	—0.1	...

[a] Based on monthly budgetary receipts and expenditure data pertaining to revenues from all sources and disbursements for all purposes of the national government for the period January 1939 to December 1948.

[b] Assuming an annual (fictitious) total of receipts and expenditures of 48 million quetzales.

The movement of the Treasury balances suggests, on the other hand, that there is no need for seasonal borrowing by the government because, as indicated above, the seasonally low rate of disbursements in the first three months of the fiscal year results in an accumulation of balances. In other words, if at any time during the fiscal year Treasury balances fall abnormally and unexpectedly low, the explanation for such an occurrence must be sought in reasons other than purely seasonal movements.

THE FLEXIBILITY OF THE TAX SYSTEM

Having discussed the relatively subordinate subject of seasonal changes in government receipts and expenditures, we shall now approach the problem of the behavior of government receipts under the impact of cyclical changes in income and prices.[2] Comments on cyclical changes in expenditures will also be presented.

The movement of tax receipts under the impact of cyclical movements of income and prices is usually referred to as the flexibility of the tax system. It is defined as the relation between changes in national income, or gross national product, and changes in tax receipts. The system is considered flexible if tax receipts fluctuate more widely than national income. Flexibility can be the result of built-in factors or structural characteristics of individual taxes; or, it may be the result of adjustments in tax rates and the imposition of new, or the elimination of old, taxes through legislative or administrative action of the government. The latter type of flexibility may be subsumed under the term, administrative flexibility.

We shall first consider the behavior of total tax receipts in relation to movements of the gross national product. As the data shown in Table 49 indicate, the expansion of tax receipts over the entire period under consideration was somewhat larger than that of the gross national product. A closer scrutiny of the figures discloses, however, that the relation between tax receipts and gross national product was rather unstable from year to year. In some years tax receipts expanded while the gross national product declined; in others, small changes in the gross national product were associated with substantial changes in tax receipts, and vice versa.

There are three reasons for this absence of a closer correlation. One is the fact that during the period under consideration important changes in the tax structure occurred that are bound to distort the statistical comparison; these structural changes will be discussed below. The second is the time lag that exists in the case of some taxes between changes in the tax base (income, turnover,

[2] The term "cyclical changes" is used here without the implication that there need be any regularity in the occurrence of business cycles. It is meant merely to denote fluctuations in income and prices of a few years' duration, in order to distinguish them from seasonal and long-run movements.

TABLE 49

CHANGES IN GROSS NATIONAL PRODUCT, PRODUCT OF COMMERCIAL SECTOR, AND TAX RECEIPTS, 1936/37 TO 1947/48

(1936/37 = 100)

Fiscal Year	Gross National Product	Product of Commercial Sector	Total Taxes[a]	Import Taxes	Export Taxes	Consumption Taxes	Direct Taxes	Property Taxes	License and Transaction Taxes
1936/37	100.0	100.0	100.0	100.0	100.0	100.0	100.0	100.0	100.0
1937/38	93.6	105.5	108.5	108.1	99.8	105.4	145.0	98.1	128.6
1938/39	82.3	94.0	106.4	102.2	108.6	104.0	131.4	89.1	132.0
1939/40	94.4	84.2	105.7	99.6	97.6	107.7	171.8	92.6	130.4
1940/41	95.7	82.1	98.2	86.3	101.1	99.4	168.8	93.2	129.1
1941/42	110.4	93.1	102.9	88.7	100.4	108.1	185.6	99.5	148.5
1942/43	148.3	105.3	116.6	80.6	156.4	133.2	233.9	107.4	150.1
1943/44	*	112.9	141.3	90.0	178.1	178.5	359.9	118.3	168.3
1944/45	....	134.3	142.4	100.9	124.5	223.2	312.3	104.0	180.6
1945/46	199.6	154.3	203.0	147.7	169.7	321.8	411.1	113.4	291.5
1946/47	....	213.3	275.2	218.8	172.4	412.3	639.4	123.2	442.9
1947/48	278.8	287.6	304.1	274.6	153.2	429.7	660.9	127.2	457.8

[a] Unadjusted data. See Table 14.
* Not available.

value of property, etc.) and changes in revenue. The third and
perhaps most important reason is the fact, mentioned in the
discussion of the national income and its composition, that fluctuations in the product of the noncommercial sector of the economy—which were largely caused by extraneous factors— affect
the level of tax receipts much less than changes in the commercial
sector.

This is borne out by a comparison between the year-to-year
changes in the index of the income of the commercial sector and
the year-to-year changes that occurred in the level of tax receipts.[3]
Such a comparison is presented in Table 50. It will be noted
that, throughout the period, the changes move in the same direction in both series and there appears to be a rough correlation
between the magnitudes of the changes.

TABLE 50

ANNUAL CHANGES IN COMMERCIAL-SECTOR PRODUCT
AND TAX RECEIPTS

(*In percent*)

| Period | Annual Changes | |
	Product of Commercial Sector	Total Tax Receipts
1936/37 to 1937/38	+ 5.5	+ 8.5
1937/38 to 1938/39	−10.9	− 1.9
1938/39 to 1939/40	−10.4	− 0.7
1939/40 to 1940/41	− 2.5	− 7.1
1940/41 to 1941/42	+13.4	+ 4.8
1941/42 to 1942/43	+11.3	+13.3
1942/43 to 1943/44	+ 7.2	+21.2
1943/44 to 1944/45	+11.9	+ 0.8
1944/45 to 1945/46	+11.5	+42.6
1945/46 to 1946/47	+38.2	+35.6
1946/47 to 1947/48	+34.8	+10.5

The Flexibility of Individual Taxes

In order to arrive at a general conclusion as to the over-all
flexibility of the tax system as a whole, it seems necessary to con-

[3] Year-to-year changes are a better measure of the correlation between the
two time series because they tend to minimize the effects of changes in tax rates
and other structural changes in the revenue system.

sider first the degree of flexibility inherent in the various groups of taxes.

Import taxes.—As indicated before, import taxes which accounted on the average for 40 percent of all tax receipts, are overwhelmingly specific, i.e., levied on the basis of weight. Only 20 percent of all import taxes, i.e., consular invoice fees and a limited number of duties, are imposed ad valorem. Assuming a stable composition of imports (at least in terms of the rate structure of the tariff schedule), import duty collections thus should fluctuate proportionately with the *volume* of imports.[4] Since it appears reasonably certain, however, that the volume of Guatemalan imports fluctuated more than proportionately with changes in the real gross national product or, more correctly, with changes in the product of the commercial sector,[5] the yield of import taxes, relative to changes in real income, is likely to show a substantial degree of flexibility. But if the gross national product is measured in money terms and if it is assumed that domestic prices (as well as prices of imports) normally move in the same direction as changes in real income,[6] the high-income elasticity of imports —and the resulting high flexibility of import tax receipts relative to the real gross national product—is obscured by the price changes implicit in the gross national product (and the product of the commercial sector) data. If we assume—and this assumption is not contradicted by the Guatemalan experience—that an expansion in real terms is almost always associated with a substantial rise in the price level, we arrive at the conclusion that import taxes levied on a specific basis are likely to be more or less neutral, i.e., their yield varies more or less proportionately with changes in the gross national product. This conclusion is partly

[4] If movements of import prices cause a change in the *value* of imports, import taxes remain virtually unaffected, i.e., they show a low flexibility relative to the value of imports.

[5] A complete verification of this proposition is difficult in view of the distortions of the war and postwar years in the level of imports. For a more detailed discussion, see chapter x.

[6] The reaction of the volume of imports to changes in import prices relative to prices of domestic goods (the price elasticity of the demand for imports) can be neglected as of decidedly minor importance in this connection.

borne out by the data shown in Table 49. If we compare the movements of the product of the commercial sector with those of import tax collections, we find a case of almost complete neutrality, particularly in recent years.

Lest this conclusion be misinterpreted, an important modification seems necessary. The yield of the import taxes was found to be neutral only because its inherent flexibility (due to a high income elasticity) was offset by price changes affecting the value of the gross national product. If in the future a gradual expansion of the gross national product should take place without inflationary price changes—certainly the most desirable form of economic evolution—it is likely, for reasons which will be presented in a later chapter,[7] that the volume of imports will expand more rapidly than the gross national product. If this is the case, the yield of import taxes will likewise rise faster than the gross national product, i.e., import taxes will be flexible. (This presupposes of course, an essentially unchanged level of duty rates and no major changes in the composition of imports.) This aspect of the taxation of imports is an important argument for the continued reliance on import taxes as a major source of government receipts, in spite of the evidence of the undesirable distribution of the burden of import taxes presented in an earlier chapter.

Export taxes.—Turning now to export taxes, we note at once that the expansion in their yield during the period under consideration has been small. The explanation for the slow and somewhat erratic movement of this group of taxes is simple. Export taxes are levied on a specific basis; thus, their yield is determined exclusively by the physical volume of exports. Since the *volume* of taxable exports is likely to show smaller changes than national income in *money* terms (of which the value of exports forms an important part), export taxes are decidedly inflexible.

Consumption taxes.—The yield of consumption taxes increased between 1936/37 and 1947/48 by 330 percent. Most

[7] See pp. 239–45.

of this increase was due to substantial changes in the tax rates applicable to liquor, beer, and cigarettes, but there is reason to believe that as a result of the quasi-luxury character of some of the taxed commodities (e.g., liquor, beer) the group of taxes as a whole is fairly flexible. According to observers familiar with Guatemalan institutions, the lowest-income groups, particularly among the rural indigenous ppoulation, consume largely untaxed home-distilled liquor and only those enjoying a somewhat higher real income are consumers of taxed liquor. A similar situation presumably obtains in the case of tobacco consumption where a shift from low-taxed cigars to higher-taxed cigarettes takes place. Therefore, the yield of consumption taxes must be considered flexible.

Direct taxes.—Collections of direct taxes increased almost sevenfold in the period between 1936/37 and 1947/48, as is shown in Table 49. This increase is accounted for by the introduction of the business profits tax in 1937/38, and the subsequent increase in rates, and by the high degree of built-in flexibility of this and other direct taxes. The built-in flexibility of the business profits tax is due to two factors. First, changes in real income of the taxpayers result in a more than proportionate change in tax liability because of the progressive nature of the tax structure. Second, changes in the price level also cause shifts in the tax liability because the basis for the assessment of the tax is money income. For the same reason, a rise in the price level also makes more business firms subject to the profits tax, since as a result of an increase in the price level their money profits exceed the level of the basic exemptions. The high degree of built-in flexibility of the direct taxes, together with their rate increases and their expanded coverage, has enhanced the importance of this group of taxes as a source of tax revenue relative to all other groups of taxes. This is shown in the percentage figures of Table 15 and is of considerable significance in the appraisal of the changes in the degree of flexibility of the tax system as a whole that have occurred in recent years.

Property taxes.—On the other end of the scale of flexibility stands the group of property and property-transfer taxes. As a result of a proportionate rate and a valuation basis that for all practical purposes is constant, receipts from property taxes proper are bound to be completely inflexible. Whatever changes of revenue occur are due to a greater degree of tax delinquency during periods of low income and to the additions to the tax base through new construction and rural improvements during periods of expansion.

In the case of the property-transfer tax, a somewhat higher level of tax revenues can be expected during periods of business expansion when the turnover of business and private real property is likely to be greater than during a period of low-level activity. But since the assessment of transfer taxes is customarily based upon assessment values, changes in the market values of transferred property are only incompletely reflected in tax revenues. Thus, the very small expansion of revenues in this category of taxes presumably was largely the result of new construction, a greater turnover of property in the last three years of high business activity, and the partial reappraisal of real property initiated in 1942.

Built-in Flexibility

The combined result of the divergent behavior of the various groups of taxes is a rather mild degree of over-all flexibility. The next step in our analysis is to determine what proportion of the observed over-all flexibility of the tax system was due to built-in flexibility and what part was accounted for by administrative flexibility. In order to obtain such a breakdown, the yield of the most important taxes of the Guatemalan revenue system was recomputed under the hypothetical assumption that the same tax rates as those prevailing in 1936/37 prevailed throughout the entire period. The results of this computation are presented in columns 5 and 7 of Table 51.

The figures indicate that between 1936/37 and 1947/48,

TABLE 51

CHANGES IN TAX REVENUE AS THE RESULT OF BUILT-IN AND ADMINISTRATIVE FLEXIBILITY, 1936/37 TO 1947/48

| Fiscal Year | 1936/37 = 100 | | | | In Millions of Quetzales | | | | |
| | Gross National Product | Product of Commercial Sector | Actual Tax Collections | Tax Collections at 1936/37 Rate Structure | Actual Tax Collections | Tax Collections at 1936/37 Rate Structure | Changes in Tax Receipts from 1936/37 | | |
							Total	Because of Built-in Flexibility	Because of Administrative Flexibility
1936/37	100.0	100.0	100.0	100.0	10.3	10.3	....	....	....
1937/38	94.9	105.5	108.5	104.8	11.1	10.8	+ 0.8	+ 0.5	+0.3
1938/39	82.3	94.0	106.4	101.9	10.9	10.5	+ 0.6	+ 0.2	+0.4
1939/40	94.4	84.2	105.7	101.0	10.9	10.4	+ 0.6	+ 0.1	+0.5
1940/41	95.7	82.1	98.2	93.2	10.1	9.6	− 0.2	− 0.6	+0.4
1941/42	110.4	93.1	102.9	97.1	10.6	10.0	+ 0.3	− 0.3	+0.6
1942/43	148.3	105.3	116.6	103.9	12.0	10.7	+ 1.7	+ 0.4	+1.3
1943/44 ......*		112.9	141.3	121.3	14.5	12.5	+ 4.2	+ 2.2	+2.0
1944/45		134.3	142.4	130.1	14.6	13.4	+ 4.3	+ 3.1	+1.2
1945/46	199.6	154.3	203.0	154.4	20.9	15.9	+10.5	+ 5.6	+4.9
1946/47		213.3	275.2	211.6	28.3	21.7	+18.0	+11.5	+6.5
1947/48	278.8	287.6	304.1	226.2	31.2	23.2	+20.9	+13.0	+7.9

* Not available.

when the gross national product increased almost 180 percent, tax collections would have expanded by only 126 percent over the base year if the tax structure of 1936/37 had prevailed. Thus, we find a built-in flexibility of the tax structure of somewhat less than unity.

Essentially, the same conclusion can be derived from a comparison of tax receipts at constant rates with changes in the income (product) of the commercial sector of the economy. Throughout the twelve years under consideration, the index of tax collections at constant rates moved in the same direction as the index of the product of the business sector, but fluctuated less on the average than the latter.

The last five columns of Table 51 show a comparison of changes in revenue which were due to built-in flexibility with those resulting from administrative flexibility. It is evident that without changes in the tax structure the system would have yielded in the three postwar years only three-fourths as much revenue as the amount actually collected. A comparison of expenditures (see chapter iv) with the amounts that would have been collected if the tax structure had not been changed reveals that the amounts collected would have been insufficient to maintain government functions at the levels which prevailed and would have resulted in prohibitively large deficits.

A comparison between actual and hypothetical tax collections (at 1936/37 rates) also provides a measure of the financial results of changes in the tax rates and other modifications of the tax structure. The largest gains in collections did not take place until the postwar expansion of prices and business activity when the business profits tax and the increased consumption taxes began to yield substantial returns.

Changes in Flexibility

In the preceding section, a distinction between built-in and administrative flexibility of the Guatemalan tax system has been made. In order to determine the degree of built-in flexibility, the tax structure of 1936/37 has been applied to subsequent years. It was found that the degree of built-in flexibility is smaller than unity, i.e., tax revenues expand (and contract) less than proportionately with an expansion (or contraction) of money income. Since for obvious reasons we are more interested, however, in the characteristics of the present than of the prewar tax structure, we must now carry our analysis one step further and attempt to determine to what extent changes in the tax structure that have occurred since 1936 have affected its built-in flexibility.

The statistical results of such an attempt are shown in Table 52 where the hypothetical yields of the Guatemalan tax system at 1936/37 rates are compared with the yields that would have obtained if throughout the last ten years the tax structure of the fiscal year 1947/48 had prevailed. An inspection of the index representing yields of the 1947/48 tax structure shows that, as a result of the administrative changes made during the last ten years, the built-in flexibility has increased somewhat. This increase in built-in flexibility very clearly was the result of the introduction of the business profits tax, as well as the subsequent rate increases in this tax and the rate changes of consumption taxes. The increased built-in flexibility may be demonstrated by comparing the indexes of the hypothetical yields of the 1936/37 tax structure with the (likewise hypothetical) collections calculated at the tax rates prevailing in 1947/48. With the presently prevailing structure the amounts of taxes collected would have expanded more rapidly (and, as the data for the first two years show, contracted more rapidly) than with the structure of the tax system prevailing in 1936/37. A comparison with the indexes of the gross national product and of the product of the commercial sector of the economy, on the other hand, indicates that even after the expansion of the more flexible parts of the tax system, the tax revenue as a whole still shows a built-in flexibility of less than unity. That is to say, collections at the 1947/48 tax structure expanded and contracted less than the money income of the economy; the basically inflexible portions of the tax structure still

TABLE 52

CHANGES IN BUILT-IN FLEXIBILITY OF TAX RECEIPTS, 1939/40 TO 1947/48

Fiscal Year	1939/40 = 100					In Millions of Quetzales		
	Gross National Product	Product of Commercial Sector	Actual Tax Collections	Tax Collections at Rate Structure in 1936/37	Tax Collections at Rate Structure in 1947/48	Actual Tax Collections	Tax Collections at Rate Structure in 1936/37	Tax Collections at Rate Structure in 1947/48
1939/40	100.0	100.0	100.0	100.0	100.0	10.9	10.4	13.1
1940/41	101.4	97.5	92.7	99.1	96.2	10.1	9.6	12.6
1941/42	116.9	110.6	17.3	91.5	103.0	10.6	10.0	13.5
1942/43	157.2	125.1	110.1	95.3	123.8	12.0	10.7	16.2
1943/44	*	134.1	133.1	102.0	139.1	14.5	12.5	18.2
1944/45	*	159.5	133.9	119.0	140.8	14.6	13.4	18.4
1945/46	211.4	183.3	190.8	127.7	176.1	20.9	15.9	23.1
1946/47	*	353.3	259.6	207.7	215.6	28.3	21.7	28.3
1947/48	295.3	341.6	286.3	222.0	238.2	31.2	23.2	31.2

* Not available.

outweigh those parts of the revenue system that possess a high degree of built-in flexibility.

The computations of hypothetical tax yields shown in Table 52 also permit a comparison of the hypothetical tax yields with each other and with actual tax collections in absolute figures. The last column of the table indicates that, for the period as a whole, tax collections at the 1947/48 structure would have been substantially larger than actual collections. Since actual collections were in effect adequate in the sense that budget deficits were avoided, the figures may be interpreted as indicating that in the years prior to the postwar expansion of prices and business activity the present tax structure would have been too severe, given the then prevailing level of government expenditures. The correctness of this conclusion obviously depends, however, to a large degree upon what is to be considered a proper level of government expenditures. As a preliminary to the discussion of this question, we now turn to a brief consideration of the flexibility of government expenditures.

FLEXIBILITY OF GOVERNMENT EXPENDITURES

Since government expenditures are subject to the budgetary controls exercised by the administrative and the legislative branches of the government, all government expenditures are, prima facie, flexible in the sense that they are periodically subject to control and review. In practice, however, it is quite obvious that despite the institutional framework of annual budget making, certain types of expenditures are more flexible than others. Although salaries and, if necessary, the entire salary schedule can be changed and the number of government positions can be theoretically increased or decreased at the will of the administration and the legislature, the salary bill of the government is notoriously inflexible in the downward direction. In the upward direction greater flexibility obtains, but as the index of the unit cost of government, presented above, shows, even changes in the upward direction are slow and small compared with increases in the general price level. Flexibility upward is enhanced, however, by an increase in the number of positions, which is in part a result of the assumption of additional functions by the government.

Payments on the public debt theoretically must be considered highly inflexible because they represent a firm contractual commitment of the government. But as a result of the extraordinary conditions that prevailed in Guatemala during most of the period under study, we find that service payments on the public debt fluctuated very widely; the data on government expenditures for debt service (presented in Table 53) show no regular pattern since the continuity of the volume of expenditures for this purpose was interrupted by the debt transactions of 1938/39 and by the retirement of the foreign debt in 1944/45.

Government expenditures of every country include, however, a certain proportion of outlays which by their nature are flexible. Such expenditures are payments for the purchase of office equipment, vehicles, uniforms, etc. They are flexible for two reasons: in the first place, they can be postponed if funds are not available; second, the prices of such commodities are likely to change proportionately with the general price level. For the same two reasons one would be inclined to consider public investment expenditures, involving the purchase of construction materials, machinery, and labor, as highly flexible. Such expenditures are clearly postponable—although the undesirability of indefinite postponement must be kept in mind—and purchase prices (including wages for unskilled labor) fluctuate. But for practical purposes, a distinction may be drawn between the initial flexibility of investment expenditures and their ultimate flexibility, once investment projects have been initiated. For technical reasons, as well as for economic reasons, many investment projects cannot be discontinued or even curtailed at the will of the administration or the legislature, since it is clearly desirable that whatever investment projects are undertaken be carried through to completion. It is this *technical* inflexibility of investment expenditures, once they have been undertaken, that must be taken into account if the over-all flexibility of government expenditures, which in-

TABLE 53

ORDINARY AND EXTRAORDINARY GOVERNMENT EXPENDITURES, 1937/38 TO 1948/49

Fiscal Year	Gross National Product, in Millions of Quetzales	Expenditures, in Thousands of Quetzales				Gross National Product	In Percent of 1937/38			
		Total	Ordinary[a]	Extraordinary	Debt Service		Product of Commercial Sector	Expenditures		
								Total	Ordinary[a]	Extraordinary
1937/38	113.6	11,141.6	6,957.4	2,311.8	1,872.4	100.0	100.0	100.0	100.0	100.0
1938/39	98.8	14,014.7	7,068.2	2,681.8	4,265.4	87.0	89.1	122.8	101.6	115.9
1939/40	113.6	11,035.5	7,168.5	2,457.4	1,409.5	99.8	79.9	96.7	103.0	106.3
1940/41	114.9	10,632.6	7,258.7	2,636.7	737.2	101.1	77.9	93.1	104.3	114.1
1941/42	132.7	10,962.8	7,446.4	2,850.8	665.6	116.6	88.3	96.0	107.0	123.3
1942/43	178.2	13,381.9	7,509.7	5,218.9	651.3	156.7	99.8	117.2	107.9	225.7
1943/44	*	18,347.7	7,886.8	5,731.6	4,729.3	....	107.0	160.7	113.4	247.9
1944/45	....	19,954.3	9,741.1	7,199.0	3,014.2	....	127.3	174.6	140.0	311.4
1945/46	239.9	29,234.4	19,485.8	8,642.7	1,105.9	210.9	146.3	256.1	280.1	373.9
1946/47	....	32,380.4	21,785.8	9,915.0	679.6	....	202.2	283.7	313.1	428.9
1947/48	335.0	45,941.0	23,984.2	21,369.5	587.3	294.6	272.7	402.5	344.7	924.4
1948/49	....	49,442.0	29,108.0	19,662.3	671.7	....	(284)[b]	433.1	418.4	850.5

[a] Ordinary expenditures excluding payments for debt service, which are considered ordinary expenditures in government accounts. Data pertain to liquidated budgetary expenditures.
[b] Crude estimate.
* Not available.

clude a high proportion of development outlays, is to be appraised.

The complex nature of the flexibility of public expenditures makes a statistical appraisal of the expenditure experience of the Guatemalan government rather difficult. The breakdown of expenditures into income payments (salaries, wages, and pensions) and purchases of materials[8] is of little avail in this connection, since a breakdown between payments for (inflexible) salaries and (flexible) wages is not available. Some indication of the flexibility of the component parts of the total government expenditures can be obtained, however, from an analysis of the breakdown of outlays classified as ordinary and extraordinary expenditures. As indicated above, the distinction is primarily of administrative significance. Appropriations for ordinary expenditures provided for in the annual budget are readily available for disbursement. Extraordinary expenditures are usually provided for in global amounts for less definitely defined purposes, such as school construction, purchase of equipment, etc.

It is in the nature of this administrative distinction, however, that the bulk of ordinary expenditures, which consist primarily of salaries, purchase of office supplies, rentals, etc., falls largely into the inflexible category of expenditures, while extraordinary expenditures are primarily of the flexible variety. This is confirmed by the movements of the two types of expenditures in the course of the last twelve years, as shown in Table 53. Ordinary expenditures, from which debt service expenditures have been excluded, rose constantly and apparently without any relation to changes in the gross national product or the product of the commercial sector of the economy. Extraordinary expenditures, on the other hand, followed more closely the movements of the gross national product and the product of the business sector, although the amplitudes of the changes in the upward direction were much larger than those in the economy's income. The most pronounced increases in extraordinary expenditures occurred in

[8] See chapter iv, Table 25.

the last three years when the investment program of the national government was initiated, thus giving an indication of the initial flexibility of investment expenditures.[9]

But it would be an oversimplification to consider the rise in extraordinary expenditures merely as a temporary expansion. The technical inflexibility of investment expenditures and even more so the policy of economic and social development under public auspices, to which the government is committed, have resulted in a movement of investment expenditures to a higher level that must be considered as permanent, barring unforeseen developments. The composite result of the expansion of government activities in recent years presumably is a growing inflexibility of expenditures in the downward direction, at least in the short run. In the final result, a decline of investment activities is, of course, possible, but it would obviously be undesirable to curtail investment activities simply because ordinary administrative expenditures prove to be inflexible. It seems of paramount importance therefore to oppose a further growth of ordinary administrative expenditures, since there is danger that such an expansion may ultimately be at the expense of flexible investment expenditures. If an expansion of the government's administrative functions are necessary, attempts should be made to obtain such an expansion through improved efficiency and not through an expansion of the public payroll.

THE PROPER DEGREE OF REVENUE FLEXIBILITY

Having reached the conclusion that a downward adjustment of administrative expenditures is unlikely, and recognizing the maintenance of an adequate level of public investment as desirable, we can now return to a further consideration of the flexibility of government receipts in order to determine what would be a proper degree of revenue flexibility.

[9] Since some investment expenditures, such as disbursements for the construction of the Roosevelt Highway and of low-cost houses, are not included in the table, the amounts involved in public investment expenditures somewhat understate the true magnitude of the expansion.

Cyclical Fluctuations

Most economists concerned with problems of fiscal policy seem to agree that, in industrial economies in which autonomous changes in the rate of investment cause fluctuations in the level of business activity and employment, a high degree of revenue flexibility is desirable. The result of such revenue flexibility is that, in a period of inflationary expansion, government revenues exceed expenditures, thus causing a budget surplus which tends to counteract the inflationary pressures in the economy. In a period of recession and less than full employment, on the other hand, the flexibility of the fiscal structure causes a budget deficit and necessitates public borrowing. The injection of new funds into the economy is designed to offset the deflationary forces and to halt and possibly reverse the downturn.

This scheme of fiscal policy is, of course, of limited applicability in a country like Guatemala where the primary cause of cyclical fluctuations is not changes in the rate of private investment but changes in the volume of exports and the level of export prices. In an expansion of export proceeds the gross national product expands and causes an expansion of imports. But to the extent to which there is a lag between exports and imports, the expansion of the money supply and of income generated in the economy's export sector is bound to exert inflationary pressures. It has been recognized that under such conditions an accumulation of Treasury balances seems desirable. Such an accumulation can be attained through an increase of revenues, a decrease of expenditures, or a combination of both. Since, as we have seen, government expenditures in Guatemala are likely to be inflexible in the short run and since the government will find it advantageous to make use of expanded foreign exchange reserves for purchases abroad, it appears highly desirable that the cyclical expansion of revenues result in a Treasury surplus that will offset, at least to some extent, the inflationary pressures of foreign origin (which, incidentally, may be accentuated by an induced expansion of private domestic investment). Thus, one is forced to the conclusion that as an instrument of anti-inflationary policy a high degree of revenue flexibility is desirable.

A consideration of the situation likely to occur as a result of declining export proceeds leads, however, to a substantial qualification of the preceding conclusion. A flexible revenue structure would result in a government deficit that presumably would have to be financed by resorting to central bank credit. But an expansion of the money supply accentuates the imbalance in the country's international accounts, resulting in a stringency of foreign exchange reserves, which in turn may easily hamper the government's investment activities[10] and adversely affect the country's international credit standing. To some extent, the exigencies of such a situation can be mitigated by the accumulation of exchange reserves during periods of an export surplus. But if balance-of-payments difficulties are not to be aggravated by central bank-financed deficits and if government expenditures are to be maintained at an adequate level, a large decline of tax receipts is decidedly undesirable.

It follows that the revenue system best suited for the economic structure of Guatemala would be one with a rather high degree of flexibility in the upward direction and a low flexibility downward. It is obviously impossible to devise an automatic system fitting these specifications. But the previously introduced distinction between built-in and administrative flexibility indicates how this impasse can be resolved. In order to cope with short-run cyclical fluctuations, it appears advisable to maintain a revenue structure with a low degree of built-in flexibility. In periods of an inflationary expansion, however, additional taxes designed primarily to curtail the expansion of consumers' expenditures may have to be superimposed upon the existing system. Taxes meeting these requirements, for example, would be sales taxes or income taxes with a low level of basic exemptions. In other words, if cyclical inflationary pressures threaten the stability and efficacy of the economy, it may be necessary to strengthen the impact of the fiscal

---

[10] In so far as they involve the purchase of imported materials and equipment.

structure upon the economy by siphoning off at least a portion of inflated consumer incomes. When the inflationary pressures subside, such additional taxes should of course be repealed.

It would be unrealistic, however, to expect any implementation of this conclusion—which comes dangerously close to being a counsel of perfection. An increase in the consumer's tax burden would of course be strenuously opposed—at any time—by the low- and middle-income groups primarily affected by such a scheme. Moreover, the experience of Guatemala, as well as that of other countries, shows that an increase in consumption taxes, once introduced, is hardly ever repealed. Therefore, the all-too-simple device of raising and lowering consumption taxes with the rhythm of cyclical expansion and contraction must be modified. In the structural and institutional framework of the Guatemalan economy, this modification can take two forms. As indicated above, the most important source of inflationary pressure is the recurrent expansion of export proceeds, particularly of coffee, which is frequently not accompanied by an increase in the unit cost of coffee production. In view of this, it seems highly desirable to make the coffee export tax more flexible by putting it on a value basis. An increase in the price of coffee would then result in increased yields of the coffee export tax.[11] A direct effect of a higher coffee tax would be a partial curtailment of consumption expenditures and, what is more important, of investment expenditures of coffee producers, who usually invest a large share of their savings in real estate or hold it in the form of bank balances abroad, thus adding little to the productive capital formation of the country.

The second method of relieving inflationary pressures must be sought outside the field of fiscal policy through monetary controls exercised by the central bank under the direction of the

---

[11] Further discussion of current proposals to raise the coffee export tax will be found in the last section of this chapter. As will be seen there, the proposals, by imposing a *temporary* surtax over and above the present rate, fit the flexibility requirements of Guatemalan public finances; by maintaining the present rate as the lower limit of the tax it adds an element of inflexibility downward and of flexibility upward.

Monetary Board. To develop here in detail methods of anti-inflationary monetary controls would take us outside the subject matter of the study; moreover, the monetary and banking legislation of Guatemala is sufficiently explicit on the question of anti-inflationary measures to make any elaboration unnecessary. It may be sufficient merely to point out that inflationary pressures can be curtailed, if not contained, through proper controls of the monetary system since, in the absence of liquid funds in the hands of the public, inflationary pressures can become effective only through an expansion of the money supply. Although the influence of the central bank is somewhat limited by its inability to control the use of Guatemalan funds held abroad and by the extension of credit by foreign exporters to Guatemalan importers (and, conversely, by foreign importers to Guatemalan exporters), a curtailment of the volume of domestic bank credit—preferably on a selective basis—undoubtedly would exercise a strong influence over the money supply and thus effectively supplement the anti-inflationary fiscal policies which, as indicated above, may prove insufficient in themselves to cope with a strong inflationary updrift.

Long-run Flexibility

Under present conditions, prospects appear to be good that, through proper fiscal and monetary policies in the principal industrial countries of the world, major cyclical fluctuations in the level of employment and prices, such as those experienced in the interwar period, will be avoided in the foreseeable future. With the dangers, inherent in such cycles, to the stability and material well-being of less developed countries such as Guatemala at least partially alleviated, the primary attention of the country's fiscal policy can be focused upon the problem of achieving a high and steadily rising rate of economic development.

Hence, we must modify our approach somewhat and inquire into the fitness of the fiscal system for the purpose of assisting in the country's economic development. As indicated above, the level of the government's fiscal revenues depends primarily upon the volume of production and consumption in *real* terms, since the most important groups of taxes are levied upon a specific basis. If the national income increases in real terms, the volume of exports, the volume of imports, and the volume of consumption—including that of taxed commodities—rise and the yield of taxes on exports, imports, and consumption likewise increases. As noted above, there are reasons to believe that real imports and real consumption (of taxed commodities) increase more than proportionately with an increase in national income. Therefore, the yields of taxes levied on imports and consumption are likewise bound to rise more than proportionately with an increase in the country's total output of goods and services. This means that, barring major changes in the tax structure, the revenue system is reasonably and adequately flexible for a process of gradual expansion of general economic activity *without* inflationary price increases. If, on the other hand, as a result of an excess of government expenditures over tax receipts or for some other reason, an increase in money income over and above that in real income takes place, the structure of the present fiscal system would prove to be unsuited to stem an inflationary tide.

In view of the fact that the present fiscal system is not likely to undergo any basic structural change in the next few years, it thus seems of paramount importance to avoid inflation. Inflationary pressures of whatever origin would either necessitate a curtailment of government expenditures or result in government deficits, which in turn would further aggravate and perpetuate inflation. In either case, the economic development process which the present government is attempting to foster would be endangered.

THE PROSPECTS FOR HIGHER TAX REVENUES

The preceding observations notwithstanding, it may become necessary to supplement the present tax system with new sources of revenue. The need for additional revenues might arise for instance if, for reasons beyond the control of the Guatemalan government, the level of imports, and with it receipts from import taxes, should sharply decline. A more immediate and compelling reason for attempting to raise the level of tax receipts, however, is the government's policy of financing development projects that require expenditures over and above the normal yield of the present tax structure.[12] The question then arises: what additional sources of revenue are available to the Guatemalan government?

A general answer to this question is impossible since it depends upon the type of fiscal emergency in which the government finds itself, and on the level of income prevailing in the various sectors of the economy. It is clear that in a period of lagging exports, for instance, the imposition of additional taxes upon exports would be inadvisable. Conversely, during a period of price increases of domestic as well as imported goods, the imposition of higher import and consumption taxes may be desirable.[13]

In this connection, there are, however, certain observations to be made which, it is believed, are of sufficiently general validity to make them meaningful. Higher revenues can be obtained through three kinds of measures: (1) an improvement of the administration of existing taxes, (2) the imposition of higher rates on existing taxes, and (3) the imposition of new taxes.

As shown in the preceding chapter, there are undoubtedly in the present system of tax administration certain areas of slack, the elimination of which appears highly desirable. Direct taxes, property taxes, and liquor taxes in particular seem to be promising sources of revenue that can be made to produce better yields through improvements in administration. As a matter of fact, the present system of administration unquestionably holds considerable areas of hidden reserves, which could be tapped through improvements in the tax administration. Needless to say,

[12] The need for larger tax revenues, on the other hand, may make it difficult, if not impossible, to repeal those components of the present tax structure which, for reasons of equity or administrative efficiency, do not appear to be desirable.

[13] Account may have to be taken, however, of the existence of international commitments regarding the maintenance of existing duty rates.

these administrative improvements are desirable from the point of view of tax morale and tax equity, even if there is no immediate need for higher tax revenues. This observation probably applies with equal, if not more, justification to nontax receipts, such as those resulting from operations of public services and enterprises.

The imposition of higher rates is preferable to the introduction of new taxes because it does not require the creation of a new administrative apparatus. There are, however, definite limits set upon the extent to which the rates on various types of taxes can be increased, because excessive tax rates may result in diminished fiscal receipts. Thus, for instance, an over-all increase in import taxes would undoubtedly cause an upsurge in smuggling activities; or the raising of liquor taxes would cause an expansion in the illegal production and sale of alcoholic beverages; or the raising of the rate structure of the business profits tax might result in more extensive evasion.

Certain tax increases, however, appear practicable. As shown above, the yield of property and property transfer taxes has declined relative to total tax receipts because neither the tax rate of three per mill nor the assessed value of real property has been changed in recent years.[14] Because of this, and because of the high cost of the collection of this tax, it would appear that an increase in the basic rate to four or five per mill would be feasible.[15]

As to the largest source of revenue, i.e., import taxes, it appears that, although the average level of duties is still quite high, an increase in the duties on certain types of imports would yield additional revenue. Thus, higher duties on such luxury goods as gold and silver watches, fancy silk goods, expensive glass and chinaware, heavy passenger cars, etc., would in all probability produce somewhat higher yields.

[14] With the exception of property reassessed since 1945.

[15] Such a rate increase could perhaps be combined to good advantage with a raising of the exemption of small holdings, as suggested above, p. 164. Moreover, if the process of reassessment cannot be speeded up, thought should perhaps be given to the advisability of raising the rates on property not yet reassessed.

The sharp rise in the level of coffee prices since the fall of 1949, which so far has not been accompanied by any major increase in the cost of production, offers quite apparently a ready opportunity for the government to increase its revenues without imposing additional strains on the economy as a whole. As indicated in preceding chapters, there are many reasons to believe that the coffee export tax is one of the few taxes in Guatemala, the main burden of which is not shifted to the low-income groups. Moreover, a comparison of coffee prices which prevail at present with those of earlier years indicates that even a substantial increase in the coffee export levy is not likely to have any significant adverse effect upon the volume of coffee exports.

The desire to provide additional government revenues, in order to lend additional financial support to the economic development of the Guatemalan economy, and the exceedingly favorable conditions prevailing in the world coffee markets have been taken into account in the preparation by the administration of two proposals to raise the coffee export tax for the crop year 1950/51. One proposal provides for a surtax amounting to Q4.35 per quintal of coffee so that the total tax per quintal, including the present tax of Q1.65, would amount to Q6.00. The other proposal establishes a surtax of Q3.35, raising the total rate to Q5.00. The proposals differ also regarding the allocation of the additional revenues to be derived from the surtaxes. The following table shows the differences in the allocation between the two proposals:

	Proposal 1	Proposal 2
a) General Treasury fund	Q2.70	Q1.30
b) Highway construction	1.00	....
c) Establishment of a coffee institute.....	.25	1.00
d) Additions to the Securities Fund of the Banco de Guatemala	.20	.35
e) Amortization of Treasury letters, notes, and bonds	.20	.35
f) Capital contribution to the Production Development Institute	....	.35
Total	Q4.35	Q3.35

If the volume of coffee exports is assumed to continue at the present level of approximately one million quintals, the increase in revenues would amount to Q4,350,000 under the first, and Q3,350,000 under the second proposal. The first proposal would provide the general fund of the government with more than 60 percent of the additional revenues, while the second would provide the general fund with a substantially smaller share.

The first proposal provides further approximately one million quetzales for road construction. The remainder of the yield of the surtax would be allocated in almost equal proportions to the Securities Fund of the Banco de Guatemala, to the amortization of government short- and long-term securities, and to the endowment of a coffee institute which is to assume the functions of the Central Coffee Office (Oficina Central de Café) and the following additional tasks: "Improvement in the production and processing of coffee with a view toward increasing their efficiency; the economic defense of the coffee producers particularly in periods of insufficient returns, and the promotion and stimulation of coffee exports." The tax proposal does not specify in what ways the proposed institute would discharge its functions but merely instructs the government to prepare legislation for that purpose.

Under the second proposal the coffee institute would obtain almost one-third of the additional revenue (or approximately one million quetzales). Approximately 350,000 quetzales would accrue to the Securities Fund of the Banco de Guatemala; an equal amount would be used for the retirement of government debt and to increase the capital of the Production Development Institute.

Since, as noted above, the primary—if not the exclusive—reason for increasing tax revenues is the need for funds to finance economic development, the second proposal, in spite of its lower yield, seems to conform more closely to the general objectives of the government's fiscal and developmental policies. Under this proposal, more than 60 percent of the tax yield would be set aside directly and indirectly for economic development purposes, because under present conditions funds accruing to the central bank and to the coffee institute could be made available to the Production Development Institute or for other development purposes in addition to the capital contribution to the institute directly provided for in the proposal.

At the time of this writing the proposed tax legislation has not yet been enacted, but irrespective of the final form which the new tax bill will take, it would appear desirable that the surtax on coffee exports be put on a more permanent basis than the present proposals contemplate. A general revision of the export tax which would put the tax on an ad valorem basis or tie it to the quotations of the New York coffee market presumably would provide for a substantial increase in revenues at least for a number of years. The same general principle of imposing a flexible surtax, applicable in periods of high export prices, could be adopted for other export taxes, although the question of contractual commitments of the government somewhat complicates the issue in this case.

As a general rule it may be advisable to make it a mandatory obligation of the Ministries of Finance and Economy to appoint a committee of experts familiar with the tax structure and the effects of the tax system upon the economy for the purpose of conducting a periodic review of tax rates.

As to the introduction of new taxes, it should be stressed that in our opinion there is considerable validity in the proverbial dogma that "old taxes are good taxes." This supreme rule of public finance is basically valid because, as has been seen, the introduction of new taxes unavoidably raises administrative difficulties, at least for a transitional period, and may disturb the functioning of the economy which is adjusted to the existing tax structure.

But under certain conditions, the price of temporarily high costs of administration and upsetting the economy may have to be paid. True, the argument of high initial costs of administration must be properly weighed in considering the introduction of a personal income tax, which has been under active discussion for some time, but there may be other reasons for the introduction of new taxes, such as considerations of equity or the need for additional revenues, that override the purely administrative aspects. The proposed personal income tax would round out, so to speak, the existing tax structure by imposing new tax burdens on non-business income in the high- and middle-income brackets, and would ease somewhat the tax burden of unincorporated business firms.[16]

It must be realized, however, that the personal income tax, because of its generous exemption provisions and the likelihood of its limited yield, particularly in the first years after its introduction, is no cure-all. Changing conditions may necessitate the introduction of other taxes, either permanently or for limited periods only. Thus, in a period of strong inflationary pressures, taxes designed to absorb excess purchasing power in the hands of the consumers may have to be introduced. Taxes suitable for this purpose would be general sales taxes, or purchase taxes on certain broad categories of consumers' goods. The lowering of basic exemptions in the proposed income tax would offer another possibility of achieving the same end. Under other conditions, such as widespread speculation in real estate, the imposition of taxes on capital gains which are now tax-free would appear desirable.

[16] See chapter vi, pp. 142–45.

IX

THE FISCAL SYSTEM AND THE NATIONAL INCOME

THE LAST four chapters have discussed the operations of the fiscal system and their impact upon various conceptually distinct sectors of the economy. We have thus laid the groundwork for the next phase of our investigation, which now proceeds to treat the interaction of the fiscal system with the economy as a whole. This chapter is devoted to a discussion of the relationship between the fiscal system and the level of national income. It is followed by an analysis of the effects of the fiscal system upon the monetary system and upon the international accounts of the economy. The final chapter of the study is devoted to a consideration of the fiscal aspects of the problem of economic development.

The fiscal system affects the national income in three distinct ways. First, the level of government expenditures and receipts is one of the factors determining the *level* of the national income. Second, the difference between government expenditures and receipts may cause an expansion or contraction of the national income. Third, the fiscal system causes a redistribution of the national income among the various income groups. We shall now discuss each one of these effects in turn.

THE SHARE OF GOVERNMENT IN THE GROSS NATIONAL PRODUCT

The Relative Level of Government Receipts and Expenditures

The level of government receipts and expenditures plays a dual role as a factor determining the size of the national income.[1] On the one hand, tax receipts take away from each household, and, in the aggregate, from the economy as a whole, a certain pro-

---

[1] In this section the differences between government receipts and expenditures are disregarded and attention is focused upon their amounts in relation to the national income.

portion of income which by necessity either would have to be spent or saved.[2] Government expenditures, on the other hand, create income through the purchase of goods and services, from firms or individuals (its employees), which forms part of the income stream of the economy. Moreover, the services that the government provides in the form of schools, roads, hospitals, police protection, national defense, etc., also accrue in the ultimate analysis to private households and form a stream of benefits which are a form of nonmonetary income.

The share of government in the the national income, in its role as a purchaser of goods and services and as the producer of government services, is shown in Table 54. If we disregard the

TABLE 54

GROSS NATIONAL PRODUCT, GOVERNMENT RECEIPTS, AND GOVERNMENT
EXPENDITURES, 1937/38 TO 1947/48

(*In millions of quetzales*)

Fiscal Year	Gross National Product	Government Receipts[a]	Government Expenditures[a]	As a Percent of Gross National Product	
				Government Receipts	Government Expenditures
1937/38 .... 113.6		14.1	12.7	12.4	11.2
1938/39 .... 98.8		15.1	15.3	15.3	15.5
1939/40 .... 113.6		14.0	13.0	12.3	11.4
1940/41 .... 114.9		13.6	12.6	11.8	11.0
1941/42 .... 132.7		14.0	12.9	10.6	9.7
1942/43 .... 178.2		16.3	15.3	9.1	8.6
1943/44 .... *		20.0	16.9	....	....
1944/45		19.9	25.8	....	....
1945/46 .... 239.9		33.6	32.4	14.0	13.5
1946/47		44.3	40.0	....	....
1947/48 .... 335.0		45.6	51.1	13.6	15.3

[a] Receipts and expenditures of all administrative authorities shown in Table 12.
* Not available.

fiscal year 1938/39, the fiscal data for which are affected by a large amount of extraordinary receipts and the retirement of bank loans, we find that the share of the government in the gross national product has increased in the postwar years by approxi-

---

[2] "Saved" in the Keynesian sense, i.e., either deposited in a savings account, invested through the net purchase of securities, or simply held idle in the form of cash or bank deposits.

mately 2 percent compared with prewar years. Compared with the war years, the increase has been 3 to 4 percent. But in interpreting these figures, we must take account of two factors: first, the decline of tax receipts relative to the gross national product during the war years, which was a result of the curtailment of imports imposed by the supply and shipping conditions prevailing abroad; and second, the inclusion of receipts from, and expenditures of, the nationalized plantations since 1945/46.[3] If allowance is made for these two factors, we arrive at the conclusion that until the end of the fiscal year 1947/48 government expenditures and receipts did not rise significantly in relation to the gross national product. Although income data for 1948/49 are lacking, there are some indications that in that year the share of the government in the gross national product rose further as a result of deficit financing. But it is unlikely that the increase amounted to more than 1 to 2 percent of the gross national product.

Another method of obtaining a quantitative appraisal of the relationship between government activities and national income is a comparison of tax receipts with the gross product of the private sector of the economy. This method of measurement of the burden of taxation on the economy disregards by implication the value of the services that the government provides to the economy and is beset by certain other conceptual difficulties, but it reflects a defensible common-sense notion that a given level of production supports a certain volume of government services.

The comparison is presented in Table 55. It confirms the previously reached conclusion that, contrary to the impression that seems to prevail in some sectors of Guatemalan public opinion, the cost of government, in so far as it is represented by taxation, has not appreciably risen in recent years. As a matter of fact, the practically unchanged ratio of taxation to the total output of goods and services of the private sector bears out the observation made at the end of the preceding chapter that an increase in the

---

[3] See chapter iii, particularly Table 15.

over-all level of taxation will be necessary if the government intends to continue its policy of fostering and actively supporting economic development.

TABLE 55

BURDEN OF TAXES ON THE PRIVATE SECTOR OF THE ECONOMY,
1937/38 TO 1947/48

(*In millions of quetzales*)

Fiscal Year	Gross Product of Private Sector[a]	Tax Receipts of National Government	Tax Receipts as a Percent of Gross Product of Private Sector
1937/38	101.8	11.1	10.9
1938/39	86.4	10.9	12.6[b]
1939/40	101.8	10.9	10.7
1940/41	102.8	10.1	9.8
1941/42	120.3	10.6	8.8
1942/43	163.3	12.0	7.3
1943/44 ....*		14.5	....
1944/45		14.6	....
1945/46	207.6	20.9	10.1
1946/47		28.3	....
1947/48	284.0	31.2	11.0

[a] Gross national product minus expenditures of the national government and municipalities, excluding debt payments.

[b] The high percentage shown in this year is a reflection of the fact that between 1937/38 and 1938/39 the product of the commercial sector which forms the primary tax base of the revenue system rose, while the gross national product fell.

* Not available.

The Fiscal System, the Level of Consumption, and the Rate of Savings

In view of the likelihood that the implementation of the government's announced development policy may necessitate an increase in government expenditures as well as receipts in the years immediately ahead—preliminary and partial data for the fiscal year 1949/50 bear out this prognostication—it appears appropriate to discuss briefly the economic consequences of such an increase relative to the level of the national income. On the basis of the estimated incidence of taxation on the various income groups and the relationship between consumption expenditures and income within individual groups, it appears that not quite 90 percent of total tax receipts in 1947/48 fell on consumption in the sense that in the absence of the tax burden the taxpayers would have spent the amount of their tax liability on the purchase of additional consumers' goods.

Conversely, slightly more than 10 percent of the total tax burden came out of savings in the sense that, had there not been any tax burden, the taxpayers would have saved an amount equivalent to 10 percent of total tax collections.[4] If we assume that the savings forgone through the collection of taxes would have been kept idle in the country or transferred abroad, the disbursement of such tax collections by the government is expansionary. That is to say, in a period of less than full employment and with a stable or receding price level, taxes obtained through a curtailment of savings will cause an expansion of employment and production. If there are inflationary pressures active in the economy, however, the expenditures of those tax receipts which curtail savings will accentuate the inflationary pressures and may lead to further price increases.

But the fact that the bulk of tax collections comes from consumption funds and thus actively curtails consumption expenditures is, of course, of greater importance. It focuses attention on the basic issue involved in the decision whether or not government receipts and expenditures should be increased. More specifically, if we take into account the government's avowed policy of fostering economic development, the question is: how large an increase in expenditures and receipts is considered desirable in view of the fact that 90 percent of all additional taxes result in a commensurate decline in consumer expenditures? An answer to this question obviously involves two sets of considerations. One pertains to the problem of the economic welfare of the population, as measured by the level of consumer expenditures, the other to the level of private production.

---

[4] Readers familiar with this method of analysis will recognize at once that the analysis implies that the average propensity to save equals the marginal propensity. This assumption seems permissible because the amounts of taxes coming out of consumption and savings, respectively, were derived not in the aggregate but by income groups. Within individual income groups, except the highest (open-end) group, the difference between the average and the marginal propensity is likely to be small.

It is clear that in the aggregate the amount of benefits derived from additional government services should at least be equal to the sacrifice involved in curtailing consumption. Any attempt to compare the benefits from government expenditures with the sacrifice of consumption involves a dual value judgment, one pertaining to the social desirability of additional government services and the other involving the social evaluation of the sacrificed consumption. Most people would agree that the construction of, say, clinics for children represents a social gain if the sacrifice of consumption necessary for this construction involves the sacrifice of expenditures for amusements. But in most instances the social evaluation of the benefits versus the losses involved in a larger volume of government activities (financed by a curtailment in private consumption) is not that simple and one-sided. An increase in the government's general administrative expenses, which may be involved in an increase in the level of the government's share in the gross national product, may be socially less desirable than the curtailment of expenditures for, say, private housing.

There exists, moreover, a basic technological and institutional difference between government and private consumption expenditures. There is a wide range of essential services that only the government can provide or that the government can provide more economically than the private sector of the economy. By their very nature, schools, hospitals, roads, courts of law, and the protection of life and property clearly can be provided only, or more advantageously, by the government. In so far as the population of the country as a whole expresses the opinion, through the democratic processes of elections and legislation, that it desires more of such government services, it expresses by implication a social choice as to whether or not it prefers more government services at the expense of curtailing its private consumption.

The second aspect of the effects of curtailing consumption through taxation pertains to the level of private production.[5] In so far as the level of production adjusts itself, immediately or

5 See also chapter v, pp. 115–19.

after a time lag, to changes in the level of demand, the curtailment of consumption results also in a curtailment of the private production of goods and services. Such a curtailment is of course offset by an increase in the production of government services, so that the aggregate of goods and services produced remains unchanged. But given a certain structure of production, with a certain allocation of fixed capital, it may happen that a reallocation of a country's human and capital resources, such as that involved in a contraction of private production of goods for the consumer and an expansion of government services, will cause at least a temporary under-utilization of some resources, particularly of fixed assets. Fortunately, the dangers of such a dislocation are remote in the case of Guatemala, because the vigorous rate of population increase, supplemented by an increase in per capita consumption, is bound to take up the slack that a shift in the composition of the gross national product may cause in some areas of aggregate demand.

Taxation and Work Incentives

There remains to be considered one more aspect of the relationship between the level of government activities and the volume of the gross national production. That is the effects of the level of taxation and government services upon the incentive to work, which is, after all, together with the availability of natural resources, the most important single determinant of the size of the national income.

The restriction of the enjoyment of income, either through direct taxation or through price increases resulting from indirect taxation, may tend to act as a deterrent to work, particularly in those instances in which marginal income is affected by a higher tax burden. This disincentive, in most instances, is not offset by the services that the government provides because most of these services do not take a form that is appreciated as his personal income by the individual consumer. The case studies on the consumer tax burden, presented in chapter vi, have shown that the incidence of the Guatemalan tax structure becomes clearly progressive only in the very highest-income brackets and is even mildly regressive in the upper-middle-income groups. It appears reasonable, therefore, to conclude that the incidence of the tax burden upon marginal effort in all but the highest-income group is not greater than the average incidence. Since the average tax burden is fairly small, its disincentive effect is on the whole likely to be unimportant.

THE EFFECTS OF BUDGET SURPLUSES AND DEFICITS

The preceding section has dealt with the relationship between the level of government expenditures and receipts and the gross national product. The purpose of this section is to discuss the effects of the *differences* between government receipts and expenditures, i.e., surpluses and deficits.

General Observations

It is hardly necessary to remind the reader of the fact that current economic doctrine in the field of fiscal policy no longer frowns upon budget deficits (or surpluses) under all conditions. On the contrary, there is substantial agreement among economists that in highly industrialized countries such as the United States or Great Britain, the appearance of a deficit or surplus in the government's finances can exert an important stabilizing influence upon the level of economic activity and prices and upon the movement of international accounts. If, other things being equal, the government pays out more money than it takes in, either by drawing down its balances or by creating new money through borrowing from banks or from private idle funds, it will cause, of course, an increase in money income, which in turn will result either in more production or, if the resources of the economy are fully employed, in an increase in the 'price level; at the same time the level of imports will increase. Conversely, if the government increases its balances or pays off bank or foreign debts, it withdraws more money from the income stream than it puts into it through disbursements. In consequence, income and consumption decline, and either the level of production recedes or, if production does not readily respond to a decline in effective demand, prices will decline; the level of imports likewise will fall.

It follows from these considerations that the government should attempt to accumulate Treasury balances in periods of inflationary expansions and of export surpluses and disburse more than it receives through tax and other regular revenues in periods of declining prices and retarded business activities.

Particular circumstances prevailing in less developed countries require certain modifications of these rules. In countries such as Guatemala, where the preponderant proportion of the gross national product consists of agricultural products, destined either for the export market or for domestic consumption, an increase in private and business income generally does not result in an immediate expansion of production but tends to cause an increase in the price level. More specifically, since it usually takes from six months to a year to expand food production and since the level of food production, being determined primarily by non-economic factors such as weather conditions and local customs, may not readily respond to a rising demand, the expansion of income through a drawing down of Treasury balances (or the disbursement of borrowings from banks) is bound to cause a short-run increase in prices.

The effects of excess government disbursements on the level of exports also are likely to be adverse, since increased cost of production may weaken the country's competitive position abroad. Fortunately, the cost-price relationship in the case of Guatemala's main export crop, coffee, has been so favorable in recent years that this aspect can be neglected. There cannot be any question, however, that such excess disbursements cause an expansion of imports which may result in a loss of foreign exchange reserves, which losses may become aggravated by an outflow of private capital.

The same line of reasoning applies, of course, to the accumu-

TABLE 56

GOVERNMENT SURPLUSES AND DEFICITS, NATIONAL INCOME, AND PRICE MOVEMENTS, 1937/38 TO 1948/49

Fiscal Year	Effective Government Surplus (+) or Deficit (−)[a] (In Q1000)	Gross National Product (In millions of quetzales)		Product of Commercial Sector (1937/38 = 100)	Price Indexes (1937/38 = 100)		Trade Balance (In Q1000)
		In Money Terms	In Real Terms (1937/38 Prices)		Wholesale Prices[b]	G.N.P. Deflator	
1937/38	+1,384	113.6	113.6	100.0	100.0	100.0	− 1,871
1938/39	+1,070	98.8	122.6	89.1	96.3	80.6	− 1,529
1939/40	+1,368	113.6	131.5	79.8	94.4	86.1	− 2,067
1940/41	+1,385	114.9	141.4	77.8	88.2	81.1	− 2,695
1941/42	+1,282	132.7	145.4	88.2	91.0	91.0	+ 2,585
1942/43	+ 433	178.2	157.9	99.8	112.5	112.6	+ 4,534
1943/44	+3,095	*	....	107.0	135.9	119.2	+ 2,727
1944/45	− 118	....	....	127.3	162.1	143.1	+ 5,120
1945/46	+ 149	239.9	152.0	146.3	190.9	157.4	+ 3,781
1946/47	+5,816	....	....	202.2	217.6	157.8	− 2,396
1947/48	−5,435	335.0	182.9	272.6	232.5	182.8	−11,738
1948/49	−3,634	....	....	....	242.5	....	−17,117

[a] Change in Treasury balances (increase +; decrease −) plus net amortization of public debt (+) or net borrowing (−).
[b] Wholesale prices of thirteen foodstuffs in Guatemala City (1937–46), linked with wholesale price index of seventy-one commodities in Guatemala City (1946–49).
* Not available.

lation of Treasury balances. In the domestic economy, an untimely accumulation of Treasury balances, i.e., one that is not offset by an export surplus or an expansion of bank credit to the private sector of the economy, will primarily lead to a contraction of prices; as to the economy's international position, a decline of imports may be expected, accompanied by the repatriation of capital held outside the country.

The Guatemalan Experience

The preceding discussion has presented a brief analysis of the effects of government surpluses and deficits in isolation, in order to clarify their significance as factors determining the level of economic activity and prices. If we turn now to a brief consideration of the actual experience of Guatemala with respect to government deficits and surpluses, it is necessary to relate the data on government deficits and surpluses to other pertinent series and factors and to take account of the fact that, in most years, the occurrence of such surpluses or deficits was accidental rather than the result of decisions based on economic policy considerations.

Table 56 compares annual data of effective government surpluses and deficits with movements of the gross national product, prices, and trade balances. In the first four years we find an accumulation of Treasury balances while the gross national product in money terms remained practically unchanged, with the exception of the temporary drop in 1938/39. This development apparently was a result of price declines in excess of the increase in the volume of production in real terms. Trade statistics for the same period indicate large import surpluses; but since the foreign-exchange reserves of Guatemala expanded during the same period, it is likely that these surpluses were due to an undervaluation of banana exports and therefore only apparent rather than real.[6] Thus, the conclusion seems warranted that the budget

6 See chapter ii, p. 32. This interpretation is borne out by a comparison of the value of banana exports, as shown in trade statistics, with the amount of foreign exchange sold to Guatemalan banks by the United Fruit Company for later years for

surpluses, which were caused, it should be emphasized, in part by the yield of the newly introduced business profits tax but primarily by the large collections of import taxes, were at least partly responsible for the decline of prices and wages which occurred at that time. This decline did not affect real income, which kept on rising, and it may have helped coffee exporters to overcome the prevailing difficulties resulting from depressed coffee prices.

Throughout the war years (1941/42 to 1944/45), export surpluses, which, as the movement of foreign exchange reserves indicates, were real as well as statistical, developed primarily as a result of the scarcity of import commodities. As a result, shortages occurred, and price increases of considerable proportions took place. The government surpluses of this period, though ineffective to stem the tide of inflation, unquestionably mitigated the upward pressures somewhat. Besides, they were put to a desirable use: the foreign debt was almost completely paid off in 1944/45 without unduly straining the country's exchange resources.

In the postwar period, a decisive change took place in 1947/48 when Treasury balances declined by 2.6 million quetzales and the government incurred an internal debt of 2.8 million through borrowings from the banking system. In spite of record exports, trade balances turned severely adverse, although in all probability not so much as the trade statistics suggest. Prices increased by 26 percent, but the upward pressure on prices subsided toward the end of the period.

It is difficult to appraise the causal role that the government deficit played in this period. The upsurge of imports was to a large extent, though perhaps not completely, accounted for by the backlog of import demand accumulated in the course of the preceding years and by the simultaneous rise in incomes through large export proceeds. Moreover, the government deficits were

which data on foreign exchange sales are available. Investment expenditures in Guatemala by foreign-owned enterprises (again primarily by the United Fruit Company) may have further increased the foreign exchange holdings during that period.

partly offset by the accumulation of sinking funds[7] in the hand of the Banco de Guatemala; these funds amounted to Q891,000 at the end of the fiscal year 1947/48, and to Q1,056,000 at the end of 1948/49.[8]

After all circumstantial evidence is considered, it appears that the government deficits in 1947/48 and 1948/49 were not primary causal factors of the inflationary updrift that took place in those years. This is indirectly also borne out by the experience of 1946/47 when, in spite of a large accumulation of Treasury balances, prices rose by 18 percent. But the deficits unquestionably contributed, as a secondary or perhaps marginal factor, to the postwar inflation.

This role of government surpluses and deficits, as an accentuating or mitigating rather than as a primary causal factor, points also to the limitations which intentional operations with surpluses and deficits will have in the future. It is clear that, in a country like Guatemala, neither a business recession originating from abroad nor an export boom caused by an increase in the foreign demand for Guatemala's exports can be "cured" by any conceivable fiscal policy. But such expansions and contractions of business activity and prices can be to some extent mitigated by proper fiscal policies.

The limited flexibility of the revenue structure, discussed in the preceding chapter, is likely to cause only relatively minor fluctuations in Treasury balances if the level of expenditures remains unchanged. Given a stable level of expenditures and an adequate equilibrium level of receipts, the built-in flexibility of the revenue system should produce relatively minor Treasury surpluses in a period of moderate expansion[9] and some deficits in a contraction. This built-in rhythm of fiscal operations can of course be accentuated, if need be, by net borrowings from the

---

[7] From assigned tax revenues; see chapter iii, pp. 64–65.

[8] At the same time, however, the banking system acquired substantial holdings of municipal bonds of the City of Guatemala. This, of course, aggravated the pressure of the government's deficits.

[9] In the case of severe inflation, the degree of built-in flexibility is insufficient. See chapter viii, p. 194.

banking system in periods of contraction and net debt retirements in a period of expansion. But it must be kept in mind that the government's freedom of action is limited—at least in the down-turn—by the movements of the country's foreign-exchange re-serves. Only to the extent to which exchange reserves are built up in step with Treasury balances during an upswing—and there are many reasons to believe that such increases will normally be the case—can the country afford an accentuation of the depletion of foreign exchange in a downturn through the incurrence of Treas-ury deficits.[10]

Fortunately, the need for anticyclical fiscal policy is less great in Guatemala than in highly industrialized countries where cyc-lical unemployment affects large groups of the population and causes hardship and social dissatisfaction. The number of indus-trial workers in Guatemala is small, in absolute terms as well as in relation to the agricultural population, which remains largely unaffected by cyclical disturbances. Their well-being is primarily determined by harvest conditions and, indirectly, by the terms of trade which determine the purchasing power of agricultural earnings over imported goods.

In conclusion, it must be emphasized that the preceding dis-cussion neglects two important aspects of the effects of govern-ment surpluses and deficits, and, indirectly, of government loan operations. In the first place, it completely disregards the pur-poses of expenditures that may give rise to deficits. This problem of the allocation of government expenditures will be dealt with in the last chapter of this study. For the purposes of this section, it may suffice to indicate that a distinction must be made between productive and unproductive expenditures in excess of govern-ment receipts. A deficit which results in a general increase in efficiency, and therefore of real income, or an expansion of ex-ports, or which makes domestic production competitive with im-ports, is obviously preferable to an unproductive deficit caused by,

[10] The avoidance of deficits in a recession may become even more important in the future if, as a result of progressive industrialization, a secular rise in the import demand occurs.

say, an increase of expenditures for government buildings or public amusements. The high proportion of the expansion of government expenditures in the last three years that was used for public investment projects holds promise that in the future a growing share of such expenditures will be devoted to genuinely productive purposes, and the sacrifices of current consumption will thus be rewarded by a multiple increase in the output of goods and services available to the economy.

The second modification of the preceding discussion is necessitated by the implicit assumption that all borrowing comes from the domestic banking system (or from abroad) and that all amortization payments are made to the banking system or to foreign creditors. This assumption seems to be in accordance with the facts as they prevailed in Guatemala in the period under discussion, perhaps with the minor modification that an unknown proportion of the Guatemalan foreign debt retired in 1944/45 was held by Guatemalan citizens.

It is to be hoped, however, that in the not-too-distant future the Guatemalan government will be able to rely at least for a moderate part of its investment expenditures on noninflationary borrowings from private savers, either through the sale of bonds outside the banking system or through the investment of savings deposits of financial institutions. In so far as government borrowings are financed by an increase in savings,[11] government deficits do not add to the income stream and thus do not affect the level of prices or production. The problem of stimulating and channeling savings for this purpose as well as for the purpose of financing private investment will be touched upon once more in the next chapter.

REDISTRIBUTION OF THE NATIONAL INCOME

The last section of the present chapter concerns itself with the effects of the fiscal system upon the distribution of the gross

[11] The tapping of idle savings for financing government deficits is, of course, inflationary.

national product. In a broad sense, this section is a continuation of the discussion of the impact of the fiscal system upon individual households (chapter vi); but here the analysis is carried one step further, taking into account not only the burden imposed by the tax system upon families but also the benefits derived from the services that the government provides. This section thus deals primarily with the welfare impact of the fiscal system in accordance with the broad principles of welfare economics which stipulate that the general welfare is enhanced by a redistribution of income in favor of lower-income groups.[12] The redistribution of income also affects certain dynamic interrelationships of the economy that determine its growth and stability, i.e., the rate of savings, the level of consumption and imports, and the productivity of the economy. All these aspects have to be taken into consideration in an appraisal of the effects of the fiscal system on the distribution of the gross national product.

The Guatemalan Redistribution: The First Model

For the purposes of this chapter we conceive of the impact of the tax system upon individual income groups in the same way in which we measured the tax burden upon individual households in chapter vi, i.e., as a sum of money that is taken away by the government from each household. This sum represents a net deduction from the income of the individual household. But in order to obtain an indication of the impact of the tax burden upon the distribution of the gross national product, the typical households of chapter vi have to be replaced by income groups or, more exactly, by classes of family income. This has been done in the computations shown in Table 57.

It must be pointed out at once that the income distribution underlying the analysis is highly tentative; but it is based upon the best sources of information at our disposal and appears to be

---

[12] These principles are, of course, subject to the important modification that the optimum distribution of income is not complete equality of income but that degree of inequality that provides sufficient incentives to assure maximum efficiency and productivity.

TABLE 57

REDISTRIBUTION OF INCOME THROUGH THE FISCAL SYSTEM IN 1947/48: FIRST MODEL

(*In thousands of quetzales*)

Family Income (*In quetzales*)	Number of Families (*In thousands*)	Original Income	Taxes Borne[a]	Benefits Received[b]	Redistributed Income	Redistributed Income as Percent of Original Income	Gain Through Budgetary Deficits[c]	Redistributed Income Including Gain Through Deficits	Redistributed Income as Percent of Original Income
0–300	174.0	37,855	1,544	5,165	41,476	109.6	1,159	42,635	112.6
301–600	213.5	90,282	5,946	9,141	93,477	103.5	2,051	95,528	105.8
601–1,200	91.0	66,531	6,219	5,689	66,001	99.2	1,276	67,277	101.1
1,201–2,000	26.1	38,223	4,349	2,856	36,730	96.1	641	37,371	97.8
2,001–5,000	11.1	36,582	4,302	2,514	34,794	95.1	564	35,358	96.7
5,001–10,000	3.9	29,045	3,353	1,920	27,612	95.1	431	28,043	96.6
10,001 and over	2.4	36,482	3,943	2,371	34,910	95.7	532	35,442	97.1
Total economy	522.0	335,000	29,656	29,656	335,000	100.0	6,654	341,654	102.0

[a] Total tax collections less assigned taxes, special taxes, and taxes borne by foreigners.
[b] Adjusted; total benefits equal total taxes borne.
[c] Equal to budget deficit plus special taxes and taxes borne by foreigners.
Note: For sources and methods of computation see Statistical Note to chapter ix.

consistent with data on tax collections, property distribution data (of the Property Tax Administration), and other pertinent figures. The tax burden of the various income groups is shown in Table 59 in the Statistical Note appended to this chapter.[13] It shows, of course, essentially the same picture as that presented in chapter vi: a tax burden that rises from a low of 4.1 percent for the lowest-income group (with an annual family income below Q300) to a peak burden of 11.8 percent in the income group with an annual family income of Q2,000 to Q5,000; thereafter the average tax burden declines somewhat (but it obviously continues to rise for those families whose income is subject to the progressive business profits tax).[14]

The diminution of the family income through the process of taxation is offset, on the other hand, by a flow of services that the government provides for the community as a whole; but in the last analysis, the benefits of these communal services accrue to the individual households in the form of police protection, educational facilities, hospitals, roads, etc. The allocation of the benefits derived from these services to individual households is fraught with severe conceptual difficulties. Furthermore, the amounts of benefits derived from government services vary not only with the level of income but also with respect to variations in the source of income, the family status of income earners (for example, the number of children enjoying free educational facilities), the amounts of property owned by each family, etc.

In the interpretation of the allocation model presented here, these conceptual and statistical limitations of its meaning must be kept in mind. However, since the direction and composition of government services are not accidental but are the result of deliberate actions by the legislature and the administration—which actions are based upon judgments as to the benefits to be derived from these services—there is ample justification for an attempt

---

[13] The note also provides information on sources of data and methods of computation.

[14] Lack of more detailed information on the income distribution in the highest-income brackets prevented a further breakdown of the open-end group of family incomes of Q10,000 and above.

to apportion the benefits of these services to individual households.[15]

In order to obtain a quantitative indication of the benefits that accrue to households in the various income groups, we make use of the distinction of government expenditures by function which was introduced in chapter iv. Administrative, national defense, and economic development expenditures are allocated proportionate to income. This method of allocation, which is admittedly arbitrary, appears to be a reasonable approximation of the true allocation, since the benefits of all services provided through these types of services are in one way or another related to the economic position that the individual beneficiaries (i.e., households) hold in the community. The benefits of police protection, for instance, accrue to property owners in proportion to the value of their property. The services of the judiciary are less important to persons in low-income brackets and presumably give greater benefits to families with higher incomes. Expenditures for economic development directly and indirectly provide benefits for all members of the community; but it seems reasonable to assume that the business community which has a larger per family income derives proportionately more benefits from better roads, new bridges, etc., than members of lower-income groups.

Only in the case of social and cultural expenditures does it seem preferable to choose a different method of allocation. Education facilities, the maintenance and expansion of which absorb the largest part of this type of expenditure, are made available to all income groups alike, irrespective of the level of income of individual families. Therefore, it appears appropriate to allocate social and cultural expenditures on a per capita basis.

The result of this allocation, together with the distribution of the tax burden by income groups discussed before, is shown in

---

[15] For a more detailed discussion of the problem of allocating benefits of government services, see John H. Adler, "The Fiscal System, the Distribution of Income and Public Welfare" (with a Statistical Appendix by E. R. Schlesinger) in Kenyon E. Poole (ed.), *Fiscal Policies and the American Economy* (New York: Prentice-Hall, Inc., 1951).

summary form in Table 57. In order to distinguish between the amounts of benefits derived from tax funds and from the incurrence of government deficits, the sum total of expenditures—and therefore of benefits—is shown in two parts. One is equal to the total of the taxes borne by the Guatemalan economy; the other equals the difference between expenditures and receipts and is allocated separately among income groups on the basis of the same allocation scheme as the first. The combined effects of the impact of the tax burden and of the accrual of benefits to the various income groups (redistributed income as a percent of original income) is a moderate redistribution of the gross national product in favor of the two lowest-income groups. The lower-middle-income class is hardly affected by the redistribution, since its share of the benefits of government services is almost equal to its tax burden. The upper three income groups bear the burden of the redistribution.

If government expenditures in excess of tax revenues are added to the distribution of benefits—on the plausible assumption that expenditures, financed by deficits, are distributed among the various types of government services in the same proportion as expenditures financed by taxes—the economy as a whole records of course a net gain. The gain accrues again primarily to the two lowest-income groups whose initial income is increased through the fiscal redistribution by 13 and 6 percent, respectively.

Table 57 appears to indicate that the economy gained through the government deficit 2 percent of the gross national product.[16] This gain, which, as pointed out in the preceding section, is real in the sense that an excess of government disbursements over receipts always results in an increase in monetary income, may be offset, of course, by the losses in material welfare incurred by certain sectors of the economy as a result of the inflationary impact which the deficit may cause. In so far as there exists a time lag between price increases and upward adjustments in the income

[16] The 1947/48 excess of government expenditures over receipts includes also a small amount of expenditures financed by tax receipts that do not cause a tax burden upon the economy, since these taxes fall on foreign investors or consumers.

receipts of wage and salary earners in the lower-income groups, the inflationary impact of the government deficit presumably offsets the gains through additional benefits by the losses in purchasing power. Conversely, the losses of the upper-income groups resulting from the redistribution of the fiscal system are offset by their windfall gains in the form of inventory and speculative profits, for instance in real estate.

In all probability, the middle classes get the disadvantages of both the redistributive effects of the fiscal system and the redistribution of income through inflationary price rises, since in their case it seems reasonable to assume that there exists a considerable time lag between price increases and income adjustments.

The Second Model: Indigenous and Nonindigenous Differences

As indicated above, the redistribution model presented in Table 57 is but a first schematic approximation of the actual distribution of the combined impact of the tax burden and the accrual of benefits from government sources. Its major defect is that it fails to take account of the differences in the tax burden and the amounts of benefits derived from government services that exist within each income group. Table 58 represents an attempt to take account of one of the major discontinuities in the Guatemalan income distribution by distinguishing between the impact of the revenue and expenditure system on the indigenous sectors of the economy, on the one hand, and its impact on the nonindigenous, fully monetary sector on the other.

The differences between the consumption patterns of the typical indigenous and *ladino* low-income family result, as indicated in a previously presented comparison, in an appreciably smaller per family tax burden upon the indigenous population than upon nonindigenous families. These differences have been taken into account in the computation of the tax burden shown in Table 58

TABLE 58

REDISTRIBUTION OF INCOME THROUGH THE FISCAL SYSTEM IN 1947/48: SECOND MODEL

(In thousands of quetzales)

Family Income in Quetzales	Original Income	Taxes Borne[a]	Benefits Received[b]	Redistributed Income	Redistributed Income as a Percent of Original Income	Gain Through Budgetary Deficit[c]	Redistributed Income Including Gain Through Deficit	Redistributed Income as a Percent of Original Income
Indigenous economy:								
0–300	37,855	1,544	3,783	40,094	105.9	849	40,943	108.2
301–600	60,174	3,671	4,603	61,106	101.5	1,033	62,139	103.3
601 and over	23,176	1,731	1,528	22,973	99.1	342	23,315	100.6
Total indigenous economy	121,205	6,946	9,914	124,173	102.4	2,224	126,397	104.3
Nonindigenous economy:								
0–600	30,108	2,275	4,007	31,840	105.8	899	32,739	108.7
601–1,200	43,355	4,488	4,637	43,504	100.3	1,041	44,545	102.7
1,201–2,000	38,223	4,349	3,398	37,272	97.5	762	38,034	99.5
2,001–5,000	36,582	4,302	2,885	35,165	96.1	647	35,812	97.9
5,001–10,000	29,045	3,353	2,165	27,857	95.9	486	28,343	97.6
10,001 and over	36,482	3,943	2,650	35,189	96.5	595	35,784	98.1
Total nonindigenous economy	213,795	22,710	19,742	210,827	98.6	4,430	215,257	100.7
Total economy	335,000	29,656	29,656	335,000	100.0	6,654	341,654	102.0

[a] Total tax collections less assigned taxes, special taxes, and taxes borne by foreigners.
[b] Adjusted: total benefits equal total taxes borne.
[c] Equal to budget deficit plus special taxes and taxes borne by foriqners.
Note: For sources and methods of computation see Statistical Note to chapter ix.

and presented in more detail in the Statistical Note to this chapter.

The lighter tax burden finds its counterpart in a smaller participation of the indigenous population in the benefits of government services. The correction of the incidence of benefits for indigenous-nonindigenous differences seems justified in view of the fact that the bulk of the indigenous population does not fully take part in the country's market economy and in its social and cultural life and progress. More specifically, the educational facilities at the disposal of the indigenous sector of the economy are unquestionably more limited than those of the prevalently urban nonindigenous sector; the same applies to hospital and social welfare facilities. In the case of developmental expenditures, it seems likewise reasonable to take into consideration that the primitive agricultural ways of life of the majority of the indigenous populations are hardly affected by road improvements and other *fomento* projects.

The limited incidence of the benefits of these expenditures has been taken into account statistically by reducing the benefits of social and cultural expenditures and of expenditures for economic development purposes more or less arbitrarily by one-third. The benefits of national defense expenditures were left unchanged; and administrative expenditures, the primary purpose of which is the administration of the other types of expenditures, were distributed proportionately to the combined incidence of three other types of government services.

The combined result of the low tax burden and the corrected incidence of benefits of government services is, in the aggregate, a substantial redistribution of income in favor of the indigenous population. Another and perhaps more important effect is that the income group with a family income of Q600 to Q1,200 now records a net gain while under the previous scheme it appeared as a net loser. The net gains of the indigenous sector as well as those of the two lowest-income brackets of the *ladino* sector are, of course, again accentuated by the additional benefits derived from deficit disbursements of the government.

The Over-all Effects of the Income Redistribution

Since a statistical appraisal of the redistributive effects of the fiscal system has been presented, it seems appropriate to offer a few brief comments on the over-all effects of this redistributive process. As indicated above, the redistribution affects the well-being of the economy as a whole, as well as its stability, rate of growth, and productivity.

Although the income derived from the benefits of government services may not be appreciated as the equivalent of money income (and by the same token, is not felt in the same way as the burden of taxes), it nonetheless must be considered real in the sense that it enhances the economic welfare of the economy as a whole. It is impossible to measure this welfare effect, since its magnitude obviously depends upon an appreciation of the difference of the usefulness of small additions to income of families with lower and higher income, respectively. But in the specific case of Guatemala, this material welfare effect certainly also influences the productivity of the economy. The social and educational expenditures in particular, which provide, in the aggregate, more benefits to the lower than to the higher-income groups, are bound to enhance the productivity of rural and urban workers by providing them with better schools, more hospitals, and similar social improvements. The productivity effects, of course, do not become apparent immediately; but they are undoubtedly of major long-run significance. This stimulation of a gradual productivity rise through social expenditures also affects, in the final result, the rate of growth of the economy.

There are, however, limits on the extent to which the redistribution of income exerts a positive influence on the rate of growth of the economy. In so far as the redistribution takes away income from the upper-income groups, whose rate of savings accounts for the bulk of total private savings in the economy, it causes a fall in total savings and, indirectly, in private capital formation. This negative aspect of the effect of the redistribution of income through the fiscal system, however, must not be overrated, since a relatively high proportion of the forgone savings presumably would take the form of unproductive investment, such as private housing construction of the luxury type. Perhaps a more important limit to the highly distributive social and cultural expenditures is the constant need for expenditures for the economic development of the country. Under the distribution scheme adopted above, economic development expenditures, it is true, result only in a mild redistribution of income; but they cause an increase in over-all output and productivity, thus enhancing the economic well-being of all income groups.

In conclusion, it should be noted that the redistribution of the national income through the Guatemalan fiscal system is relatively moderate. Lack of comparable studies makes broad international comparisons impossible. But a study of the redistributive effects of the American fiscal system indicates that in the United States the redistribution of the national income has assumed much greater proportion than that prevailing in Guatemala. It must be added, however, that this is primarily the indirect result of the high per capita income of the United States, which permits the imposition of high taxes and thus a large volume of social and cultural expenditures.

STATISTICAL NOTE

Income Distribution

The family income distribution presented in Table 59 is based on the Arias study, the Goubaud Carrera study, and the tax declarations submitted by business firms to the Control Office of the Profits Tax (Contraloría del Impuesto sobre Utilidades). The estimates, originally prepared to conform to a 1947/48 population estimate of 3,300,000[17] (660,000 families of five members each), were revised to conform to the results of the 1950 census, which indicated a 1947/48 population of 2,610,000 (522,000 families). Although the census classified 68.4 percent of the population as rural, it employed a very loose definition of urban, and it was therefore assumed that two-thirds of the families

---

[17] Unofficial estimate of the General Statistical Office (Dirección General de Estadística) prepared prior to 1950 population census.

TABLE 59

Burden of Taxes by Income Groups, 1947/48[a]

(In thousands of quetzales)

Family Income	In Quetzales							
	0-300	301-600	601-1,200	1,201-2,000	2,001-5,000	5,001-10,000	10,001 and over	Total
Number of families (in thousands)	174.0	213.5	91.0	26.1	11.1	3.9	2.4	522.0
Total income	37,855	90,282	66,531	38,223	36,582	29,045	36,482	335,000
Consumption taxes	799	2,606	1,833	857	776	547	586	8,004
Import duties on consumers' goods	139	768	1,346	1,110	1,208	993	1,063	6,627
Import duties on business goods	340	1,415	1,210	728	659	464	498	5,314
Other shifted business taxes	237	1,082	978	621	562	396	424	4,300
Unshifted business profits tax	…	…	91	228	325	331	549	1,524
Other unshifted business taxes	…	…	639	564	539	428	538	2,708
Consumers' property tax	4	15	28	23	24	25	44	163
Inheritance and gift tax	…	…	8	11	12	12	44	87
Miscellaneous taxes[b]	25	60	86	207	197	157	197	929
Total tax burden[c]	1,544	5,946	6,219	4,349	4,302	3,353	3,943	29,656
Tax burden as percent of income	4%	7%	9%	11%	12%	12%	11%	9%

[a] For classification of taxes, see Tables 31 and 35.
[b] Includes stamp tax on salaries, radio tax, air and rail transportation taxes, consumers' motor vehicle taxes, life insurance premium tax, consumers' property transfer taxes, entertainment taxes, and consumers' miscellaneous taxes.
[c] Excludes special taxes and those borne by foreign investors and consumers (see text).

(348,000) were indigenous and one-third *ladino*. Fifty percent of the indigenous families (174,000) were placed in the lowest-income group, while 142,300 were assigned to the Q300–600 group and 31,700 were estimated to have incomes in excess of Q600.

Distribution of the Tax Burden

In order to obtain a figure for the total burden of taxes in 1947/48 which would be meaningful from the standpoint of studying the redistribution of income through the fiscal system, taxes borne by foreign investors and consumers and certain special taxes were first deducted from total collections. This adjustment amounted to 1,578.1 thousand quetzales and included the *ausente* tax, import duties on business goods paid by major foreign companies, chicle export and exploitation taxes, a portion of the banana export tax, the central bank income tax, the Electric Company income tax, the sugar and *panela* sales taxes, and certain minor export taxes. The estimates of the distribution of the burden of the remaining taxes (see Table 59) were then derived by the following methods.

Consumption taxes.—The total physical consumption of alcoholic beverages and tobacco products by the indigenous sector was estimated from the Goubaud Carrera study. The tax burden for each of the three indigenous income groups was then computed on the basis of the 1947/48 tax rates. The resulting total for the indigenous population was subtracted from consumption tax collections to obtain the total *ladino* burden, and this was allocated among the various income groups on the basis of a percentage distribution of *ladino* family expenditures for alcoholic beverages and tobacco products, which was derived from the Arias study.

Import duties on consumers' goods.—Ad valorem equivalents of the import duties on major imported consumers' goods were computed, and by assuming that domestic profit margins and handling costs were equal to 75 percent of imports (c.i.f.), the burden (in quetzales) of these duties on the three indigenous income groups was obtained on the basis of the Goubaud Carrera study. Utilizing the Arias study, the same procedure was used in the case of *ladino* families, but in this case the figures were adjusted to conform to total collections.

Import duties on business goods.—The same procedure which was followed for import duties on consumers' goods was used in obtaining the burden of these duties on the indigenous sector as a whole, but it was not possible to allocate this total directly among the three indigenous income groups on the basis of the Goubaud Carrera study. As an alternative, the total was distributed in accordance with estimates of total consumption expenditures by the various indigenous income groups in the market economy. This was assumed to be 40 percent of total consumption in the 0–300 group, 60 percent in the 301–600 group, and 70 percent in the 601-and-over indigenous group. In the case of the *ladino* population, the residual (i.e., total collections minus indigenous burden) was distributed among the various income groups on the basis of total consumption expenditures.

Other shifted business taxes.—These taxes were distributed among all income groups on the basis of total consumption, for no more exact statistical basis for apportioning these taxes between the indigenous and *ladino* sectors was available. The same adjustment for the degree of the participation of the three indigenous income groups in the market economy was made here as in the case of the import duties on business goods.

Unshifted business profits tax.—The percentage *ladino* income distribution was weighted by the business profits tax rates and then adjusted to take account of the Q500 exemption allowed under this tax. The resulting percentages were applied to one-half of the 1947/48 collection.

Other unshifted business taxes.—The burden of these taxes was allocated proportionately to income among *ladino* families with incomes of Q601 or over.

Consumers' property tax.—A distribution of real estate ownership by size of holdings was derived from a sample of 1,413 cases taken from the property tax rolls of the General Revenues Office (Dirección General de Rentas). These figures were adjusted to obtain a percentage distribution of real estate by income groups, and the resulting percentages were then applied to consumers' property tax collections for 1947/48 (assumed to be equal to one-third of total collections).

Inheritance and gift tax.—The percentage distribution of real estate by income groups was weighted by the rates of the inheritance and gift tax and then adjusted to take account of the exemption allowed under this tax. The resulting percentages were applied to the 1947/48 collections.

Miscellaneous taxes.—The burden of this group of taxes was allocated on three different bases. The stamp tax on salaries was distributed proportionately to income among *ladino* families with incomes over Q600; the air and rail transportation taxes, consumers' motor vehicle taxes, radio tax, consumers' property transfer taxes, life insurance premium tax, and entertainment taxes were allocated proportionately to income among all families with incomes over Q1,200; and the consumers' miscellaneous taxes were apportioned proportionately to income among all families.

Distribution of Expenditure Benefits

In order to determine the redistributive effects of a balanced budget, total 1947/48 government expenditures were adjusted downward to the level of the total burden of taxes in that fiscal year. The percentage composition of government expenditures by purpose (exclusive of debt payments) [18] was then applied to this figure, and the various types of expenditure benefits were allocated among the income groups by methods described in the text of this chapter. The redistributive effects of total budgetary operations were obtained by adding the benefits gained from the 1947/48 cash deficit and the taxes borne by foreign investors and consumers, and assuming that these additional benefits were distributed in the same manner as those under the balanced budget.

[18] During 1947/48, amortization and interest payments could be disregarded for the purposes of studying the redistribution of income, for they were made almost entirely to foreigners or government-owned agencies.

X

FISCAL OPERATIONS AND THE MONETARY SYSTEM

THE PRECEDING chapter discussed the effects of the fiscal system on the national income. The present chapter continues the analysis of the interaction of the government budget with the economy as a whole and studies the influence of fiscal operations upon the monetary system and the international accounts of the Guatemalan economy.

THE CURRENCY AND THE FISCAL SYSTEM

In Guatemala, as in most other countries at a comparable stage of economic development, domestic government borrowing has been effected almost exclusively through the banking system and has thus had an important influence on the money supply. This section explores the relationship between budgetary operations and the monetary system which has existed in recent years; it then examines factors in the Guatemalan economy which so far have prevented the establishment of an effective market for government bonds among the savers of the country.

Government Financing and the Money Supply

In Guatemala, as in other countries, government financing is one of the three major sources of the money supply, and, along with the balance of payments and business financing, it determines the aggregate means of payments of the economy. A part of the *gross* money supply that is derived from these three sources is, of course, neutralized within the banking system in the form of time and savings deposits owned by the public and by the foreign currency liabilities, capital, and other nonmonetary accounts of the banks. These neutralizing factors must be deducted in order to arrive at the *net* means of payments in the hands of the public and government.

The method of analysis shown in Table 60 makes immediately apparent the *gross* contributions made to the money supply since 1936 by the international, government, and domestic business sectors of the Guatemalan economy, respectively. It is conceptually impossible to determine the *net* contribution of each of these sectors, since the amounts that are neutralized within the banking system cannot be definitely allocated to either the government, the balance of payments, or private business.

The government's contribution, as may be seen, has been made in two ways:[1] (1) seigniorage in the Treasury coin issue, and (2) borrowing and repayment of loans to the banking system. For certain analytical purposes, however, it is the net means of payments in the hands of the public which is the important economic variable; from this point of view Treasury cash balances and the deposits of the government and autonomous agencies constitute a special neutralizing factor, and they are shown as such in the table.

Seigniorage profits on the subsidiary coin issue have been of little quantitative importance in recent Guatemalan fiscal and monetary experience. The data given in Table 60 show that the total value of the subsidiary coins minted and put in circulation by the Treasury increased from 1.8 million quetzales to 2.6 million between June 30, 1937, and June 30, 1946. Since the intrinsic value of the metals used in these coins amounted to 50 percent of the token value, the seigniorage profits of the government during the period were actually only 0.4 million quetzales. These represented the normal by-product of minting operations and, in view of their limited size, were undoubtedly not consciously employed as a fiscal device.

Since July 1, 1946, the coinage powers have been in the hands of the Banco de Guatemala, and the government no longer obtains

---

[1] The budget, of course, also influences the balance of payments and money of external origin. This subject is discussed in the second section of this chapter.

TABLE 60

FACTORS AFFECTING THE MONEY SUPPLY

(In millions of quetzales)

As of End of June	Balance of Payments[a] (1)	Treasury Coin Issue[b] (2)	Fiscal and Nonfiscal Borrowing from Banks[c] (3)	Government Contributions Total (4=2+3)	Financing of Business[d] (5)	Total Created (6=1+4+5)	Savings and Time Deposits (7)	Deposits and Other Liabilities in Foreign Currency in Banks (8)	Banks' Capital Reserves and Non-monetary Accounts[e] (9)	Total Neutralized (10=7+8+9)	Net Means of Payment (Total Created Less Total Neutralized) (11=6-10)	Total Deposits and Cash Holdings of Government and Autonomous Agencies (12)	Money Supply in Hands of Public (13=11-12)
1937[f]	4.87	1.84	3.44	5.28	17.80	27.95	0.80	2.63	6.56	9.99	17.96	4.21	13.75
1938[f]	8.21	1.88	3.46	5.34	19.08	32.63	0.76	0.55	13.28	14.59	18.04	5.37	12.67
1939	9.45	1.88	1.59	3.47	19.31	32.23	0.66	0.56	11.86	13.08	19.15	5.15	14.00
1940	11.07	1.88	1.54	3.42	18.67	33.16	0.46	0.47	10.66	12.59	20.57	6.95	13.62
1941	13.49	1.88	1.51	3.39	19.06	35.94	0.68	0.48	11.57	12.73	23.21	7.93	15.28
1942	21.00	1.88	1.58	3.46	18.05	42.51	0.45	0.48	12.00	12.93	29.58	9.34	20.24
1943	30.00	1.88	1.47	3.35	17.91	51.26	0.44	...	12.93	13.37	37.89	9.84	28.05
1944	41.63	2.24	1.17	3.41	17.47	62.51	0.95	4.65	11.67	17.27	45.24	10.43	34.81
1945	42.97	2.41	1.16	3.57	16.73	63.27	1.13	...	15.14	16.27	47.00	6.09	40.91
1946	48.96	2.64	1.04	3.68	19.74	72.38	0.42	...	19.28	19.70	52.68	5.01	47.67
1947	54.19	2.64	1.85	4.49	25.44	84.12	0.93	...	21.32	22.25	61.87	11.04	50.83
1948	50.27	2.64	5.86	8.50	30.67	89.44	1.07	...	25.70	26.77	62.67	10.99	51.68
1949	45.43	2.64	8.49	11.13	37.62	94.18	1.24	1.16	28.16	30.56	63.62	4.50	59.12

[a] International reserves of the banking system.
[b] Since 1946, liability of bank of Guatemala (see text).
[c] For detailed breakdown of these government liabilities to the banking system, see Table 61.
[d] All other assets of the banking system, excluding deposits at central bank, holdings of notes and coins, and nominal accounts such as the local-currency contribution to the International Monetary Fund, the Bond for the Consolidation of the Coinage System, and government securities issued to and still held by INFOP.
[e] Does not include offset to local currency contribution to International Monetary Fund.
[f] Adjusted end-of-year data, except in case of financing of government for which midyear data were available.

seigniorage profits. The coins which were issued by the Treasury prior to that date have become a liability of the Banco de Guatemala, the government having reimbursed the central bank for this added obligation by giving it a special bond of Q2.6 million.

Changes in the value of government liabilities to the banking system have been far more significant for the money supply. Data pertaining to these obligations are presented in detailed form in Table 61. As may be seen, government liabilities to the banks are of three different types: direct fiscal obligations of the national government, contingent liabilities of the national government, and obligations of municipal governments. In addition, a distinction is drawn between government debts to the central bank and its debts to the other banks. Under conditions of business prosperity, credits to the government by commercial banks may not always represent a net addition to the money supply, for these funds, in the absence of the government credit, could presumably have been lent to private borrowers. In the case of the central bank, however, loans to the government undoubtedly are a net contribution to the means of payments.

Two distinct phases are evident in the case of fiscal borrowing by the national government. Between June 1937 and June 1941, all fiscal obligations to the banking system were retired, with a correspondingly deflationary influence on the money supply. No new borrowing was effected until the fiscal year 1947/48, but during that and the following year the government borrowed 5.9 million quetzales. The full inflationary impact of these credits was not reflected in an expansion of the money supply because money of external origin declined by almost nine million quetzales during these two fiscal years. This decline, however, must be attributed partly to government borrowing.

The contingent obligations of the national government to the banking system take the form of the system's holdings of the government-guaranteed mortgage bonds (*bonos hipotecarios*) issued by the National Mortgage Credit Institute (Credito Hipotecario Nacional), a government-owned institution. The entire pro-

TABLE 61

LIABILITIES OF THE GOVERNMENT TO THE BANKING SYSTEM

(In millions of quetzales)

As of End of June	Direct Fiscal Borrowing of National Government			Contingent Liabilities of National Government			Municipal Borrowing			Total Government Borrowing
	Central Bank[a]	Other Banks	Total	Central Bank[a]	Other Banks	Total	Central Bank[a]	Other Banks	Total	
1937	0.14	2.00	2.14	0.50	...	0.50	0.80	...	0.80	3.44
1938	0.09	2.07	2.16	0.50	...	0.50	0.80	...	0.80	3.46
1939	0.09	...	0.09	0.70	...	0.70	0.80	...	0.80	1.59
1940	0.04	...	0.04	0.70	...	0.70	0.80	...	0.80	1.54
1941	0.01	...	0.01	0.70	...	0.70	0.80	...	0.80	1.51
1942	...	...	...	0.80	...	0.80	0.78	...	0.78	1.58
1943	...	...	...	0.70	...	0.70	0.77	...	0.77	1.47
1944	...	...	...	0.40	...	0.40	0.77	...	0.77	1.17
1945	...	...	...	0.39	...	0.39	0.77	...	0.77	1.16
1946	...	...	...	0.27	...	0.27	0.77	...	0.77	1.04
1947	...	...[b]	...	0.67	0.27	0.94	0.91	...	0.91	1.85
1948	1.39	1.80[b]	3.19	1.35	...	1.35	1.32	...	1.32	5.86
1949	2.10	3.84[b]	5.94	1.39	...	1.39	0.81	0.35	1.16	8.49

[a] Banco Central de Guatemala through June 30, 1946, Banco de Guatemala thereafter.
[b] Does not include a credit of 0.4 million for contribution to Bretton Woods institutions.

ceeds of earlier issues were used to finance public works and housing projects, and clearly form part of the government contribution to the money supply. A portion of the proceeds of later issues were employed for general banking operations, whose character was of a purely commercial nature and may thus be considered to represent business financing. But since all activities of the National Mortgage Credit Institute are deemed in the public interest and since the bonds carry the government guaranty, it appears justified to consider all of the banking system's holdings of these bonds as government financing.

The monetary and fiscal aspects of the municipal bonds are similar to those of the issues of the Mortgage Institute. These bonds are also guaranteed by the national government and were used in their entirety to finance public works. The bank holdings of both types of obligations remained fairly constant during most of the period under review but increased moderately during the last two fiscal years, this increase coming at the same time as the renewal of fiscal borrowing by the Treasury.

When the government neutralizing factors (Treasury cash holdings and deposits of the government and autonomous agencies) are considered in conjunction with these expansionary factors, the conclusions reached with respect to the influence of changes in the money supply on price and income movements are essentially the same as those obtained in the preceding chapter in connection with the discussion of the influence of the government's surpluses and deficits on the national income.[2] In fact, the monetary analysis of the budget which is presented in this chapter is to a certain extent merely another way of looking at the national-income analysis of the last chapter. Each of the two approaches is, of course, relatively more useful for different purposes. The central bank authorities, for example, would probably find the money-supply approach of greater value in formulating policy, whereas government officials who are responsible for development policies would be more concerned with the analysis of national

[2] See pp. 210–14.

income series. However, until such time as the country develops a
system of making current estimates of the national product, the
use of money supply data to analyze the influence of fiscal operations on incomes and prices will be important in such policy decisions.

It does not seem necessary to repeat the findings of chapter ix
in detail. The basic conclusion, it will be recalled, was that
changes in government liabilities to the banking system and in
official deposits and cash holdings have acted as an accentuating
and mitigating rather than a primary causal factor in the Guatemalan price and income movements since 1937. Since the government surpluses and deficits influence these variables through the
medium of changes in the net means of payments, the same conclusion, of course, applies to the influence of budgetary operations on the monetary system.

Savings and the Government Bond Market

Although the absence of a fully developed government securities market did not materially affect the stability of the currency
during the period under review, there is no guaranty that continuous borrowing from the banking system may not do so in the
future. For this reason, we turn now to an examination of those
forces which have tended either to retard or further the development of a government bond market in Guatemala. In this analysis,
attention is directed particularly to the policies of the government
which were designed to foster savings habits and to create an interest in government securities among private individuals. Moreover, since private persons also save collectively through the
mediums of savings banks, life insurance companies, and the
Social Security Institute, the analysis also includes a discussion of
the government's role in fostering the development of these collective savings institutions.

At the present time, the general public holds none of the direct
fiscal debt of the national government but does own a moderate
amount of securities which have been guaranteed by the govern-

ment. As of the end of 1949, five such issues, with a total par value of 1,305.8 thousand quetzales were outstanding.[3] These consisted of Q2,100 of 3 percent mortgage bonds of 1929, Q924,400 of 5 percent mortgage bonds of 1946, and three series, totaling Q379,300, of 5 percent municipal public works bonds, which were issued in 1947 and 1949. Most of the early issue of mortgage bonds had already been retired, and the entire issue will be redeemed by 1953. All the other issues are for fifteen-year terms.

The limited acceptance of government securities by Guatemalan savers reflects the decided preference that they, like savers in other Latin-American countries, have normally shown for tangible investments and sending their funds abroad for safekeeping. This attitude is accounted for by three principal factors which can be counteracted by government action: (1) a deep-rooted fear of the effects of inflation, occasioned by the devalorization of fixed denomination savings in liquid form that occurred during the period of continuous government deficits beginning in 1899 and ending in 1924 during which the then existing gold peso depreciated to one-sixtieth of its former international value; (2) the higher yields which may be obtained from other forms of domestic investment, particularly during periods of rising prices;[4] and (3) the relative illiquidity of government securities which results from the underdeveloped state of the government bond market.

The government has taken steps to encourage investment in its securities by counteracting two of these factors; it has attempted to increase their liquidity by price-supporting operations in the open market and has acted to raise their effective rate of return by granting favorable tax treatment. The deficits of re-

---

[3] A portion of these securities are held by nonbank investors like the Social Security Institute and San Carlos University.

[4] If the changes in the price index of domestically produced construction materials are taken as an approximation of the capital gains which can be earned on real estate and if the wholesale price index is assumed to measure the opportunities for making inventory profits, the average annual rates of return on these two forms of investment since 1937 would have been 14.1 and 12.3 percent, respectively—figures that are highly favorable when compared with the 5 percent now being earned on government-guaranteed securities.

cent years appear to indicate, however, that the authorities have not as yet attacked the root of the trouble, namely, the fear of the danger of inflation.

The law establishing the Banco de Guatemala established the Fund for the Regulation of the Bond Market (Fondo de Regulación de Valores), whose policy is "directed toward the stabilization of the quotations on securities issued or guaranteed by the State or by public entities, and of such other official or semi-official obligations as may be decided upon by the Securities Commission."[5] Such stabilization is to be accomplished through the purchase and sale of securities in the open market, the funds for purchase consisting of the profits of the *fondo*, the profits of the Banco de Guatemala, and any budgetary appropriations or surpluses so assigned. At the present time, the fund is supporting the mortgage bonds of 1946 and the municipal public works bonds of 1947 and 1949 at prices slightly above par. This policy appears to have been moderately successful in encouraging public confidence in the securities, but inflationary pressures seem to have offset this progress to some extent. Limited purchases of bonds in the open market can, under conditions of price stability, significantly widen the market for government securities, but a rising price level tends to turn such a support program into an indirect method of selling the securities to the supporting agency.

The policy of increasing the effective return on government obligations through favorable tax treatment has so far apparently not been successful in stimulating interest in this form of investment. At the present time, the ownership, transfer, and income from all government and government-guaranteed securities are exempt from all existing taxes (even including the stamp tax) and all taxes that may be levied in the future.[6] But because of the absence of a tax on capital gains and the apparently sporadic enforcement of the tax on returns from capital, this tax inducement to the owners of government securities has not had much practical

[5] The Securities Commission (Comité de Valores) is composed of the president and manager of the Banco de Guatemala and the Ministers of Finance and Economy.
[6] Congressional Decree 450 of November 14, 1946.

significance. As tax administration is improved, and if and when the proposed income tax law is passed, the government's tax-exemption policy should prove more effective and create additional incentives to invest in government bonds.

The government has also played a major role in the development of collective savings institutions. With the exception of insurance companies, most of which are the agencies of foreign firms, all such institutions are at present directly sponsored by the government. They consist of the Savings Department of the National Mortgage Credit Institute, the Savings Section of INFOP, and the Social Security Institute. From the standpoint of creating savings habits, the work of the Savings Section of INFOP, which began operations in March 1949, is particularly important. This organization pays an interest rate of 3 percent and has established savings plans among school children and the employees of business firms. Considering the short period of time in which they have been in effect, these plans appear to have been quite successful. By the end of the first year of its existence (February 28, 1950), the Savings Section of INFOP had Q193,077 of savings deposits, or 13.7 percent of the country's total. Its most significant work in the savings field, however, must be considered to be of a long-run nature—i.e., the slow but important task of educating the population to the value of thrift.

THE BUDGET AND THE BALANCE OF PAYMENTS

As the preceding section indicated, the balance of payments rather than government financing has been the principal determinant of the Guatemalan money supply throughout most of the country's recent history. But fiscal operations also had, of course, an important influence on the money of external origin, and it is with this effect of the budget that the present section is concerned.[7]

[7] Obviously, the significance of the balance of payments extends beyond its purely monetary effects, since it is one of the principal determinants of the size and composition of national income and the rate of growth of the Guatemalan economy. But in order to simplify the exposition and avoid repetition, it has been considered preferable to discuss the balance of payments in connection with the monetary system.

The influence of the fiscal system on the balance of payments is twofold: (1) the government, through its expenditures abroad, is an important user of foreign exchange,[8] and (2) the size and composition of government receipts and domestic expenditures indirectly affect the level of exports and imports and may induce a capital outflow if the government borrows from the banking system.

The Government as a User of Foreign Exchange

The government's expenditures abroad in selected fiscal years since 1937/38 are shown in Table 62.[9] As may be seen, they consisted of external debt payments, purchases of imported merchandise, diplomatic and consular expenditures, and other payments for such miscellaneous purposes as students' scholarships and contributions to international agencies. Foreign expenditures have ranged from 6 to 19 percent of total government expenditures and have been relatively less important since 1946/47 than they were in earlier years. It is apparent that the major explanation of this decline is the heavy payments for the retirement of the external debt which were made in 1937/38, and again in 1944/45. If these two years are disregarded and the last two years are compared with 1942/43, when the external debt payments consisted almost entirely of normal interest and amortization charges, it is clear that government expenditures abroad for purposes other than debt service have increased to approximately the same extent as the debt service has declined.

The largest part of the increase in these other expenditures was due to an expansion of purchases of imported merchandise. Diplomatic and consular expenditures have, as might be expected, grown to a lesser extent than total government expenditures, and other payments abroad have exhibited no definite trend. The

[8] The government, through its ownership of the nationalized farms, is also an important foreign-exchange earner, but since these operations are not fiscal in the strict sense of the word, they are not considered in the discussion.

[9] Government expenditures abroad are measured by its foreign payments from domestic accounts. Changes in the Treasury's balances abroad are effected through the domestic banking system and therefore reflected in the government's purchases and sales of foreign exchange to domestic banks.

TABLE 62

RELATION OF GOVERNMENT EXPENDITURES ABROAD AND TOTAL GOVERNMENT EXPENDITURES IN SELECTED YEARS

(In thousands of quetzales)

Fiscal Year	Purchases of Imported Merchandise	Diplomatic and Consular Expenditures	External Debt Payments	Other Expenditures Abroad	Total Government Expenditures Abroad[a]	Total Government Expenditures[b]	Expenditures Abroad as a Percent of Total Government Expenditures
1937/38	307.2	213.8	1,398.3	173.4	2,092.7	10,979.0	19.1
1942/43	596.1	244.7	569.8	133.0	1,546.3	12,766.4	12.1
1944/45	401.4	167.2	2,678.8	75.7	3,323.1	22,944.1	14.5
1946/47	868.1	783.1	160.0	398.2	2,209.4	36,226.6	6.1
1947/48	1,103.5	1,001.5	120.0	272.8	5,497.8	46,759.5	11.8
1948/49	4,846.4	771.8	.....	202.2	5,820.4	47,403.4	12.3

[a] Foreign payments from domestic accounts.
[b] Budgetary expenditures, including interest and amortization payments.

increase in imports has been associated with the government's expanded investment program, and if the government continues to follow its announced policy of fostering economic development, it would seem that changes in government commodity imports will, for all intents and purposes, be the only important factor determining the direct influence of the government on the balance of payments.

Table 63 presents the ratio of real government imports to total real government expenditures in the years since 1936/37. Purchases of imports, it will be noted, averaged about 3.5 percent of government expenditures in the prewar and early war years and then declined to an average of about 2 percent in the late war and early postwar years, reflecting the scarcities of this period. In 1947/48 and 1948/49, they rose to a new plateau and averaged 9.5 percent of total expenditures, measured in real terms. This growth reflects the expansion of government investment activities connected with the increasing proportion of government expenditures going to schools, hospitals, and economic development. The government also obtains imported goods through private importers, but all except a small proportion of these purchases appears to be included in the foreign expenditure accounts of the government.

In order to determine the net effect of the increase in government expenditures which has taken place in recent years on the propensity of Guatemala to import, it is also necessary to take account of the ratio of real private imports to the real gross product of the private sector. These data are also presented in Table 63. A trend similar to that found in the case of the government is evident. A decline in the war and early postwar years, as compared with the prewar period, was followed by an expansion in the more recent years. In this case, however, the 1947/48 ratio, although still substantially higher than that in the government sector, appears to be about the same (20 percent) as in the prewar years, and it appears that in Guatemala, unlike many other countries with a similar economic structure, an expansion in real national income does not induce a more than proportionate increase

TABLE 63

RELATION OF GROSS PRIVATE PRODUCT, GOVERNMENT EXPENDITURES, AND IMPORTS, IN REAL TERMS

(In thousands of quetzales; at 1937/38 prices)

Fiscal Year	Government Sector			Private Sector		
	Real[a] Government Expenditures	Real Government Imports	Real Government Imports as a Percent of Real Government Expenditures	Real Gross Product of Private Sector (In millions)	Real Private Imports[b]	Real Private Imports as a Percent of Real Private Product
1937/38	10,099.0	307.2	3.0	101.8	20,633.0	20.3
1938/39	11,228.9	432.4	3.9	107.2	20,287.1	18.9
1939/40	10,417.5	420.7	4.0	118.2	17,108.6	14.5
1940/41	10,622.2	429.5	4.0	126.8	14,590.5	11.5
1941/42	9,825.5	406.1	4.1	132.2	11,825.1	8.9
1942/43	11,410.7	422.2	3.7	145.0	10,739.7	7.4
1943/44	12,873.0	321.6	2.5	*	11,754.3	....
1944/45	12,344.1	235.8	1.9	....	12,705.2	....
1945/46	19,254.4	338.0	1.8	131.9	18,031.0	13.7
1946/47	20,817.0	514.0	2.5	....	27,171.9	....
1947/48	25,107.4	2,176.4	8.7	155.4	31,121.4	20.0
1948/49	24,749.4[c]	2,554.8	10.3	....	33,906.4	....

[a] Cash expenditures, excluding transfer of assigned revenues and interest and amortization payments.
[b] Deflated by import price index. Data are actual for years shown in Table 62 and interpolated for other years.
[c] Index of unit cost of government in 1948/49 estimated at 190, as compared with 185.8 in 1947/48.
* Not available.

in imports. Two important factors help to explain this difference. In the first place, imports during 1937/38 and 1938/39 were abnormally large because of the commencement of large-scale operations at the United Fruit Company's Pacific coast installations. Second, a significant part of the increase in real income is explained by a growth in the indigenous population, among whom the demand for imported goods is limited.

For this reason, we turn now to an investigation of the relationship between commercial sector income and private imports. As Table 64 clearly indicates, imports in this case have expanded more than income, the index of the ratio of money imports to money commercial-sector income having risen from 100 to 109 between 1937/38 and 1948/49. Moreover, since a complete income series is available for the commercial sector, it is now possible to appraise the influence of the war and postwar scarcities on the volume of private imports. In 1946/47, the index was at 110, presumably because of the backlog of deferred demand; it declined to 104.4 in the following year and then rose again as the result of the increase in the value of exports and income.

In order to obtain a valid comparison, a similar index in money terms is presented for government imports. As would be expected from the previous analysis, the index of the ratio of government imports to total government expenditures is much higher in the last two years than the corresponding private index. Moreover, a comparison of the rates of increase of the two indexes since the end of the war indicates that the marginal propensity of the government to import is at present significantly higher than that of the private sector. Although the statistical evidence is not absolutely conclusive, it suggests that, to the extent to which taxation curtails consumption of imported goods, additional government purchases abroad offset the curtailment of private imports by a considerable margin and thus result in a higher total volume of imports.[10]

[10] Notwithstanding the fact that the average propensity of the private sector to import is still substantially higher than that of the government. It is, of course, the net change in imports associated with increases or decreases of income in the two sectors which is important.

TABLE 64

RELATION OF GROSS COMMERCIAL PRODUCT, GOVERNMENT EXPENDITURES,[a] AND IMPORTS

(1937/38 = 100)

Fiscal Year	Index of Gross Product of Commercial Sector	Index of Private Imports	Ratio of Index of Private Imports to Index of Commercial Product	Index of Total Government Expenditures	Index of Government Imports	Ratio of Index of Government Imports to Index of Total Expenditures
1937/38	100.0	100.0	100.0	100.0	100.0	100.0
1938/39	89.1	95.1	106.7	105.9	136.1	128.5
1939/40	79.8	82.7	103.6	96.6	136.5	141.3
1940/41	77.8	75.2	96.6	99.0	148.6	150.1
1941/42	88.2	69.7	79.0	103.2	160.9	155.9
1942/43	99.8	73.5	73.6	122.3	194.0	158.6
1943/44	107.0	90.8	84.9	143.4	166.9	116.4
1944/45	127.3	104.8	82.3	163.4	130.7	80.0
1945/46	146.3	141.7	96.9	285.2	178.4	62.6
1946/47	202.2	222.4	110.0	357.4	282.6	79.1
1947/48	272.6	284.6	104.4	461.9	1,335.8	289.2
1948/49	(284)[b]	311.7	(109)	465.6	1,577.6	338.8

[a] Cash expenditures, excluding transfer of assigned revenues and interest and amortization payments.
[b] Estimate.

Indirect Effects of the Budget on the Balance of Payments

The sources of the government's receipts and the composition of its domestic expenditures also influence the movements of Guatemala's international accounts. Unfortunately, however, most of the indirect effects of the budget on the balance of payments are not statistically measurable and are touched upon only briefly in this study.

Fiscal operations may influence the volume of Guatemala's exports in two ways. In the first place, the taxes levied on export industries are cost-increasing and may thus at times impede their ability to compete effectively in the world market. Second, budgetary deficits and surpluses, through their inflationary or deflationary effects on the prices, also influence the costs of export industries and affect the relative profitability of investment in the export and domestic sectors of the economy.[11]

In most instances, these influences have had little significance in Guatemala during the period under review. The cash surpluses of the late 'thirties were undoubtedly of some benefit to coffee producers during that period of a relatively unfavorable cost-price relationship for coffee; but since the beginning of the war, the cost-price structure of the coffee industry has improved so greatly that neither the deficits of the last two or three years nor the coffee export tax has tended to divert resources from the coffee sector. In fact, it may be argued that the export tax has probably been of some positive benefit to the country's balance of payments, for coffee producers and exporters have been forced to return a larger share of their profits to Guatemala.

Budgetary operations have also been neutral in the case of banana exports, but the same conclusion cannot be reached with respect to chicle. Although the withdrawal of the two American companies from production in 1949 was primarily the result of the advent of competition of synthetic product and of large inventories in the United States, the chicle exploitation and export taxes

[11] In view of the specialized nature of Guatemalan export production, price movements do not cause any significant diversion of sales between the export and home markets.

probably had some influence on their decision to curtail operations in Guatemala.

The indirect effects of the budget on the level of imports have also been relatively mild. As has been indicated earlier, cash surpluses and deficits have acted as a mitigating or accentuating rather than a primary causal factor in the country's money income and price movements since the late 'thirties. As a consequence, changes in the demand for imports have been associated with government credit operations and movements in Treasury balances to only a limited extent, although some capital outflow may, of course, have been induced by government borrowing from the banking system.

Because of the composition of Guatemalan tax receipts, the decline in private income resulting from tax collections has caused a relatively large decrease in the private demand for imports. The high proportion of import duties on consumers' goods (21.2 percent in 1948/49)[12] has meant that more than one-fifth of all taxes has been withdrawn from households and income groups which are direct consumers of imported products. It is not likely, moreover, that the price increases which have resulted from the shifting of most other taxes have caused more than a moderate substitution of foreign for domestic goods, for the most heavily taxed products, cigarettes and alcoholic beverages, are adequately protected by import duties.

In both the immediate future and the long run, the primary impact of fiscal operations on Guatemala's international accounts will probably take place through the government's economic development program. The higher incomes which are likely to result from government investment expenditures are bound to lead to an expansion of imports, over and above the increase that is due to the government's direct expenditure of foreign exchange. An estimate of the magnitude of these investment-induced balance-of-payments pressures and a discussion of various methods of relieving them are included in the following chapter, which considers the fiscal system and economic development.

[12] See Table 60.

XI

THE FISCAL SYSTEM AND ECONOMIC DEVELOPMENT

THROUGHOUT the entire text of this study, the impact of the fiscal system upon the rate of capital formation[1] has intermittently held our attention. This is only natural, since there is hardly any aspect of the tax structure that does not directly or indirectly, through its impact on the level and composition of consumption and the rate of savings, affect the rate of private investment. The level and the direction of government expenditures likewise are important determinants of the pace and the composition of private investment activities. Moreover, a certain proportion of government expenditures itself represents capital formation, because the additions to the existing plant of public highways, hospitals, schools, and government buildings obviously form part of the process of capital formation.

There are two reasons, however, that make it appear desirable to devote a separate chapter to the problem of economic development—capital formation in the broadest meaning of the term—and the role which the govermnent, through the fiscal system and nonfiscal activities, has played, and intends to play in the future, as an active force influencing the rate and guiding the direction of economic development. One reason is the obvious need to present a quantitative appraisal of the capital formation experience of recent years. The second is the desirability of discussing the prospects of economic development, through both public and private initiative, and how they are affected by the fiscal system. This discussion also presents an opportunity to comment on problems closely related to the central theme of economic development,

---

[1] The term "capital formation" pertains, of course, to the creation of real capital, such as houses, plants, machines, etc., not to the accumulation of capital funds by business firms, private individuals, or the government.

such as the effects of *fomento* on the balance of payments and the role of foreign capital in the growth of the Guatemalan economy.

PRIVATE AND PUBLIC CAPITAL FORMATION

One of the major difficulties besetting any analysis of capital formation and the level and rate of economic development is the scarcity of data that prevails in this field in almost every country; Guatemala, unfortunately, is no exception. If, nevertheless, some data on public and private capital formation in Guatemala are presented here, it must be kept in mind that they are little more than estimates of the order of magnitude of the true quantities. It is believed, however, that they reflect quite accurately the year-to-year movements of the magnitudes involved.

The Volume and Composition of Capital Formation

Estimates of the total capital formation in Guatemala in the years 1937/38 to 1948/49 are shown in Table 65. The figures on private capital creation are based on the value of private construction and on the value of capital goods imports; their deriva-

TABLE 65

ESTIMATES OF TOTAL CAPITAL FORMATION, 1937/38 TO 1948/49

(In thousands of quetzales)

Fiscal Year	Private Capital Formation	Government Capital Formation	Total Capital Formation	As Percent of Total Capital Formation	
				Private Capital Formation	Government Capital Formation
1937/38	4,620	1,214	5,834	79.2	20.8
1938/39	4,280	944	5,224	81.9	18.1
1939/40	3,880	1,213	5,093	76.2	23.8
1940/41	4,780	1,529	6,309	75.8	24.2
1941/42	3,610	1,731	5,341	67.6	32.4
1942/43	3,200	2,448	5,648	56.7	43.3
1943/44	4,240	1,642	5,882	72.1	27.9
1944/45	7,300	3,055	10,355	70.5	29.5
1945/46	12,260	4,918	17,178	71.4	28.6
1946/47	14,860	5,469	20,329	73.1	26.9
1947/48	17,800	16,522	34,322	51.9	48.1
1948/49[a]	(18,500)	(17,000)	(35,500)	52.1	47.9

[a] Preliminary estimates.

tion is explained in the Statistical Note appended to this chapter. The data on government capital formation were specially compiled for this study by the research staff of the Banco de Guatemala from government expenditures records. They consist of outlays for public construction; repair and maintenance expenditures were excluded.[2]

The figures show that, with the exception of one year, private investment accounted for two-thirds or more of total capital formation until 1946/47. In 1947/48 and 1948/49, however, when both private and public investment rose to record levels, government investment came close to accounting for one-half of total capital formation. If the effects of price changes which occurred in the period under consideration are eliminated in order to arrive at the composition of the real volume of investment, the share of private investment increases somewhat. In Table 66 the amounts of investment expenditures have been deflated by the price indexes of construction materials and imports of manufactured goods in the case of private investments, and by the construction materials index in the case of government investment.[3] The resulting estimates of real capital investment show that as a consequence of the sharp price increases in the cost of construction, compared with the increase in machinery prices, the real share of the government in total capital formation was appreciably smaller than its money share. Conversely, the data seem to indicate that, given the amount of total investment, it would have been preferable from the point of view of the economy as a whole if private

[2] It should be noted that in most years they differ considerably from the figures shown for economic development expenditures in chapters iv and ix. The differences are due to the restricted definition of capital formation applied here and to the different purposes of the two classifications. School construction, for instance, is shown under social and cultural expenditures in Table 25 (p. 78) as well as in investment expenditures in Table 65. Road repair outlays, on the other hand, are considered as economic development expenditures in Table 25 but do not appear in the investment figures.

[3] Private investment consisted of construction and machinery imports in proportions that varied considerably from year to year. (See Table 73 in the appended Statistical Note.) Government investment included relatively insignificant amounts of machinery, although the share of imported construction materials in total expenditures was quite large, particularly in the later years. But the price rise of imported construction materials is covered by the construction cost index.

investments had been larger and the volume of government investments correspondingly smaller. But since the volume of government investment probably had a stimulating rather than a negative effect upon the volume of private investment, it does not follow that a smaller volume of government investment would have resulted in a larger volume of more economical private investment. It seems certain, however, that the large combined volume of construction activities of 20 million to 24 million quetzales in the last two years was one of the reasons for the sharp increase in the cost of construction, the other being the scarcity and slow delivery of imported construction materials.

TABLE 66

ESTIMATES OF REAL CAPITAL FORMATION, 1937/38 TO 1948/49

(In thousands of quetzales at 1937/38 prices)

Fiscal Year	Private Capital Formation	Government Capital Formation	Total Capital Formation	As Percent of Total Capital Formation	
				Private Capital Formation	Government Capital Formation
1937/38	4,620	1,214	5,834	79.2	20.8
1938/39	4,340	955	5,295	82.0	18.0
1939/40	3,870	1,231	5,101	75.9	24.1
1940/41	4,640	1,552	6,192	74.9	25.1
1941/42	3,340	1,620	4,900	67.3	32.7
1942/43	2,500	1,940	4,440	56.3	43.7
1943/44	3,390	1,098	4,488	75.5	24.5
1944/45	4,140	1,728	5,868	70.6	29.4
1945/46	6,250	2,251	8,501	73.5	26.5
1946/47	7,590	2,156	9,746	77.9	22.1
1947/48	8,330	6,311	14,641	56.8	43.2
1948/49[a]	(8,500)	(6,500)	(15,000)	56.7	43.3

[a] Preliminary estimates.

The Rate of Capital Formation

There are two ways in which the significance of the annual amounts of capital formation can be appraised. One is to relate the amount of capital formation to the amount of capital in existence, thus obtaining a measure of the rate at which capital grows. Needless to say, the application of this conceptually simple measure is in practice almost always impeded by the difficulties of appraising the value of capital in existence. Therefore, it is necessary to rely upon the second method of measurement, which relates the volume of capital formation to the level of the gross national product. Table 67 shows this relationship as it obtained in

TABLE 67

RATE OF CAPITAL FORMATION, 1937/38 TO 1947/48

Fiscal Year	As Percent of Gross National Product			As Percent of Real Gross National Product		
	Private Capital Formation	Government Capital Formation	Total Capital Formation	Real Private Capital Formation	Real Government Capital Formation	Real Total Capital Formation
1937/38	4.1	1.1	5.1	4.1	1.1	5.1
1938/39	4.3	1.0	5.3	3.5	0.8	4.3
1939/40	3.4	1.1	4.5	2.9	0.9	3.9
1940/41	4.2	1.3	5.5	3.3	1.1	4.4
1941/42	2.7	1.3	4.0	2.3	1.1	3.4
1942/43	1.8	1.4	3.2	1.6	1.2	2.8
1943/44	...*	...	...	...	...	...
1944/45	...	...	...	...	...	...
1945/46	5.1	2.1	7.2	4.1	1.5	5.6
1946/47	...	...	...	...	...	...
1947/48	5.3	4.9	10.2	4.6	3.5	8.0

* Not available.

Guatemala between 1937/38 and 1948/49. In the prewar years, when a considerable proportion of private capital formation was accounted for by imports of machinery and capital equipment financed by an inflow of foreign capital,[4] total capital formation amounted, on the average, to 5 percent of the gross national product. Unavailability of foreign capital equipment and construction materials caused a decline of capital formation in the war years. Thereafter a rigorous expansion took place, first in the private sector which apparently attempted to make up the depletion of equipment and the small volume of construction of the war years, and then from 1946/47 onward in the government sector. In 1947/48 total capital formation exceeded 10 percent of the gross national product in money terms. Although no national income

[4] The United Fruit Company expanded its plantation operations on the Pacific Coast during this period.

data for 1948/49 are available, the level of private and government investment expenditures suggests that this rate was well maintained in that year. It should be noted, however, that a portion of this increase is again accounted for by the fact that increases in investment costs exceeded the rise in the general price level. As a result, the share of capital formation in the gross national product in real terms reached only 8 percent.

It need hardly be emphasized that a high rate of capital formation is not only a sign of the economic vitality of any country, but, in the case of Guatemala as in that of all other less developed countries, it is also one of the basic prerequisites for a rise in the standard of living and economic well-being; another equally important precondition is a rise in the productivity of human effort, achieved through better training, better supervision, and an improved diet without the application of additional capital in the usual sense of the term. Therefore, economic and fiscal measures designed to foster and maintain a high rate of capital formation must form an essential part of government policy. But since the country's natural and human resources set definite limits to the share of real production that can be spared from consumption and the preservation of existing human and capital resources, a concentration upon the most desirable forms of investment becomes of paramount importance.

The Productivity of Investment

Whether a particular form of investment is considered more desirable than another is a question that in certain respects is decided by the price mechanism of the economy which rewards the successful investment with high profits and penalizes the unsuccessful one with financial failure. In the case of government investment, with respect to which the market mechanism is largely inoperative,[5] the process of deliberate selection through budget appropriations and, in the specific case of Guatemala, through

[5] Unless excessive unit costs deter some types of public investment and favor others.

the control processes of public bids and the approval of specific expenditures through the *acuerdos de erogación* takes the place of the price and profit system. But from the point of view of the rate of economic development itself, an additional criterion must be considered, namely, the contribution that each unit of capital formation makes to the country's productive resources as distinct from less productive or unproductive forms of capital accumulation.

The distinction between productive and less productive or unproductive investment necessarily must be somewhat arbitrary, since the objective of all capital investment is the increased production of goods and services. The distinction is usually based, at least in part, on social value judgments. But the influence of social (or political) value judgments can be kept to a minimum, if the criterion of the *direct* effect of the various types of investment on the level of production and the productivity of the economy is applied. Thus, private investment may be considered to be directly productive if it adds to the sum total of the means of organized production, i.e., to real business capital; by the same token, government investment is directly productive if it enhances directly the productivity of private business capital. In other words, investment in plant, machinery, tools, storage facilities, sales outlets, etc.,[6] are considered directly productive, whereas residential housing, whether for the owner's own consumption or for rental purposes, is unproductive or, at least, less productive.

In the case of government investment, the distinction is less clear, since the government's investment activities aim not only at the creation of more productive capital, but also at the increase of social and cultural service capital, such as hospitals, schools, and libraries. In a certain sense, all these forms of government investment are productive. The "product" of hospitals is improved health; the "output" of schools, better education—"products" that in turn affect the efficiency and productivity of the economy.

[6] In United States national income and investment statistics, productive investment is usually subsumed under the headings of nonresidential construction and capital equipment.

But in the case of other government investment, such as the construction of the Olympic Stadium,[7] the connection between investment expenditures and increased productivity of the economy is more remote. It therefore seems permissible to consider as directly productive investment only such outlays as those for highways, bridges, and certain other construction, and to consider investment expenditures for social and cultural development and national defense as indirectly productive.[8] In order to obtain an estimate of the net directly productive capital formation of the business sector, it has been assumed, on the basis of information that appears to be reliable, that 20 percent of total construction is nonresidential and that one-fourth of private machinery imports represents replacement of obsolete and worn-out equipment.

In Table 69, the time series of directly productive capital formation, thus derived, is compared with total private capital formation. The figures indicate that in the period under consideration only one-third to one-half of total private capital formation is accounted for by productive investment. Only in the first two years was the share of productive in total investment larger than 50 percent. As indicated above, this was due to the high volume of capital-goods imports by the United Fruit Company. Large capital goods imports likewise account for the high incidence of productive private investment in the postwar years, but in view of the cumulative depreciation in the war years the replacement-ratio of four to one may be too low for this period. The increases in construction cost in excess of the rise of machinery prices is again responsible for the larger share of directly

---

[7] Only a small part of the expenditures incurred in connection with the construction of the Olympic Stadium is included in figures on government expenditures shown in this study, since the construction was not completed until 1950. According to data provided by the superintendent of the stadium, total expenditures amounted to 4.7 million quetzales, of which 1.6 million were disbursed during 1948/49.

[8] A breakdown of government investment expenditures is shown in Table 68. The distinction between directly and indirectly productive capital expenditures is of course somewhat artificial; a more or less arbitrary decision has to be made in order to draw a line between the two types of expenditures. Actually, a complete range of various degrees of productivity of government expenditures exists, descending from, say, agricultural machinery purchases of INFOP (see pp. 263–68) to expenditures for parks and statues.

TABLE 68

GOVERNMENT INVESTMENT EXPENDITURES, BY PURPOSE, 1937/38 TO 1947/48

(In thousands of quetzales)

Fiscal Year	Total Government Investment Expenditures		Economic Development Investment		Social and Cultural Development Expenditures		Capital Expenditures for National Defense	
	In Q1,000	In Percent of Total	In Q1,000	In Percent of Total	In Q1,000	In Percent of Total	In Q1,000	In Percent of Total
1937/38	1,214	100.0	1,046	86.2	168	13.8		
1938/39	944	100.0	944	100.0				
1939/40	1,213	100.0	1,213	100.0				
1940/41	1,520	100.0	1,413	92.4	116	7.6		
1941/42	1,731	100.0	1,561	90.2	170	9.8		
1942/43	2,448	100.0	2,272	92.9	175	7.1		
1943/44	1,642	100.0	1,557	94.8	85	5.2		
1944/45	3,055	100.0	2,868	93.9	188	6.1		
1945/46	4,919	100.0	3,451	70.1	1,467	29.9		
1946/47	5,469	100.0	3,561	65.1	1,527	27.9	381	7.0
1947/48	16,522	100.0	11,614	70.3	4,607	27.9	300	1.8
1948/49	(17,000)	100.0	...*		...		...	

* Not available.

TABLE 69

Net Directly Productive and Total Private Capital Formation, 1937/38 to 1948/49

(In thousands of quetzales)

Fiscal Year	Private Capital Formation			Real Private Capital Formation		
	Total	Net Directly Productive Only	Net Directly Productive as Percent of Total	Total	Net Directly Productive Only	Net Directly Productive as Percent of Total
1937/38	4,620	2,370	51.3	4,620	2,370	51.3
1938/39	4,280	2,220	51.9	4,340	2,250	51.8
1939/40	3,880	1,880	48.4	3,870	1,850	47.8
1940/41	4,780	2,200	46.0	4,640	2,130	45.9
1941/42	3,610	1,220	33.7	3,340	1,060	31.3
1942/43	3,200	1,040	32.5	2,500	790	31.8
1943/44	4,240	1,480	34.9	3,390	940	27.7
1944/45	7,300	2,730	37.3	4,140	1,550	37.4
1945/46	12,260	4,760	38.8	6,250	2,660	42.5
1946/47	14,860	6,880	46.3	7,590	3,760	49.5
1947/48	17,800	8,730	49.0	8,330	4,460	53.5
1948/49[a]	(18,500)	(9,200)	49.7	(8,500)	(4,500)	52.9

[a] Crude preliminary estimate.

productive in total private capital in real terms, i.e., if the effects of price increases are eliminated.[9]

Combining now directly productive government and private investment (Tables 70 and 71), we find that, with the exception of 1946/47, the share of productive government investment in total productive capital formation has been higher in recent years than before the war although as a result of the above-cited adverse price condition, the increase was somewhat less pronounced in real terms.

If unproductive and indirectly productive investment is excluded from the estimates of capital formation, the rate of investment in 1947/48 amounted to 6.1 percent in money terms and 4.9 percent in real terms, compared with an average level of 2.5 percent in earlier years. Although the government has continued in the last two years to make large investment expenditures, it is by no means certain whether the 1947/48 rate can be maintained. Even if the government should succeed in maintaining a large volume of investment expenditures and devote a large share of this total to directly productive purposes, an objective appraisal of present conditions must take into account that during 1947/48 the level of capital equipment imports, which make up the bulk of private productive capital formation, was unusually high and that it is therefore unlikely that it will be maintained—even if the rate of total private capital formation remains high.

This conclusion leads directly to the question how far government fiscal and monetary policy can, and should, exert an influence over the rate of private productive capital formation. This problem will be commented on in the next section.

The low rate of net productive capital formation in the course of the last decade, relative to the level of the gross national product and to the capital formation experience of other countries[10] in recent years, is, of course, a direct reflection of the low per

[9] See the last three columns in Table 69.

[10] The comparable rates for the United States in the last four years (1946 to 1949) were: 8.4 percent; 10.0 percent; 10.8 percent; and 10.7 percent. Comparable data for other countries are not available. But the high rate of gross capital formation

capita income of Guatemala. But it also calls attention to one important fact frequently overlooked in discussions of economic development in Guatemala and elsewhere: although the rate of capital formation is small, the per capita income in real terms has risen (see chapter ii, Table 5) by an average of 2 percent per year in the course of the last twelve years. This strongly suggests that capital formation, though of great importance as a determinant of the rate of material progress, is only one of the factors governing the rhythm of the country's growth, the other—and equally important one—being the increase in real productivity, which apparently has been enhanced not only through more favorable terms of trade but also through gradual improvements in the techniques of production, particularly in agriculture.

THE FISCAL SYSTEM AND PRIVATE CAPITAL FORMATION

The impact of the fiscal system upon private capital formation has been commented upon in earlier sections of this study, particularly in chapter v; thus little need be added here. Since statistical and institutional evidence suggests that only a small portion of the total tax burden is borne by business and since the progression of the incidence of taxation on income derived from business ventures is very mild indeed, it has been concluded that probably not more than 10 percent of total taxes come out of savings, i.e., would be saved in the absence of taxation. Therefore, it seems certain that the accumulation of business capital is affected hardly at all by the tax structure. To the extent, however, to which taxation curtails consumption, it affects business opportunities by restricting the markets of new as well as old business firms.

The absence of any taxation on capital gains, which would seem to offer a positive incentive to investment in risky business ventures (the financial success of which is rewarded by capital

in most European countries suggests that the postwar rate of productive capital formation there was at least as high as in the United States. It is likely, however, that the rate of productive capital formation in most other Latin-American countries is of the same general order of magnitude as that of Guatemala, if not somewhat lower.

TABLE 70

VOLUME AND RATE OF DIRECTLY PRODUCTIVE CAPITAL FORMATION, 1937/38 TO 1947/48

(Actual values)

Fiscal Year	Directly Productive Capital Formation						Directly Productive Capital Formation as Percent of Gross National Product		
	Total		Net Private		Government Economic Development Investment		Total	Net Private	Government Economic Development Investment
	In Q1,000	In Percent of Total	In Q1,000	In Percent of Total	In Q1,000	In Percent of Total			
1937/38	3,416	100.0	2,370	69.3	1,046	30.7	3.0	2.1	0.9
1938/39	3,164	100.0	2,220	70.2	944	29.8	3.2	2.2	1.0
1939/40	3,093	100.0	1,880	60.8	1,213	39.2	2.7	1.7	1.1
1940/41	3,613	100.0	2,200	60.9	1,413	39.1	3.1	1.9	1.2
1941/42	2,781	100.0	1,220	43.9	1,561	56.1	2.1	0.9	1.2
1942/43	3,311	100.0	1,040	31.4	2,271	68.6	1.9	0.6	1.3
1943/44	3,037	100.0	1,480	48.7	1,557	51.3	...*	...	...
1944/45	5,598	100.0	2,730	48.7	2,868	51.3	3.4	2.0	1.4
1945/46	8,211	100.0	4,760	57.9	3,451	42.1	...	...	...
1946/47	10,441	100.0	6,880	65.9	3,561	34.1	...	...	3.5
1947/48	20,344	100.0	8,730	42.9	11,614	57.1	6.1	2.6	3.5

* Not available.

TABLE 71

REAL VOLUME AND RATE OF DIRECTLY PRODUCTIVE CAPITAL FORMATION, 1937/38 TO 1947/48

(*At 1937/38 prices*)

Fiscal Year	Real Directly Productive Capital Formation						Real Directly Productive Capital Formation as Percent of Real Gross National Product		
	Total		Net Private		Government Economic Development Investment		Total	Net Private	Government Economic Development Investment
	In Q1,000	In Percent of Total	In Q1,000	In Percent of Total	In Q1,000	In Percent of Total			
1937/38	3,416	100.0	2,370	69.4	1,046	30.4	3.0	2.1	0.9
1938/39	3,205	100.0	2,250	70.2	955	29.8	2.6	1.8	0.8
1939/40	3,081	100.0	1,850	60.0	1,231	40.0	2.3	1.4	0.9
1940/41	3,564	100.0	2,130	59.7	1,434	40.3	2.5	1.5	1.0
1941/42	2,521	100.0	1,060	42.0	1,461	58.0	1.7	0.7	1.0
1942/43	2,589	100.0	790	30.5	1,799	69.5	1.6	0.5	1.1
1943/44	1,981	100.0	940	47.4	1,041	52.6	...*	...	...
1944/45	3,172	100.0	1,550	49.0	1,622	51.1	...	...	...
1945/46	4,239	100.0	2,660	62.9	1,579	37.1	2.8	1.8	1.0
1946/47	5,164	100.0	3,760	72.8	1,404	27.2	...	...	...
1947/48	8,896	100.0	4,460	50.1	4,436	49.9	4.9	2.4	2.4

* Not available.

gains), does not appear to have had the same effect. Its primary result appears to have been a concentration of investment activities in quite riskless residential construction and not in business ventures along untried lines.

Incentive to business investment is provided by the industrial development law, which offers tax exemptions to firms that avail themselves of the privileges that the Ministry of Economy is authorized to grant to them.[11] The relatively small number of enterprises that have made use of these provisions and the relative insignificance of these enterprises in the structure of the Guatemalan economy suggest, however, that other factors determining the rate and direction of private capital formation are more important than the burden of taxes or the relief therefrom. Investments in coffee plantations, in commercial ventures, particularly in the import trade, and, as indicated before, in residential real estate, continue to be the preferred and—so far as can be judged on the basis of largely nonquantitative circumstantial evidence—the most profitable outlets of private investment.

As indicated in the preceding section, the rate of economic development in Guatemala is adversely affected by the high proportion of capital formation that is absorbed by less productive and nonproductive forms of investment. The large volume of residential building—a substantial portion of which, incidentally, is not rental property but is used by the owner—is the main cause of this phenomenon, but the slow rate of growth of productive capital in the form of mechanical equipment is undoubtedly also the result of the low wage rates which prevail in many sectors of the economy and make the employment of additional capital equipment uneconomical from the point of view of the individual entrepreneur; in part it is also due to the limited availability of technical training and skill that make the use of complicated machinery and equipment expensive and in a technical sense risky. To what extent can these elements of retardation (which Guatemala has in common with many other underdeveloped coun-

[11] See chapter v.

tries in the Western Hemisphere and elsewhere) be remedied through the fiscal system?

Two lines of action suggest themselves. On the revenue side, it appears that the taxation of capital gains in unproductive real estate could conceivably be used as a partial deterrent to the high rate of residential construction of the type of housing that does not enhance the mobility of labor and does not constitute an improvement of social and living conditions of the broad masses of the urban and rural population. One of the results of the taxation of capital gains in real estate would be a reduction of the competition for building materials that occasionally are diverted from essential to less essential uses in the course of intermittent building booms. Moreover, the greater use of capital equipment in manufacturing as well as in agriculture could be fostered by granting more generous depreciation allowances for such equipment.[12]

On the expenditures side, the wider use of capital equipment could be facilitated by broadening the scope of technical training for mechanics, machine operators, etc., through the school system. The establishment of mechanization centers by the Production Development Institute[13] is obviously of significance in this connection.

ECONOMIC DEVELOPMENT THROUGH GOVERNMENT INSTITUTIONS: THE PRODUCTION DEVELOPMENT INSTITUTE

The limited scope of private initiative outside the customary investment channels was one of the main reasons for the establishment of the Instituto de Fomento de la Producción (Production Development Institute), which was created by Act of Congress on July 29, 1948, and began operations in 1949. The INFOP was

---

[12] An earlier draft of the income tax law accorded specially favorable tax treatment to business profits reinvested in fixed (as distinct from working) capital. Under existing legislation, the absence of business profits taxation on nonincorporated agricultural enterprises would make the direct introduction of large depreciation allowances in agriculture impossible. But in certain cases, these allowances could take the form of partial refunds of other taxes (e.g., of the coffee export tax).

[13] See the next section.

established with an initial capital of 6.5 million quetzales, 1.5 million of which represented the revaluation profit of the gold holdings of the Banco de Guatemala, realized at the time of the establishment of the bank in 1947; 5 million quetzales were paid to the *instituto* in the form of Treasury letters. By the end of 1949, the institute had sold bonds in the amount of 2.5 million quetzales to the Banco de Guatemala. The capital of the institute was further increased by the acquisition, through transfer of ownership, of two national farms. The INFOP law also provides that in the absence of a securities market where the institute could sell its own bonds, the government will raise the capital of the institute by annual appropriations of from 2 to 6 percent of the budget receipts of the Treasury. The 1949/50 budget provides Q650,000 for this purpose. By the end of May 1950, however, the institute had received only two monthly installments of the appropriated funds.

The institute is organized in three departments: (1) the Agricultural and Industrial Credit Department, (2) the Development Department, and (3) the Housing Department. In accordance with the provisions of the law establishing the institute, a basic plan was prepared that defined the objectives of the institute's activities in 1949 as follows: (a) to increase the production of essential foodstuffs in order to combat the high cost of living, (b) to introduce modern techniques in existing industries in order to bring down production costs, (c) to expand promising export industries and to create new ones, (d) to reduce the volume of certain classes of imports which can be economically replaced by national production, (e) to incorporate in the economy national resources thus far unutilized, (f) to make credit more easily accessible to small borrowers,[14] and (g) to initiate studies and activities preliminary to the improvement of the living standard of the population.

By the end of 1949, the activities of the institute had covered almost all of the fields outlined in the basic plan. The institute had

[14] This, we were assured, is the sense of the phrase "orientation of credit as a democratic function."

extended 619 loans totaling Q2,084,059. Approximately two-thirds of the credits had been granted to agricultural enterprises and processing industries, the remainder to manufacturing industries and commercial enterprises and for housing construction (Table 72). Among the more important manufacturing industries supported by INFOP credits were a bag factory and a paper factory using waste of citronella oil production as raw material.

TABLE 72

CREDIT OPERATIONS OF THE PRODUCTION DEVELOPMENT INSTITUTE
IN 1949[a]

	Number of Loans	Amount in Quetzales	Percent of Total
Production of basic foodstuffs......	285	396,850	19.0
Cattle and dairy industry..........	97	352,250	16.9
Fishing industry	1	20,000	1.0
Coffee production	18	13,080	0.7
Other agricultural credits	71	359,831	17.3
Housing construction and building materials	22	46,550	2.2
Processing and trade of agricultural products	24	169,425	8.1
Various manufacturing industries...	99	710,073	34.1
Hotel and tourist transportation....	2	16,000	0.8
Total	619	2,084,059	100.0

[a] Based on the preliminary report of INFOP for the year 1949.

Although these and similar investments in other lines of manufacturing production represent promising departures into new fields of private industrial activities, the most important activities of INFOP were devoted to the field of agriculture. In addition to the extension of credits, INFOP established, in connection with the operation of one of its farms, the country's first agricultural mechanization center, with which a school for tractor drivers is affiliated. It co-operated with foreign agricultural specialists in the production and distribution of hybrid seed corn, and it contracted for the construction of a 15,000-ton grain elevator in Guatemala City. In addition, it financed the technical training of Guatemalan personnel in foreign countries and undertook, partly with the aid of foreign technicians, several production studies in agriculture and forestry.[15]

A detailed analysis of the activities and future plans of the institute would take us beyond the intended scope and frame of reference of this study. Moreover, the limited duration of the institute's activities does not permit more than a very preliminary appraisal. But since the institute, though administratively autonomous, is a government institution, financed so far exclusively from public sources, and since its activities obviously have an important bearing upon the economic development activities of the government itself, a few brief comments may be in order.

Perhaps the most noteworthy phenomenon is the fact that the institute has been accepted by the business and financial community as a valuable and useful addition to the institutional framework of economic development. Commercial, financial, and agricultural interests, often critical in their comments on government activities, seem to agree in their appraisal of the institute as a desirable and so far successful undertaking. One of the points generally emphasized is the absence of direct government intervention in the operations of the institute, which apparently has managed to translate into reality the legal concept of administrative autonomy.

This favorable publicity must be ascribed in part to the concentration of the institute's credit and development activities in the field of agricultural production which, as the introductory chapter of this study has shown, forms the broad foundation of the country's economic structure. Observers believe that the institute has acted intelligently in staying away from major manufacturing ventures of the spectacular and political-appeal variety and avoiding capital investment that would strain its limited resources. Its efforts to increase productivity in the production of basic foodstuffs (corn, rice) and agricultural raw materials (cotton) through the application of limited amounts of capital inputs

---

[15] For an account of the activities of the institute in the field of collective saving see chapter x.

—mostly in the form of improved tools, mechanized equipment, and better seeds—go to the core of the economic-development problem in Guatemala.

In its credit operations the institute seems to have avoided direct competition with other financial institutions whose primary activities consist of the financing of export crops and of commercial imports. As Table 72 shows, INFOP concentrated on small loans to producers of foodstuffs for the domestic market and on loans to manufacturing enterprises whose access to other credit facilities is limited.

On the basis of its credit activities in the first year of its operation, INFOP holds promise of becoming an important addition to the institutional credit structure of Guatemala. A study of the Guatemalan credit structure, initiated in connection with this study of the fiscal system and to be completed, it is hoped, by the Research Department of the Banco de Guatemala, leads to the conclusion that a large proportion—perhaps too large a proportion—of Guatemalan credit facilities serves the financing of consumption rather than the financing of production. Lack of commercial organization and the small size of individual production units in the agricultural sector (with the exception of coffee, sugar, and foreign-owned banana production) have made the financing of food production for the domestic market a somewhat neglected field. The creation of warehousing facilities together with the expansion of credit in the food-producing sector by INFOP would go a long way toward stabilizing the production of basic foodstuffs and thus mitigating their sporadic scarcities.

The administrative autonomy of INFOP, which essentially has worked to good advantage, is not without certain negative aspects, however. Although there exists close and effective cooperation between INFOP and the monetary authorities — the Monetary Board, which directs the activities of the central bank, has a representative on INFOP's executive directorate—the experience of the first year seems to indicate that the fiscal policy of the government, particularly with respect to the timing and financing of public works, has not taken into account the credit and investment activities of INFOP. True, disbursements by INFOP for loans and direct purchases form only a relatively small proportion of the total money creation of Guatemala; but since—as the above-mentioned credit structure study will point out in greater detail—the credit control exercised by the country's monetary authorities is effective in only a limited sector of the economy (because of the large amount of self-financing, credit extension between importers and retailers, and the financing of exports through foreign purchases and financial institutions), it is the more imperative that full co-ordination be achieved within the sector that can be effectively controlled by the monetary authorities. The adverse movements of the balance of payments in the course of the fiscal year 1949/50 and the failure of the price level of basic foodstuffs to recede seasonally indicate that the sum total of credit creation was larger than the expansion of the physical volume of production of consumer goods. If it is assumed that the credit and direct purchase activities of INFOP were all high-priority operations—and there are indications that most, if not all, of them were—it would have been advisable to curtail direct government investment expenditures or, alternatively, to tighten private credit; the high unit cost of public and private construction in the last twelve months seems to bear out this contention. Fortunately, the inflationary pressures created by the investment bulge of the last two years were not strong enough to upset the economy seriously. The experience of this period points, however, to the need for continued co-ordination between the developmental activities of INFOP and the related actions of the government. The promising start which INFOP has made seems to confirm the appropriateness of the mixed approach for Guatemala—i.e., the support and fostering of private initiative through government institutions. What remains to be done is to establish an effective co-ordination of the government's developmental endeavors, in the form of expenditures for roads, schools, hospitals, etc., with the *fomento* activities of INFOP.

It appears of paramount importance that the resources of INFOP be systematically maintained and replenished by carrying out the government's commitment to allocate to the institute a certain proportion of the annual receipts of the Treasury. Only if these annual contributions become established as a firm and unavoidable expenditure of the government, can the progress of INFOP be considered assured.

This does not mean, however, that the rate of disbursement for loans and direct purchases by INFOP should be maintained at a constant level. To the contrary, changes in the rate of disbursements by INFOP can and should be made an important tool of the monetary and general economic policy, which can exercise a valuable stabilizing influence upon the level of production and real income and assure an adequate rate of economic growth.

"FOMENTO" POLICY AND THE BALANCE OF PAYMENTS

In an earlier section of this chapter, it was pointed out that in Guatemala a large proportion of total capital formation—and an even larger share of productive investment—takes the form of imports of various types of capital goods, particularly machinery and construction materials. Moreover, it was concluded in chapter x that a rise in national income results in a more than proportionate rise in the volume of imports. These two facts lead to the conclusion that the rate of foreign-exchange earnings on current account (augmented temporarily by the stock of gold and foreign currency reserves) is a significant factor limiting the rate of capital formation which even a concerted and co-ordinated economic development policy can achieve. The loss of foreign-exchange reserves in the course of the last year (1949) indicates that these limits are not merely hypothetical, but real in the sense that they pose important questions of current policy.

Private capital expenditures and government expenditures for economic development affect the balance of payments adversely in two distinct ways.[16] The initial outlays for capital formation purposes include a high proportion of expenditures abroad, since machinery and certain classes of construction materials have to be imported. Besides, the disbursements for domestic capital formation in the form of wages, salaries, and purchases of domestically produced materials cause an expansion of income which results in an increased demand for imported consumers' goods.[17] The wide range of investment projects financed from public and private sources does not permit an exact appraisal of the foreign exchange content of Guatemalan investment. But the experience of recent years suggests that this content probably does not lie very much below 50 percent of total investment expenditures. To this figure must be added the additional demand for imported goods that is indirectly induced by the investment. The extent of this additional demand depends on the domestic income expansion caused by the investment expenditures; a rough calculation indicates that in the absence of a rise in the savings ratio and in the proportion of national income absorbed by taxes, the additional demand is likely to amount to more than 20 percent of the initial investment outlay.[18]

The combined balance-of-payments effect of investment expenditures and their secondary impact on consumers' expenditures can be illustrated by the following hypothetical example.

[16] In the longer run, when construction has been completed and operations commence, an investment project may, of course, be import-reducing or export-increasing.

[17] If the expansion of real income is associated with the urbanization or "ladinization" of indigenous workers, the increase in the demand for imports is greater than otherwise.

[18] The highly tentative figure of 20 percent was arrived at on the basis of the following assumptions and calculations. The marginal propensity to import is approximately .18 (equal to the average propensity) ; the marginal propensity to save .10; and 12 percent of additional income is taxed away. This leaves a propensity to consume domestic goods and services of approximately .60. From the parameters an income multiplier (which indicates by how much income expands as a result of an expansion in investment expenditures) of 2.5 can be derived, since the multiplier k is equal to $\dfrac{1}{1-d}$, where d denotes the propensity to consume domestic goods. Thus, a domestic investment outlay of 50—which remains after allowing for capital goods imports of 50—causes an income expansion of 125. This income expansion in turn induces an increase of imports of $125 \times .18$, or 22.5 percent.

With a gross national product of 400 million quetzales and a balance of international transactions on current account at a level of 70 million quetzales, an increase of gross investment expenditures from 32 million to 40 million quetzales (or from 8 to 10 percent of the gross national product) would result in an increased import demand of 5.8 million quetzales.[19] Under present conditions, a loss of foreign-exchange reserves of this order of magnitude would put a severe strain on the country's monetary system and might, by inducing capital flight, endanger exchange stability.

This example is not to be interpreted as a counsel against an expansion of investment activities, both public and private. Quite the contrary: a reasonably high rate of capital formation is obviously the pre-eminent desideratum of Guatemalan economic policy. But it points up the serious limitations that balance-of-payments considerations impose on a vigorous investment policy.

There are, in theory, four major ways in which these balance-of-payments pressures may be relieved: expansion of exports in step with the over-all growth of the economy; borrowing abroad and the encouragement of private foreign investment; curtailment of imports through exchange or trade controls; and devaluation of the quetzal.

The development and expansion of export industries is unquestionably the most desirable of these methods. In Guatemala, the necessity of providing additional sources of foreign-exchange income has been recognized for some time, and the law establishing the Production Development Institute specifically mentions the expansion of export industries as one of the major objectives of economic policy. This task is by no means an easy one, since for reasons of stability and diversification, it appears preferable

[19] Of the 8 million quetzales of additional investment expenditures, 4 million would be absorbed by additional capital goods imports; the domestic disbursement of the remaining 4 million would cause an income expansion of 10 million which in turn would induce additional imports of 1.8 million. If, however, the rise in investment involves a commensurate decrease in consumption expenditures, this increase would be partly offset by a decrease in consumer demand for imports of 1.5 million quetzales.

to establish new export industries rather than to rely upon the growth of the traditional export production of coffee, bananas, and chicle.

The more or less unchanged volume of coffee production in recent years seems to indicate that possibilities for expanding coffee acreage are decidedly limited. This is not to say, however, that more intensive and efficient utilization of the areas now under cultivation, particularly the national farms, would not result in larger crops and export proceeds. But since the production of coffee does not seem to lend itself very readily to any large degree of mechanization, the wage rates and earnings of coffee workers are not likely to expand so as to make additional improvements of their material welfare easy. In the case of banana production, mechanization and improved processing techniques have brought substantial benefits to the workers employed on banana plantations. But while an expansion of the banana production is feasible from the standpoint of soil resources and manpower and promising from the point of view of social welfare, the large-scale initial capital input, which apparently is required to make banana production profitable, will probably prevent this industry from becoming a major outlet for domestic capital. The advent of synthetic chicle production holds little promise that the output of the natural product can be significantly expanded.

Guatemala's resources, however, undoubtedly offer numerous opportunities for the development and growth of new export industries. Any attempt to appraise these opportunities or even to enumerate them would lead us beyond the framework of this study. But the possibilities of opening up the country's tropical regions and of exploiting its practically untapped forestry resources, when considered in conjunction with the technological advances which have been made in tropical agriculture in recent years, justify the expectation that a vigorous search for new export industries will be successful. In such a research and experimental program, the government—and particularly the Production Development Institute—has, of course, an important role to play.

The second method of mitigating the balance-of-payments pressures caused by public and private investment outlays is partial reliance upon foreign capital, either through loans or in the form of direct investments. Since this subject will probably be of major practical significance in the years immediately ahead and falls to a large extent within the scope of the government's fiscal operations, it will be dealt with in some detail in the next section.

The third cure of an investment-induced balance-of-payments deficit would be the introduction of exchange or quantitative import controls, or a combination of both. Unquestionably, the "art" of devising and administering exchange and quantitative trade controls has made considerable progress in the course of the last few years. Many of the inadequacies of earlier control schemes have been eliminated in those countries which because of adverse circumstances and, in some instances, unfortunate policies have been forced to restrict the freedom of foreign exchange and international trade transactions. It must be realized, nevertheless, that the introduction of exchange controls in Guatemala would inevitably cause dislocations of business activity, distortions of trade patterns, and severe problems of administration.

Guatemala has been fortunate indeed that at no time has it been found necessary to impose exchange restrictions upon international trade and capital transactions; the application of quantitative restrictions against imports has been sporadic and, in the aggregate, unimportant. Together with a very limited number of other countries, Guatemala has managed to keep its foreign-exchange market free from normative interference, thus ensuring that allocation of its foreign-exchange resources which the dynamic forces of the market economy require. The absence of exchange restrictions has placed Guatemala in the category of preferred markets for foreign exporters, and there cannot be any question that the Guatemalan business community and indirectly the Guatemalan consumer have benefited from this preferred position.[20]

Up to now, the maintenance of a free-exchange market has apparently not resulted in an appreciable acceleration of the rate of economic progress in Guatemala, as compared with that of countries with a similar economic structure and history. But its significance for the future must not be underestimated. Admittedly, the absence of exchange restrictions is not the only (and perhaps not even the most important) factor determining the standing of Guatemala as a customer and debtor in the international financial and commercial community, but its effects upon the willingness of foreign capital to utilize the investment opportunities that Guatemala offers may be of decisive importance in the long-run development of the country.

The fourth way in which balance-of-payments pressures may be relieved—through currency devaluation—would obviously be the least desirable method of remedial action. The supply of major Guatemalan export commodities would not increase to any significant extent as a result of a devaluation of the quetzal; the primary effect of a lowering of the exchange value of the quetzal would be a decline of the volume of imports. Since the bulk of Guatemalan imports consists of more or less essential consumer goods, an increase in the price of such commodities in terms of domestic currency would in effect result in a lowering of consumption, i.e., a deterioration of economic welfare. Increases in the price of imported goods could, of course, be offset by increases in money income; but to the extent to which such increases occurred automatically or through concerted action, either by trade unions or by the government itself, they would only undo the corrective action of the devaluation. At the same time, they might set into motion inflationary forces the control of which would only add to the cornucopia of monetary and fiscal problems.

[20] The recent attempts of several European countries to re-enter the Guatemalan market and to compete price and qualitywise with American exports are an indication of the world-wide preference for an export market free of exchange restrictions.

THE ROLE OF FOREIGN CAPITAL

The entry of foreign capital into Guatemala would strike at the heart of the *fomento* problem in two ways: the attraction of the savings of other nations would increase the rate of total capital formation in the Guatemalan economy; at the same time it would ease the balance-of-payments pressures which are induced by a high rate of domestic investment.

Private foreign capital, as has been indicated in various parts of the study,[21] has had a major role in the past economic life of the country. There appears to be no reason why it should not continue to do so. As the distortions of the war and the great depression of the 'thirties gradually disappear from the international economic scene, the prospects for a gradual expansion of foreign investment are improving. With suitable domestic policies, Guatemala should be able to obtain a fair share of the flow of international investment funds. Fiscal and monetary policies, of course, are only two of the factors which determine the attractiveness of Guatemala as an area for foreign investment; political conditions and official labor policies are obviously of equal, or greater, importance in this respect.

The major influences of the government's fiscal operations on the attitudes of foreign investors have already been traced in this and preceding chapters. Three factors appear to be of sufficient importance to be emphasized again: (1) the maintenance of a free and stable foreign-exchange market, (2) the co-ordination of Guatemalan tax policies with the tax laws of other nations, particularly those of the United States, and (3) the avoidance of double taxation of corporate dividends, at progressive rates as stipulated in the proposed new income tax law and the proposed reinterpretation of the absentee tax.

Private foreign direct investment is, of course, not the only form of foreign assistance to economic development; public borrowing from abroad may be at present more important, particularly since the Guatemalan economy is reaching a stage of de-

[21] See particularly chapters ii and v.

velopment in which large outlays for social overhead capital appear unavoidable. Private capital is governed by the profit motive and cannot be expected to create social overhead capital in the form of improved transportation, communication, power, and warehousing facilities, unless the risks and yields of such investments compare favorably with those of other outlets for private funds. There are, however, forms of social overhead investment (e.g., road construction, technical training facilities, irrigation projects, etc.) which are not readily susceptible to commercial exploitation. Thus far, major activity in these lines of development investment has been impeded by the absence of an over-all development plan and a schedule of priorities. When the Production Development Institute completes its basic development plan, such a schedule should be available. For the gradual implementation of this, Guatemala's ability to obtain foreign loans is likely to become a decisive factor.

As of the end of the fiscal year 1948/49, Guatemala's external debt amounted to only $670,000,[22] and the interest and amortization charges were of negligible size. In view of this, Guatemala could undoubtedly absorb the foreign-exchange cost of servicing new foreign loans of relatively large amounts, provided that the projects financed from these funds were accompanied by an expansion of exports or replacement of imports. Moreover, an increase in social overhead capital made possible by such loans may tend to attract additional private funds from abroad, and may also act to encourage private domestic productive investment.

STATISTICAL NOTE

The derivation of the estimates of private capital formation is shown in Table 73.

Private construction in Guatemala City.—Data are based on the value of building permits issued in Guatemala City for all construction and repair in excess of Q500. Data for 1944 to 1949 published in *Boletín del Banco de Guatemala*; earlier data partly estimated.

[22] Aside from foreign claims for payment on sterling bonds which were declared invalid in 1945. See p. 88.

Total private construction.—The estimate is based on the assumption that throughout the entire period the relationship between private construction permits in Guatemala and total construction (including repairs, residential and nonresidential rural construction, and profits on the sale of new construction) was the same as in the fiscal year 1947/48.

TABLE 73

ESTIMATES OF PRIVATE CAPITAL FORMATION, 1937/38 TO 1948/49

(In millions of quetzales)

Fiscal Year	Private Construction in Guatemala City	Total Private Construction and Agricultural Improvements	Machinery Imports, f.o.b.	Machinery Imports, c.i.f., Adjusted	Total Private Capital Formation
1937/38	865	2,000	2,430	2,620	4,620
1938/39	775	1,800	2,235	2,480	4,280
1939/40	810	1,880	1,780	2,000	3,880
1940/41	1,040	2,410	2,130	2,370	4,780
1941/42	1,170	2,710	802	900	3,610
1942/43	1,065	2,470	647	730	3,200
1943/44	1,335	3,090	1,020	1,150	4,240
1944/45	2,155	4,990	2,015	2,310	7,300
1945/46	3,480	8,060	3,982	4,200	12,260
1946/47	3,835	8,880	6,842	6,000	14,860
1947/48	3,625	8,400	10,223	9,400	17,800
1948/49	4,710	10,910	....*	....	(18,500)ᵃ

ᵃ Crude estimate.
* Not available.

Machinery imports, f.o.b.—The data for machinery imports were obtained from official import statistics. The following commodity groups are completely or partly included: transportation equipment, electrical machinery, other machinery and mechanical equipment, and agricultural machinery and equipment. Consumer durables, such as passenger cars, refrigerators, etc., are excluded.

Machinery imports, c.i.f., adjusted.—The data on f.o.b. imports have been adjusted for ocean freight, insurance, and import duties, minus government purchases.

INDEX

Alcoholic beverage tax, administration of, 165, 166

Appropriation procedure and expenditure control:
administration and control of expenditures: budget controls, 85; disbursements, 83, 84
budgetary process: legislative enactment, 80, 81; modification after enactment, 81–83; preparation of budget, 77, 80

Ausente tax (*impuesto sobre beneficios de ausentes*), 122, 133, 227

Autonomous entities: Production Development Institute, 17, 19, 42, 43, 68, 69, 263–69; San Carlos University, 42, 43, 68, 69; Social Security Institute, 42, 43, 66, 67–69, 161, 239

Balance of payments: and economic development, 269–74; principal components, 34–36

Bananas: export tax, 52, 56; in the national product, 24; share in total exports, 33, 34

Barna, Tibor, 97

Brazil, comparison, 30

Budget:
of autonomous entities: control of, 85; relation to general budget, 80
influence on balance of payments, 239–46

Budgetary process: with respect to expenditures, 76, 77, 80–83; with respect to revenue, 53–55

Budget surpluses and deficits, effects of, 207–15

Business licenses and transactions taxes, cost of collection, 157

Business profits tax: administration of, 160–62; cost of collection, 157, 159; description of, 51; effects of price changes on burden of, 152–54; flexibility of, 179; principal exemptions, 51, 52; general characteristics, 51

Canada, comparison, 30

Capital, foreign, role in economic development, 275, 276

Capital formation:
government, 17–20, 248–59, 263–69
private: basis of estimates, 276, 277; and the fiscal system, 259–63
rate of, 251–53; in relation to national income, 252
in "real" terms, 250, 251
volume and composition of, 249–51

Chicle, share in total exports, 32–34

Chile, comparison, 57–62, 91–94

Coffee: export tax, 52; in the national product, 24; share in total exports, 32–34

Colm, Gerhard, 97

Compañía Agrícola, 87; *see also* United Fruit Company

Consumption, effect of fiscal system on, 204–7

Consumption taxes: cost of collection, 157; description of, 50; flexibility of, 178, 179

Contraloría del Impuesto sobre Utilidades, 160, 161; *see also* Business profits tax, administration of

Cost of government: salaries and employment policy, 168–70; unit cost, 167, 168

Cuba, comparison, 30

Denmark, comparison, 57, 59–62, 90–92, 94

Direct taxes: cost of collection, 157, 159, 160; description of, 51, 52; flexibility of, 179

Dominican Republic, comparison, 30

Economic development: and the balance of payments, 269–74; role of fiscal system, 17–20, 248–77; role of foreign capital, 275, 276

Ecuador, comparison, 30

El Salvador, comparison, 30, 57–60, 62, 90, 91, 93

Expenditures:
national government: administration and control of, 83–85; budgetary estimation of, 76, 77, 80; classified by type of payment, 76, 78, 79; for cultural and social services, 70–75;